OUR BRAVEST AND OUR BEST

OUR BRAVEST AND OUR BEST

THE STORIES OF CANADA'S VICTORIA CROSS WINNERS

Arthur Bishop

Foreword by The Honourable Henry N.R. Jackman

McGraw-Hill Ryerson Limited

Toronto New York Auckland Bogotá Caracas Lisbon London
Madrid Mexico Milan New Delhi San Juan Singapore Sydney Tokyo

1 2 3 4 5 6 7 8 9 0 TRI 4 3 2 1 0 9 8 7 6 5

First published in 1995 by
McGraw-Hill Ryerson Limited
300 Water Street
Whitby, Ontario, Canada
L1N 9B6

Canadian Cataloguing in Publication Data

Bishop, William Arthur, 1923–
    Our bravest and best

Includes Index.
ISBN 0-07-552619-0

1.Victoria Cross. 2.Canada–Armed Forces–Biography. 3.Canada–
History, Military–20th century–Biography. I.Title

CR4885.B57 1995   355'.1342'0922   C95-931658-2

The assistance of the Canadian War Museum and Public
Archives of Canada is gratefully acknowledged.

Publisher: Joan Homewood
Production Coordinator: Sharon Hudson
Editor: Don Loney/Word Guild
Cover Design: Steve Eby
Text Design: Dianna Little
Layout/formatting: Pamela Charlesworth
Cover photo: Courtesy of National Archives of Canada (C46606)

Printed and bound in Canada

To my grandson,
William Douglas Bishop

Brave men, and worthy patriots
dear to God, and fame to all ages.

John Milton

And when the strife is fierce, the warfare long,
Steals on the ear the distant triumph song
And hearts are brave again, and arms are strong.

Bishop William Walsham How

CONTENTS

FOREWORD

When Arthur Bishop asked me to write a foreword to his new book on the Canadian winners of the Victoria Cross, I felt greatly honoured.
This book is being published coincident with the fiftieth anniversary of the ending of World War II.

During the course of my duties as Lieutenant Governor, I have had the privilege of attending many celebrations honouring Canada's landing in Normandy in 1944 and the final victory of the Canadian Forces and their Allies in 1945.

Although World War II was a very real experience to those who lived through it, our younger Canadians have no personal recollection of those days. The attitude of our youth to these commemorative ceremonies is instructive. Our young people seem to be asking how is it possible that over a million Canadian men and women put on their country's uniform and were prepared to lay down their lives to preserve our freedoms and the values of decency and tolerance? Would Canadians respond now if similarily challenged?

Veterans, on the other hand, find it difficult to realize that they are now becoming objects of curiosity and interest. Veterans of our wars have always minimized their contribution: "I only joined up because all of us were joining up." Or when asked to explain the medal for valour which they received, veterans seem strangely silent or dismissive and answer with some self-deprecating remark, "I was the one who was foolish enough to volunteer."

Real heroes have always been modest and they are always reluctant to talk about their accomplishments. However, they remain our heroes and their stories must be told. These stories of Canadian heroism can inspire us all and help to define us as a nation.

Arthur Bishop, one of Canada's foremost military historians, has done us a great service by recording in such dramatic fashion the stories of our Victoria Cross winners. I can say nothing more about the heroic exploits recounted in these pages. They speak for themselves.

Colonel the Hon. Henry N.R. Jackman
Lieutenant-Governor of Ontario

TRIBUTE

This is a long overdue salute to the bravest and best of our Canadian war heroes. For gallantry in battle, Canadians take second place to no one. Between 1854 and 1945, ninety-five Canadians were awarded the British Commonwealth's–née Empire's–highest award for valour: the Victoria Cross. Taking the country's average population over this period, Canadians won more VCs per capita than any other nation in the Commonwealth.

At the outset, it must be asked "What constitutes a Canadian VC in the first place?" This question is best answered by an authority on the subject, Bruce Beatty of the Chancellery Branch of Government House. Beatty applies the following criteria as the standard:

(1) Was the individual a member of the Canadian forces at the time of the deed?
(2) Was the person born in Canada or its territories (i.e. pre-Confederation)?
(3) Did the person have a permanent residence in Canada at the outbreak of the war?
(4) If not born in Canada, did the person establish a permanent residence in Canada or its territories?

These criteria leave some latitude, but another standard might well apply, and that is did the person consider himself to be a Canadian? This falls into somewhat clearer perspective when the countries of birth are examined.

Fifty-two of the Canadian VCs were born in Canada, thirty-four in the United Kingdom, four in the United States, two in Newfoundland (this was prior to joining Canada), one in Denmark, one in India and one in Russia. Seventeen of those VC winners born outside Canada settled here.

Of the Canadian-born VCs, one came from Alberta, five from British Columbia, six from Manitoba, three from New Brunswick, three from Nova Scotia, twenty-one hailed from Ontario, one from Prince Edward Island and six from Quebec.

All but five of those in the army served with Canadian regiments. Three served with the Royal Navy and one with the Royal Naval Fleet Air Arm. Three flew with the Royal Flying Corps, three with the Royal Canadian Air Force and one with the Royal Air Force. Twenty-eight of the Canadian VCs were killed in action and seven died of wounds sustained in the action for which the VC was awarded.

Both individually and collectively, the Canadian Victoria Cross winners established the foundation of this nation's military heritage–one in which all Canadians can, and should, take undeniable pride.

Arthur Bishop
Toronto

ACKNOWLEDGEMENTS

O
ur Bravest and Our Best was made possible to a great extent through the generosity and support of the Henry N.R. Jackman Foundation. I am also grateful to the Ontario Lieutenant-Governor for consenting to write the foreword to this work. I would also like to thank his executive assistant, Jean Taylor, and his Aide-de-camp, Captain Thomas Amell, for their help.

It would not have been possible to produce this book in the form it has taken without the enthusiastic help of the Canadian War Museum. Vic Suthren, Dan Glenney, Bernard Portier, Fred Gaffen and Carmen Pulsifer were of assistance in various ways, including providing access to their files. It is my hope that this book will, on their behalf, ignite new interest in and a better understanding of Canadian Victoria Cross recipients.

To qualify this, out of ninety-five Canadian VC holders, twenty-two of the medals are either in the possession of, or on loan to, the Museum. Unfortunately, this organization, unlike some of our other government-funded institutions, lacks the funds to purchase the medals from those still in the hands of next of kin. As frequently happens, they are often put on the block for auction. In the pages that follow, the reader will see how this state of affairs was on occasion overcome.

If there is one person responsible for my interest, and that of the Museum's, in the Victoria Cross, it is Dick Malott. A graduate historian of the University of Western Ontario and a former member of the Canadian Forces (air crew and logistics) working with the Museum, his interest in VCs arose from a friendship with the widow of one of the Canadian recipients. As a favour to her, he researched the facts surrounding her late husband's medals. This produced a thirst for knowledge that led to Dick becoming the chief curator for the Canadian War Museum and the acquisition of the Victoria Crosses.

Dick was of enormous assistance to me. I was able to lean on his experience and pick his nimble brain. He was kind enough to vet the manuscript in draft form and to check the galley proofs for accuracy and detail. I appreciate the many suggestions he offered.

In the same breath, I must tender my thanks to Kay DesRochers, former Curator of Archival Resources at the Museum, for her enthusiastic and diligent help with my research.

This work probably would have never got off the deck without the advice, help and moral support of my literary agent, Frances Hanna (Acacia Publishing Services Ltd.). In Frances I enjoy a "two for the price of one" benefit in that in addition to being a top agent, she is an experienced, knowledgeable and qualified editor.

In connection with Hampton Gray's VC, I would like to thank Charles Rolfe of the Hampton Gray Chapter of the Canadian Naval Air Group as well as Stuart Soward for supplying the picture of the Japanese memorial at Sakiyama Park.

On the editorial side, I wish to acknowledge my publisher, Joan Homewood, and my editor, Don Loney.

Finally, my wife Cilla, who was her usual helpful self both as a critic and, well, as my wife.

Prologue

FOR VALOUR

The whole was conducted in full state....
It was a beautiful sight and everything admirably arranged....
The road all along was kept clear and there was no pushing or squeezing.
Constant cheering and noises of every kind,
but the horses went beautifully.

Queen Victoria

NEVER was such a momentous salute to valour so richly or royally endowed. On the bright sunny summer day of June 26, 1857, at a resplendent ceremony in Hyde Park, London, replete with the martial airs of military bands, a full dress parade, a Buckingham Palace honour guard and booming artillery salutes, Her Imperial Majesty, riding side-saddle on horseback, conducted the first investiture of the Victoria Cross by pinning the decoration to the tunic of sixty-two of the original recipients.

An historic occasion, indeed, and one that had its genesis two years earlier when, in January of 1855, the Duke of Newcastle, then the British Secretary for War, wrote to Albert, the Prince Consort, to remind him of a conversation they had had a year ago in which he had suggested that a new medal for gallantry in the field or at sea should be struck that would be eligible for all ranks. Queen Victoria who, after the Light Brigade debacle was moved to declare that "the brilliance of the charge and the gallantry and discipline evinced by all have never been surpassed by British soldiers under similar circumstances," agreed that such a new award of recognition should be coined.

What evolved was a Cross Formy or Cross Paty design — heraldry experts have never agreed which (it is described in the Royal Warrant as a Maltese Cross, which it definitely is not — nearly one and one-half inches square, attached to a ribbon by a wide "V" to a bar on which there is a sprig of laurel, the token of victory. Obverse a Royal Crown is surmounted by a lion with a scroll which reads "For Valour." When originally submitted to the Queen, it read "For the Brave"; however, Her Majesty felt this would imply that no one was brave save those who received the medal and the wording was duly changed by Royal Command.

The cross, the sign of self-sacrifice, hung from a ribbon one and one-half inches wide, red for the army and blue for the navy. With the formation of the Royal Air Force in 1918, the colour of the ribbon was decreed, by Royal Warrant signed by the then Secretary of State for War, Winston Churchill, as red for all three services.

The act or acts of valour, the date or dates and the name of the recipient were to be engraved on the back. Though the design won royal sanction, it could hardly be called attractive. Solemn and meaningful yes, but in fact rather drab. *The Times* of London was moved to describe it as "poor-looking and mean in the extreme."

The award was to carry the Queen's name, but the first proposal was a clumsy, long-winded title: "The Military Order of Victoria." Prince Albert put his pencil through it and made a notation to "treat it as a cross granted for distinguished service which will make it simple and intelligible," and promptly shortened it to the "Victoria Cross."

Lord Panmure, the new Secretary of War, took the design to the jewellers Hancocks & Company in London and commissioned them to make up a prototype. Though the firm's expertise lay in silver, it had been decided that the medal would be struck in base metal. But the Queen was far from happy with the result, as reported by her secretary:

> The Cross looks very well in form, but the metal is ugly; it is copper not bronze and will look very heavy on a red coat with the Crimean Ribbon. Bronze is, properly speaking, gunmetal; this has a rich colour and is very hard; copper would wear very ill and would soon look like an old penny. Lord Panmure should have one prepared in real bronze and the Queen is inclined to think that it ought to have a greenish varnish to protect it; the raised parts would then burnish up bright and show the design and inscription.

This led to the thought that it might be appropriate to take the bronze from Russian guns captured at Sebastopol, the last battle of the Crimean War. Engineers were dispatched to Woolwich Barracks where two 18-pounders were placed at their disposal. The cascabels — knobs on the breech of the cannon that secured restraining ropes during firing — were sawed off. Hancocks used the metal from these to produce the first batch of the newly authorized medals.

Many years later, it was learned that the guns were of Chinese origin — not Russian. The bronze was of such poor quality that it would not cool evenly, so that the Victoria Cross had to be sand cast instead of produced from a die. This meant that the details on the obverse side had to be hand-crafted. In a way, it is fitting that, in a sense, each medal is different since it was awarded for *individual* acts of valour.

The Victoria Cross is the most coveted and highly prized decoration of military service for Britain and the Commonwealth, in keeping with the Queen's express desire.

Victoria Cross

Alexander Dunn's grave, Senafe, Ethiopia

Chapter One

THE HEROIC HUSSAR

When can their glory fade?
O the wild charge they made!
All the world wonder'd.
Honour the charge they made!
Honour the Light Brigade,
Noble six hundred!

Alfred, Lord Tennyson,
"The Charge of the Light Brigade," 1854

HIS coffin and headstone lie enshrined on a grassy slope sheltered by a large rock at Senafe along the border of Ethiopia and Eritrea. He reportedly died accidentally while hunting game. Rumours suggest, however, that he committed suicide, or perhaps was even murdered. The grave, restored in 1984 by the Commonwealth War Graves Commission, is isolated and attracts little attention. The Canadian government has shown no interest whatsoever in repatriating his body.

His medals, along with a portrait, are displayed in the halls of Upper Canada College (UCC) in Toronto, Ont. where he took his early education. In the daily school-day bustle, they receive only a cursory glance from students and teachers.

In the same city, a commemorative plaque erected in 1966 by the Archaeological and Historical Board of Ontario stands at the northwest corner of Clarence Square, near the foot of Spadina Avenue, south of King Street and close to where he spent his youth. It is headed

"CANADA'S FIRST VICTORIA CROSS," yet it draws scant notice from passersby.

Such disregard for our military traditions is becoming commonplace in this country. It is also becoming fashionable — and indeed profitable — to couple that with disrespect. But if Alexander Roberts Dunn were alive today, the six-foot three-inch blond-headed hussar with the drooping moustache probably wouldn't give a damn one way or the other. He might even see some humour in the situation. Handsome, courageous and dauntless, the hero of the Valley of Death was a soldier for soldiering's sake, not for the fame his honours and bravery won him.

Born on September 15, 1833 at York (later renamed Toronto), Dunn was the fifth son of the receiver general of Upper Canada. He began his education at UCC, but when his mother died, his father returned with the family to England where Dunn attended Harrow School. While in Ireland, on March 12, 1852, at nineteen years of age, he purchased a commission as cornet (2nd lieutenant) in the prestigious 11th Hussars (Prince Albert's Own Regiment of Light Dragoons, nicknamed "The Cherry Pickers"). Dunn proved to be an outstanding horseman. In his resplendent royal blue tunic and crimson trousers, chin-strapped helmet, gold epaulets and black jack boots, the tall Canadian cavalryman with the fair beard and cool blue eyes cut a dashing, romantic figure. To accommodate his height and reach, Wilkinson's Swords had to fashion a custom-made four-foot-long sabre for him, several inches longer than regulation size. Dunn was to use the extra length to advantage in battle.

A strict disciplinarian, Dunn was nevertheless not only respected but admired and liked by the men under him. When in 1854 his regiment sailed for the Crimea, where Britain and France sent armies to preserve the balance of power in Eastern Europe by halting Russia's advance on Turkey, Dunn at twenty-one, by now a full lieutenant, was placed in charge of "F" Troop.

The morning of the Charge of the Light Brigade, October 25, 1854, was gray and chilly, unsettling and foreboding. That fit. What was about to transpire was one of the stupidest, most ill-conceived and scandalous tactical blunders in the annals of military deployment. When the order came, 637 British cavalry charged into the valley flanked by slopes heavily defended by Russian troops and artillery and a solid twelve-gun battery placed wheel to wheel at its end. Dunn was about to go into action for the first time.

The French general Pierre Bosquet best described the folly that ensued when he proclaimed, somewhat tragically, "*C'est magnifique, mais ce n'est pas la guerre! C'est la folie.*" It wasn't war, it was sheer suicide. The British were hacked to pieces. Out of 110 men making up the 11th Hussars, only twenty-five survived. Overall, the attackers lost 156 killed and missing, 134 wounded and fourteen taken prisoner. In the Valley of Death, however, Dunn was in his element.

The Canadian horseman led his troops in attack after attack around the enemy guns. Finally, when the 11th Hussars were forced to withdraw, they came under relentless fire from Fedouikine Hill to their right. A sergeant, Robert Bentley, was struggling with his horse that had been hit so badly it was near collapse. The Russians singled Bentley out as a straggler, knocked him out of the saddle, and were about to finish him off. Seeing this, Dunn wheeled about to ride back to him.

Through the maelstrom of dead and dying, and with riderless horses tearing off in all directions crazed with pain from their wounds, Dunn fended off Bentley's marauders, cutting down three Russian dragoons with his giant-sized sabre. All the while, Bentley had been clinging to his horse by a stirrup. Dunn dismounted and lifted him into his own saddle, then belted the horse smartly on the rump to send it galloping towards the British lines. On foot, he went to the aid of another of his troop, Private Harvey Levett, who had lost his mount. By dispatching another Russian hussar with his sword, Dunn rescued the private from almost certain death. He then approached a downed Russian steed, but the animal's hind legs were shot away. Undaunted, he and Levett made their way back to their own lines without having suffered a scratch.

When he saw the pitiful number of men in his regiment who had survived the fool-hardy massacre, Dunn broke into tears. As it turned out, he alone had slain more Russians that day than anyone else in an action for which he was recommended for a medal for bravery. It turned out to be in the form of the Victoria Cross.

Altogether, 111 Victoria Crosses were awarded in the Crimean War. Dunn was the only officer in the Charge of the Light Brigade to receive the medal and the only cavalry officer in the entire Crimean campaign to win it. (He was also awarded the Crimean Medal with four clasps as well as the Turkish Medal.) The citation read:

> For having in the Light Cavalry Charge on the 25th October, 1854, saved the life of Sergeant Bentley, 11th Hussars by cutting down two or three Russian Hussars, who were attacking him from the rear, and afterwards cutting down a Russian Hussar, who was attacking Private Levett, 11th Hussars.

Dunn was awarded his VC two years later, in 1856. In the meantime, he sold his commission and returned to Canada, having "eloped" with the wife of a fellow officer, Lieutenant-Colonel Andrew Douglas, who refused to give his cuckolding spouse a divorce.

Dunn, along with his companion VCs, was at the same time awarded a stipend of £10 annually for the rest of his life (later, in the 1950s, this was increased to £100 pounds — tax free). Fortunately, his family was affluent and Dunn retired to his estate near Toronto — but only temporarily.

During the Indian Mutiny, which took place between 1857 and 1859, Britain, with armies extended all over the world, called on her colonies for enlistments for the first time. Dunn helped form the 100th Prince of Wales Own Royal Canadian Regiment which arrived in England in 1858. In 1861, he paid £10,000 to become a lieutenant-colonel. However, the regiment never did participate in the Indian Mutiny, but instead was posted to Gibraltar as a garrison unit. In 1864, Dunn reached the rank of full colonel to become the first Canadian to command a regiment and the youngest colonel in the British army. But he soon tired of the static role into which he and his unit had been cast and, restless for the excitement of battle, he transferred to the "hard drinking" 33rd Duke of Wellington's Regiment of Foot. *The Times* wrote of him: "His career had already given promise of sufficient distinction to justify the belief of his friends that the highest military appointments were within his reach." But, in fact, his days were numbered.

The 33rd was sent first to Malta, then to India, and late in 1867 to Abyssinia (the country was renamed Ethiopia) where it joined in Napier's march on Magdela against the Emperor Theodore. On January 25, 1868, during this expedition, Dunn lost his life near Senafe, the true circumstances of which have never been resolved. Conjecture is wide over how he died. The only consensus is that it happened while he was hunting game.

Was it suicide? Purportedly, Dunn dismounted from his horse to sit down on a rock to rest and sent his servant to a nearby stream for some water. When the valet returned, he found his master dead from gunshot wounds. Did he kill himself accidentally? The official 33rd Regiment version is that Dunn was trying to uncork a brandy flask when his gun slipped between his legs and fired off both barrels into his chest. In his death throes, Dunn gasped, "Run for a doctor!" to his manservant, but by the time help arrived he was dead. Was he murdered? Though there appears to be no proof, this possibility cannot be lightly dismissed. Dunn is known to have reversed his will in favour of his valet, leaving the manservant open to suspicion as a probable assassin. But, more likely, it might have been either a jealous suitor or husband who shot him — or had him shot. Dunn, the dashing, handsome VC hero figure was known for his romantic affairs (he had run off with a fellow officer's wife in the Crimea), and such a demise would have surprised no one. That his body was never returned to Canada or England adds greater depth to the mystery. In 1885, seventeen years after his death, the *Canadian Military Gazette* summed up the dilemma in this fashion:

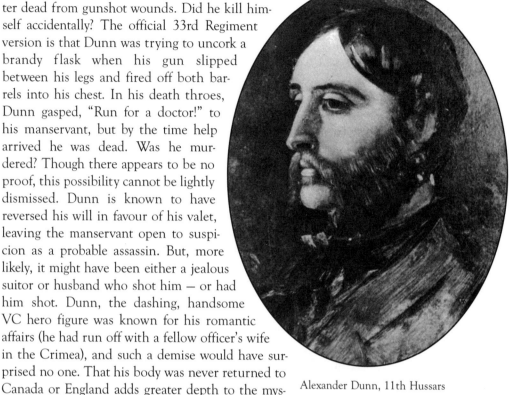

Alexander Dunn, 11th Hussars

> Colonel Dunn died of a gunshot wound in Abyssinia. It is generally supposed that his fowling-piece was accidentally discharged while he was crossing some obstruction, though some believe his servant murdered him, and a few that he committed suicide. The truth will probably never be known.

None of this in any way tarnishes his record as a warrior, nor should it.

In July 1894, Dunn's VC, along with his other medals, was sold at auction at Sotheby's in England. Canadians in London, upset by the transaction, brought it to the attention of the Canadian minister of militia, John Patterson. Patterson cabled Sir Charles Tupper, then Canadian high commissioner in London, authorizing him to buy the medals from the purchaser at the market. The medals reached Canada in time to be put on display at the Quebec Exhibition that year. Later, they were transferred to Upper Canada College. Dunn's sword and his campaign stool are on display at the Canadian War Museum on Sussex Drive in Ottawa.

In 1945, Reg Rimmer, a regular soldier with the British army, was leading a patrol of Eritrean Mounted Police along the border with Ethiopia when he came across a tiny cemetery near Senafe, which had obviously been long abandoned. Among the neglected plots, one grave appeared to have been well tended — this by the Italian army during the Fascist occupation. On the headstone, which showed signs of weathering, the engraved name "A.R. Dunn VC. Colonel" nevertheless stood out clearly. Information concerning the location of Dunn's grave did not reach the British trade commission until 1974, and it was then that the Department of Veterans Affairs began an investigation. However, no work could be undertaken until eight years later, due to military activity in Ethiopia. Restoration was begun and the commission now monitors the grave every two years.

Somewhat reassuring, but unsatisfactory nonetheless. Our first Victoria Cross winner has lain too long in a foreign soil to which neither he, nor we, have any real or significant attachment. He belongs here, at home. This is not to suggest that our other war dead, buried in cemeteries all over the world, should likewise be disturbed. No. Far from it. They must be allowed to rest in peace where, or close to where, they fell on the sword. Dunn's case is different. His death in Abyssinia did not occur in battle. It is time to bring our heroic hussar back to his native land and honour him with the salute he so richly and rightly deserves as one of our bravest and best.

The Charge of the Light Brigade, The Crimean War

Chapter Two

THE SURGEON AND THE SAILOR

CANADA's second and third Victoria Crosses were won on the frontier during the Indian Mutiny — a bitter, bloody revolt of native Sepoy troops against the British West India Company for imposing its will on the Hindu way of life. Both recipients played crucial roles in two principal actions that helped the British army quell the rebellion: the lifting of the siege of Delhi and the relief of Cawnpore and Lucknow. Yet, at face value, a more unlikely pair to accomplish such heroic feats would be hard to imagine. One was a surgeon, the other a sailor. And in training and background they were as different as day and night.

Herbert Taylor Reade hailed from Perth in Upper Canada where he was born on September 2, 1828. His father, an Irish veteran of the Napoleonic wars, had retired to Canada as apothecary to the Imperial Army, but was recalled to the militia when the Rebellion of Lower Canada broke out. He was posted to the Quebec Citadel where Herbert spent his early youth. When his father was moved to Dublin, Ireland, Herbert attended university where he graduated with his Doctor of Medicine degree in 1850. In November of that year, he was appointed assistant surgeon to the 61st Gloucestershire Regiment of Foot and later joined the unit at Peshawar, on the northwest frontier of India, where he spent the next six years. When the Indian Mutiny started on May 10, 1857, Reade was stationed at Ferozepore (now Firozpur) in Punjab, the ancient capital of Hindustan that lay 250 miles northwest of Delhi.

By contrast, William Edward Hall had little to no education. He was a Black whose mother and father had been slaves. His father had been freed during the War of 1812 when the British frigate *Leonard* intercepted a slave ship bound from Africa for the United States and forced it to deposit its "ivory cargo" in Halifax. His mother, who was a slave on a plantation near Washington, escaped her bondage when the British attacked and burned the city. She boarded one of the Royal Navy ships which ended its expedition by putting in to Halifax. There Hall's parents, Jacob and Lucinda, were married.

With the help of the Nova Scotia government, they found employment as cook and gardener on the property of Sir William Cunard, the shipping magnate, at Hantsport in the Annapolis Valley, before moving to Horton Bluffs where Jacob farmed for Peter Hall (from whom he took his surname).

On April 18, 1827, Lucinda gave birth to a son whom the couple named William Edward. The lad developed his love of the sea at an early age and was only in his teens when he signed on with the merchant marine serving on a number of trading vessels as a deck hand. When he turned twenty, he enlisted in the Royal Navy, his first ship being *Rodney*. Hall is reported to have deserted the navy around January of 1856; his name is marked in *Rodney's* ship's book as "R" (Run) dated March 12, 1856. Under military regulations, he would have had to forfeit all rank, pay and property. Whatever the circumstances, he was allowed to re-enlist and joined the warship *Shannon* soon after the vessel was commissioned in October of that same year.

Hall subsequently became a marine, and as a member of *Shannon's* crew he served with distinction in the Crimean War, earning two British medals with Sebastopol and Inkerim clasps, and the Turkish Medal. (In the early days of the Victoria Cross the campaign medals, if awarded first, were worn ahead of the new decoration.) When the Indian Mutiny broke out, Hall held the rank of captain of the foretop for *Shannon*. Along with another British warship, *Pearl*, the vessel diverted from Hong Kong where she had been escorting troops in anticipation of a Chinese insurrection, to Calcutta. They sailed with a force of 450 Royal Marines, Hall among them, their weaponry consisting of six 8-inch guns, two 24-pounder howitzers and a pair of field guns.

The Indian Mutiny began at the musketry depot at Meerut, sixty miles north of Delhi. There the Sepoys unleashed their pent-up wrath by killing most of their officers and slaughtering all white women and children. Native prisoners were released from jail, and then the Sepoys marched on Delhi.

Three days later, on May 13, 1857, three Sepoy regiments revolted at Ferozepore resulting in a brief but bloody skirmish with the Gloucesters.

Meanwhile, the native mutineers took possession of Delhi, repeated the massacre of Meerut, and proclaimed the King of Delhi as emperor. Later, the British garrisons at Cawnpore (now Kanpur) located on the Ganges River about 250 miles southwest of Delhi, and Lucknow, about fifty miles northeast of Cawnpore, came under siege. The Sepoys were taking full charge.

Inside the walled capital of Delhi, there were 40,000 well-armed rebels, highly trained and seething with hatred and revenge. With only 6,000 troops, among them Reade's 61st Gloucesters, the British were sorely outnumbered. All they could do was keep the mutineers occupied around a seven-mile perimeter until they could organize a proper assault. This task took several months.

The British attacked at three o'clock in the morning of September 14, 1857. Once through the Kashmir Gate and pressing deeply into the city with its tortuous, winding alleys, Reade began ministering to the wounded. Suddenly, a large number of rebels appeared; they scrambled up to the rooftops where they levelled murderous fire on the British. The bloodthirsty act of firing on the injured raised the hackles on Reade's neck. Temporarily discarding his role as a non-combatant, he marshalled ten troops around him and drove off the Sepoys. Two of his group were killed and six were wounded, but Reade was able to continue his work treating the wounded without further interruption.

That incident seemed to have fired in him a fierce hatred for the barbaric mutineers. Two days later he once again exchanged his scalpel for a sword. By that time the British had reached the Royal Palace and Reade led an attack by Gloucesters on the breach of the city's powder magazine in the face of enemy cannon fire. Slashing and lunging with his sword, Reade fought his way through, dispersing the Sepoys. In the hand-to-hand fighting, he managed to spike one of the enemy

Herbert Reade, 61st Regiment of Foot

guns. This action, coupled with his feat of two days earlier, earned him the title "Fighting Surgeon" — and the VC. In taking the enemy cannon out of operation, he was credited with being largely responsible for the fall of Delhi five days later.

Meanwhile, in mid-August *Shannon* and *Pearl* had reached Calcutta and the former, with its complement of Royal Marines, proceeded up the Ganges River taken in tow by the steamer *Chunbar*. Their objectives were the recapture of the British army headquarters at Cawnpore, by then in Sepoy hands, and the relief of the British garrison at Lucknow. Possession of the two vital positions gave the Sepoys control of the mutiny.

On September 2, *Shannon* reached Allahabad, 800 miles upriver from Calcutta. There the force disembarked to continue the trek to Cawnpore. Progress was slow and difficult. With sporadic fighting along the way, the heavy 18-inch guns had to be left behind. The force reached Cawnpore on October 28, by which time the British had recaptured it. According to Hall, there was still "women's blood on the walls." There the marines joined forces with reinforcements from England.

Several days later, the historic march across the dusty Indian plain began to relieve the besieged city of Lucknow where, in September, a British relief force had fought its way through to the residency, where the beleaguered British garrison was holding out against 50,000 Sepoys. Then the relief force itself was cut off.

The second relieving force, numbering 5,000, was now on the march. It was made up of Royal Marines, a Highland regiment and Sikh troops. The contingent reached the outskirts of Lucknow on November 16 and the assault began. The key to the city was the Shah Nulliff Fort, a former temple with seven-foot-thick stone walls pocked with holes for muskets, enclosed within a walled avenue fortification called the Sekandarhagh that had to be taken first. By early afternoon, this had been accomplished at bayonet point and the troops moved on to the Shah Nulliff Fort, a half mile to the west.

That strategic position and vital centre of resistance was defended by 30,000 vengeful mutineers. The "*Shannon* Brigade" dragged its guns to within 200 yards of the walls to lay down the preliminary bombardment. The crew of one of the 24-pounder howitzers was one man short, so William Hall, who had been in charge of a gun aboard ship, volunteered as a replacement.

At 4:00 p.m., the order came to lay down the barrage and the detachment began pounding shells against the wall, but to no avail. All the while the Sepoys laid down a curtain of fire through the rifle holes, inflicting appalling casualties. Clearly a crisis had been reached and the wall had to be breached without delay. There was only one answer — a close range barrage.

The two 24-pounder howitzers were moved to within twenty yards of the wall, but the crew of one of them was mowed down by the mutineers. That left only Hall and a badly wounded gunner with a single howitzer to force the wall. Undeterred, the two of them methodically sponged out and reloaded the gun in the face of relentless fire from the rebels. Finally, a shell blew a hole in the wall. The Highlanders advanced into the mosque through the gap to find the Shah Nulliff deserted. The Sepoys had fled in disarray, leaving Lucknow in British hands — but only temporarily. The British were soon forced to retreat, and it was not until March of 1858 that they were strong enough to return to Lucknow and clear out the mutineers once and for all. The Indian Mutiny did not end until November.

For his heroic action, Hall was awarded the Victoria Cross (as was his gunner). The citation read in part:

> Finally, in one of the most supreme moments in all the age long story of human courage, Hall fired the charge which opened up the walls and enabled the British to push through to the relief of the garrison and ultimately to the quelling of the mutiny and the restoration of peace and order in India.

HERBERT Reade was eventually appointed to the rank of surgeon-general. He retired from the army on pension in 1887 and became honourary surgeon to Queen Victoria in

1895. He died two years later at Sunnyland Park Gardens, near Bath in Somerset, at the age of sixty-eight. He was buried in Locksmith Cemetery. Reade's Victoria Cross was presented to the Gloucestershire Regiment in July 1939. In 1966, a memorial plaque erected in his honour was unveiled at the new Legion Building at Beckwith Street East in Perth, Ont.

William Hall did not receive his VC until October 25, 1859 when it was formally presented to him at an investiture aboard *Donegal* at the port of Queenstown in Ireland. That made him not only the first Black to receive the award, but also the first person from any British Dominion to receive it. Nova Scotia had yet to join Confederation.

After twenty-one years on active service and seven years as a gunnery

William Hall, Naval Brigade, Royal Navy

instructor, Hall retired from the Royal Navy on June 10, 1876 with the rank of petty officer first class and a certificate of good conduct. After turning down an honourary
appointment at Whitehall in London, he returned to Nova Scotia and purchased a farm
at Hantsport overlooking the Minas Basin, close to where he was born, to raise cattle and
poultry. For recreation he engaged in his favourite pastime of shooting crows. There he
lived quietly with his two sisters.

In 1901, the "Forgotten Hero" temporarily came out of obscurity to take part in a ceremony at which the Duke of York, the future King George V, unveiled a memorial to
South African War veterans on the grounds of the provincial Parliament Buildings in
Halifax. Hall was provided with a carriage and invited to join in the Royal Procession,
which delighted the crowds who thronged the streets.

He died of paralysis three years later, on August 25, 1904, at age seventy-seven, and
was buried without honours in an unmarked grave at Lockhartville. In 1945, his remains
were reinterred in the grounds of the Hantsport Baptist Church. Two years later the
Hantsport Branch of the Royal Canadian Legion, British Services League, erected a cairn
in his honour bearing a bronze replica of his VC, and at Halifax the "coloured" branch
of the Legion was named after him. At Cornwallis Street United Church in the city, a
memorial plaque stands in his memory.

Hall's Victoria Cross was presented to the Nova Scotia Museum along with his other
medals. The VC was on display at the Canadian War Museum in Ottawa, on loan from
the Nova Scotia government for several years, but it is now back on display in the Nova
Scotia Museum, Halifax.

The Indian Mutiny

Campbell Douglas, 24th Regiment of Foot

Chapter Three

ARMY SURGEON CUM SEAFARER

THE fourth Canadian to be awarded the Victoria Cross was an army doctor, who ironically had the audacity, both figuratively and literally, to win the coveted decoration for bravery in a marine action.

Late in April 1867, the British naval vessel *Assaw Valley* put in at the island of Little Adaman in the Bay of Bengal, then part of the British protectorate of Burma (officially called Myanmar since 1898). Some of the crew went ashore to reconnoitre the area. When after some days they did not return, it was assumed they might have been murdered by natives. The chief commissioner for Burma ordered an army detachment sent ashore to investigate.

A contingent of the 2nd Battalion of the 24th Regiment of Foot sailed from Rangoon and, on arrival on May 7, some landed on the island only to be immediately set upon by natives. Then a heavy storm blew up that turned the surf into a raging sea. This put the soldiers ashore in grave peril.

A rescue force consisting of four troopers led by the regimental assistant surgeon Campbell Mellis Douglas of Quebec City was quickly put into operation. Manning the oars of a gig, a skiff-like craft, they plunged into the boiling surf. But the light little boat proved to be no match for the churning sea and rain. Several times it threatened to capsize and, when it half filled with water, the team had to abandon the attempt.

An hour later the party tried again. This time Douglas stood in the bow of the boat directing his four oarsmen and balancing the vessel by shifting his weight from one leg to the other as if he'd been a man of the sea all his life. Successfully landing on the shore, the small contingent took off five of the *Assaw Valley* crew and returned to the ship. They then turned back to rescue the rest. For the feat, Douglas and the privates with him all were awarded the VC. The *London Gazette* commented on Douglas's leadership as being "in an intrepid and seamanlike manner, cool to a degree, as if what he was doing then was an ordinary act of everyday life." In addition to the VC, he was also awarded the Royal Humane Society Silver Medal.

Douglas was born in Quebec City on August 5, 1840 and educated at St. John's College and Laval University. He later attended the Edinburgh School of Medicine where he received his Doctor of Medicine and became a Fellow of the Royal College of Surgeons. He joined the British Army Medical Service in 1862 and was posted to the 24th Regiment the following year. At the time of the Burma action, he held the rank of major. In 1872, he transferred to the Royal Artillery.

In 1876, he was made surgeon-major and, in 1882, surgeon lieutenant-colonel. He retired in October of that year with the honourary rank of brigade surgeon. Returning to Canada, he married Eleanor McMaster, the niece of an admiral, and set up a medical practice in Lakefield, Ont. But his days of heroics were far from over.

Early in April 1885, the minister of militia and defence authorized the organization of a medical service in connection with the North-West (Riel) Rebellion. Two field hospitals were organized, one of them commanded by Douglas who arrived at Swift Current with the rest of the hospital team by rail — Canada's first "hospital train." On April 25, the stern-wheeler steamer *Northcote*, carrying medical and hospital supplies and a detachment from the hospital, left Saskatchewan Landing for Saskatoon to remove the wounded. Two days later, concerned over its progress, Douglas set off downriver in a twelve-foot-long canoe that weighed a mere forty-five pounds, which he nicknamed "Saskatoon." There was always the danger it might get snagged and also that rebels might take potshots at him from the riverbanks.

As Douglas had feared, *Northcote* did become wedged among the sandbars some twenty miles downriver. Douglas reached Saskatoon in May where he was joined by another medical officer who had travelled overland from Swift Current. That same afternoon, the wounded from the Battle of Fish Creek were being brought in and were billeted among the residents. Finally, *Northcote* arrived with the medical and hospital supplies.

The wounded from the Fish Creek battle of May 3 and the Battle of Batoche on May 14 were treated in houses requisitioned as hospitals. Under the direction of Douglas, who had by then been appointed director of the ambulance corps, the wounded were evacuated from Saskatoon to a base hospital at Moose Jaw, first taken aboard *Northcote* as far as Elbow, then transferred to carts. But Douglas considered the journey too severe and he had the remaining wounded sent by barge directly to Winnipeg via the Saskatchewan River, Lake Winnipeg and the Red River, a 1,100-mile trip that took from July 1 to July 14 to complete. For his part in the rebellion, Douglas received the North-West Canada Medal.

Following the Riel Rebellion, Douglas retired to England, taking "Saskatoon" with him. A boating enthusiast to the last, in 1895 he crossed the English Channel in the little canoe. Douglas died at Wells in Somerset on December 31, 1909 at age sixty-nine.

In May 1988, Douglas' widowed daughter-in-law, Frances, donated his Victoria Cross along with his other decorations to the Canadian Forces Medical School and Canadian Forces Base Borden, Ont. They were later transferred to the Canadian War Museum in Ottawa.

Arthur Richardson, Lord Strathcona's Horse

Chapter Four

THE SOLDIERS OF THE QUEEN

... so when we say that England's master
Remember who has made her so.

It's the soldiers of the Queen M'lads
Who've been M'lads, Who've seen M'lads
In the fight for England's glory Lads
Of its world wide glory let us sing.

And when we say we've always won
And when they ask us how it's done
We'll proudly point to every one
Of England's soldiers of the Queen.

Military March

A ND Canada's too! During the Boer War in South Africa, fought between 1899 and 1902, five Victoria Crosses were awarded to Canadian soldiers of the Queen. Three of the VCs were won in the same action and by members of the same regiment. Four of these acts of valour were by soldiers of the Canadian army (the other recipient served with the British army), and they not only highlighted the role and mettle of the 7,000 volunteers from the Dominion who served in the conflict — Canadians forced the first Boer surrender — but also the fact that the country had for the first time acted as one nation in aiding England. The feats also had a strong bearing on the fact that participation in the war had given the country its first sense of military maturity. This resulted in the organization of a proper army militia.

The war broke out over a conflict of

interests between the Dutch Boers (farmers) and the British in the cape colony when the English discovered diamonds in the Transvaal. The Boers feared the British would take over the country, while the English were convinced the Boers (supported by Germany, politically at any rate) were bent on driving them out.

The first Canadian to win the VC in South Africa served every day of the Boer War from August 11, 1899 to May 31, 1902. William Henry Snyder Nickerson of the Royal Army Medical Corps was attached to the Mounted Infantry when the British assaulted Bwab's Hill. At nearby Wahkersteroom, a trooper from the Worcestershire Regiment had been wounded — his stomach had been ripped open, his entrails protruding — and lay exposed in the open. The Boers were concentrating their fire on that very spot to prevent reinforcements from coming up to support the Mounted Infantry. The wounded soldier could not be moved and stretcher-bearers were unable to reach him until the fire slackened.

That evening, during an assault by infantry to assist the mounted troops, Nickerson went forward and under heavy shell and rifle fire stitched up the man's stomach and stayed with him until he could be moved to safety. For this act of bravery, Nickerson was awarded the VC and was also Mentioned-in-Dispatches.

The son of a British army chaplain, Nickerson was born in St. John's, N.B. on March 27, 1875. He received his education at Portsmouth Grammar School and his medical training at Owens College, Manchester University in England. He enlisted in the RAMC on July 27, 1898 as a lieutenant and subsequently was promoted to the rank of captain. In 1909, he became a major, and in World War I served with the cavalry in Europe and Salonika where he was three times Mentioned-in-Dispatches. In the latter part of the war, he served as assistant surgeon of the Second Division. Nickerson was later attached to

Liliefontein gun on display at the Canadian War Museum

the Scots Guards in the London District and then the Horse Guards at Whitehall. He died on April 10, 1954 and was buried at Cours, Kintyre in Argyll, Scotland.

The second Canadian VC of the war, an English immigrant, was a former North-West Mounted policeman. Arthur Herbert Lindsay Richardson of the Lord Strathcona's Horse also became the first colonial to be gazetted for the decoration in that conflict. In one of the most daring feats of the entire war, Richardson, who was weak with fever at the time, rescued one of his comrades in the face of relentless enemy fire, keeping him from being crushed to death when his horse fell on him.

This deed took place on July 5, 1900, at Wolve Spruit where a party of thirty-eight Strathconas became engaged with an enemy force that outnumbered them two-to-one. After a brief skirmish, the Strathconas were forced to retire. But Alex Mcarthur (so spelled in *Canada's Sons on Kopje and Veldt*) was shot in the arm and leg. Then his horse, which was also wounded, stumbled and fell on top of him. Richardson wheeled around to within 300 yards of the Boers who kept up a steady fire, dismounted and pulled his comrade out from under his disabled steed. And although Richardson's horse was hit by rifle fire, he managed to mount and hold Mcarthur across his saddle and ride back to camp, so saving his life.

Born in Southport, England, Richardson was brought up in Liverpool. When he was twenty-one years old, he came to Canada where he worked as a rancher prior to joining the North-West Mounted Police. (A letter from the assistant adjutant of the RCMP, on March 3, 1970 to Dick Malott, still a major in the Canadian Forces but later to be the chief curator of collections for the Canadian War Museum in Ottawa, stated that Richardson's "previous occupation was shown as a dentist." This hardly seems credible, but it is no more strange than the mystery and circumstances surrounding his life later on.) At the outbreak of war, he took "leave" from the force to join the Canadian army.

After the war, Richardson returned to serve with the Mounties, but in 1907 was forced to retire due to poor health and was made town constable of Indian Head, Sask. However, for both financial and health reasons, he lost that job and for some time depended on the welfare of the townsfolk. During this time he married and had a daughter.

In 1908, he returned to Liverpool. That much is known as fact, but the next sixteen years of his life are clouded in mystery. Apparently his wife died around 1910. The *Liverpool Post and Mercury* of December 16, 1932 described Richardson as the "Shy V.C." and reported that he had worked as "a tramway ganger, cinema attendant and so on, unknown to his relatives who believed him to be dead." That a message to that effect had been sent to his mother from a nurse in Montreal only deepens the mystery. Apparently Richardson again fell on hard times and went into seclusion until 1924 when, as the newspaper report continues, "There was a happy reunion between the long-lost V.C. and his mother and eldest brother." Richardson later found employment with the Edge-lane tram depot as a foreman.

Although Richardson preferred seclusion, a namesake had been impersonating him in Scotland, where he was fêted and honoured wherever he went. This imposter even had the effrontery to attend a garden party for VC holders hosted by King George V at Buckingham Palace. His role as a fake was not discovered until after the real Arthur Richardson VC died in Millroad Hospital, Liverpool, was buried with full military honours on December 15, 1923.

THE other three Canadian Victoria Cross winners in the South African War were Hampden Zane Churchill Cockburn, Edward James Gibson Holland and Richard Ernest William Turner, native sons all and all serving with the Royal Canadian Dragoons (RCDs) during the Battle of Liliefontein on November 7, 1900. The part played by the RCDs in which three VCs were won was a rearguard action on the Komati River to prevent the Boers from seizing two 12-pounder guns, the ammunition for which they had captured some days earlier. This was the only full-scale cavalry charge the Boers ever mounted, involving 1,200 troops.

When the attack began, Dick Turner ordered his troops to dismount and hold the line with the exhortation, "Never let it be said Canadians let their guns be taken." It never was. The main body of Boers went straight for him, wounding him in the neck and badly shattering one arm. As the Boers veered off to go after Eddie Holland, who was in charge of the Colt machine gun on the Dragoons' left flank, Turner stayed his ground until the artillery could be pulled away.

Holland's horse was blown right out from under him. Stooping, he disconnected the barrel of the Colt and staggered off towards a gun carriage that was pulling away. Someone shouted, "Wait for Eddie Holland!" One of the gunners jumped down from his seat, ran to Holland, heaved him aboard, then ran alongside the gun as the driver drove off. Holland's hands were a mess — the barrel had been almost white-hot when he dismantled it.

When the Boers reached the position, at first they thought they'd captured the gun, but when they saw that the barrel was missing they became so infuriated they set fire to the carriage.

Though the enemy came within seventy yards' range, Hampden Cockburn and his party deliberately sacrificed themselves by standing their ground to allow the artillery to get away. Cockburn was badly wounded and most of his men were killed or taken prisoner.

Cockburn was born in Toronto on November 19, 1867 and was educated at Upper Canada College, as well as Rugby School and London University in England, and the University of Toronto. At war's outbreak, he had a law practice which he promptly gave up to enlist in the Canadian Mounted Rifles, later incorporated into the RCDs. During the Boer campaign, he took part in forty-five different engagements, and in addition to winning the VC, earned the Queen's South African medal with clasps for Cape Colony, Diamond Hill, Johannesburg and Orange Free State.

Cockburn was invested with the VC in Toronto on October 11, 1901 by the Duke of York and Cornwall, and on the same occasion was presented with a sword of honour voted to him by the city council. In recognition of his services, he was appointed a major in the Governor General's Bodyguard. He later moved to Western Canada and on July 13, 1913 was killed in a riding accident on his ranch at Maple Creek, Sask. Under the terms of his will, his VC along with his sword are displayed in the lobby of the main entrance to Upper Canada College.

Edward Holland was born in Ottawa on February 2, 1878 and received his education at the Model School and the Ottawa Collegiate Institute. At age seventeen, he joined the militia and served with the 43rd Regiment and the 59th Princess Louise Dragoon Guards from 1895 to 1897. In 1899, he served with the 1st Canadian Mounted Rifles Battalion (later part of the RCDs). In 1901, he was granted a commission in the Princess Louise

Richard Turner, The Royal Canadian Dragoons

Dragoon Guards and became a full lieutenant the following year. In addition to winning the VC, Holland's service in South Africa earned him the Queen's Medal with clasps for Belfast, Cape Colony, Diamond Hill, Johannesburg and the Transvaal.

In 1904, he became a major in the 13th Scottish Light Dragoons, and in 1914 was given command of the Borden Motor Machine-gun Battery which he took to France on September 14 of the following year. In October of 1916, he returned to Canada and was transferred to the Corps Reserve. After retiring from the army at the end of World War I, in 1932 he became postmaster of Cobalt, Ont. where he died on June 18, 1948 at age seventy.

On October 19, 1969, a memorial plaque was unveiled on the grounds of Trafalgar House, the headquarters of the Ottawa Branch of the Canadian Legion on Argyle Street. Holland's Victoria Cross and medals are in the custody of the Base Museum (RCDs) at the Canadian Forces Base, Gagetown, New Brunswick.

Dick Turner had one of the most distinguished and most remarkable careers of any Canadian. A native of Quebec City, he was born on July 25, 1871 and attended Quebec High School as well as a private school before joining his father in the family wholesale grocery business. An ardent horseman, he showed an early interest in soldiering and in 1892 joined the militia as a 2nd lieutenant in the Queen's Own Canadian Hussars (QOCH). By 1895, he held the rank of captain. In 1900, when the Special Force was organized for service in South Africa, Turner joined the Canadian Mounted Rifles, later amalgamated into the RCDs.

During the Boer War, in addition to winning the VC he was also awarded the Distinguished Service Order as well as earning the Queen's Medal with clasps for Belfast, Cape Colony, Orange Free State and South Africa. Just before sailing for South Africa, Turner married a young Englishwoman, Hettie Goodday, and they later had three children.

Turner was given a hero's welcome on his return to Quebec City, and on September 17, 1901, on the Plains of Abraham, received his VC, a sword of honour and an engraved sterling silver tray, subscribed by the citizens of Quebec, from the Duke of York and Cornwall. His military career subsequent to the Boer War was just as impressive.

In 1902, by which time he had reached the rank of lieutenant-colonel, he commanded the Mounted Wing of the Coronation detachment. In 1905, he was given command of his old regiment, the QOCH. From 1907 to 1912, he was brigade commander of the 3rd Eastern Townships Cavalry Brigade, and in June 1914, just prior to the start of World War I, was promoted to full colonel. When the conflict broke out in August, Turner was appointed commander of the 3rd Infantry Brigade. On September 29, he was again promoted, this time to the rank of brigadier-general.

In April of 1915, Turner played a key role in the desperate Second Battle of Ypres when, as British prime minister Lloyd George said, "The Canadians saved the British Army!" The Canadian Division had been sent forward to help in holding the dangerous Ypres salient which jutted out like a sea cape in the Allied line stretching from Switzerland to the English Channel. The Canadians occupied the centre sector. On the 22nd, in an effort to break the stalemate and force their way to the Channel ports, the Germans unleashed 160 tons of poison chlorine gas into a light east wind. The French defenses on the left flank crumbled and their troops fled. That left a gap in the line. The Canadians attacked and tried to close it. Two days later the Germans launched another gas attack, but the Canadians held. Turner had been in the midst of the action, and to prevent the Germans from cutting around behind his brigade through the gap he had to bend his line almost as far back as St. Julien, nearly a mile away. All through the night the Canadians fought desperately to keep the Germans at bay until dawn the following morning when a British detachment finally arrived to close the gap.

On August 17, Turner was given command of the Second Canadian Division and promoted to temporary major-general. For a short period in 1916 he was made temporary commander of the Canadian Corps, and that December he took command of Canadian forces in the British Isles. On June 14, 1917, he received a knighthood and a year later was elevated to the rank of lieutenant-general. In May 1918, he was appointed Chief of the General Staff, Overseas Military Forces of Canada. By this time his decorations included six Mentions-in-Dispatches, the French Legion D'Honneur (Croix Commander), Croix de Guerre avec Palme and the Russian Order of White Eagles.

On November 22, 1919, Turner was struck off strength from the Canadian Expeditionary Force. After being transferred to the reserves, he returned to the family business in Quebec City. However, he also continued to serve the country in a variety of capacities. He was honourary colonel of several regiments and took an enthusiastic interest and part in their activities. He was also one of the founders of the Canadian Legion of the British Empire Service League and, until his retirement on July 14, 1941, was a member of the Canadian Services Commission.

On June 19, 1961, Turner died at St. Foy Veterans Hospital in the city of his birth, at age ninety, and was buried in Mount Hermon Cemetery with full military honours. His VC, medals, sword and silver tray are proudly displayed at the CFB Gagetown Museum.

Chapter Five

NO NOBLER A NATION

MEASURED in terms of the valour that Albert, the Prince Consort, insisted be inscribed on the face of the Victoria Cross, Canadians took second place to none in the Great War. Between August 1914 and November 1918, seventy Canadian VCs were awarded, an incredible achievement for a country with a population of less than 10 million at the time, one that fielded nearly a tenth of its manhood into battle.

Of those seventy Canadians who were awarded the Victoria Cross, twenty-nine were born Canada, seventeen in England, nine in Scotland, seven in Ireland, four in the United States, two in Newfoundland (which joined Confederation in 1949), and one in each of Denmark and Russia. All but one served with Canadian units and his is a case in point.

Michael O'Leary, the first Canadian VC of the conflict, was born in Ireland. Before the war, O'Leary came to Canada and joined the North-West Mounted Police. When he rejoined the Irish Guards, with which he earned his VC, he was given leave from the NWMP while officially still on strength. It is a moot point, perhaps, but since he was still technically serving as a Canadian law officer at the time he won his decoration, surely this classifies him as a Canadian VC. Also, O'Leary was among the seventeen VC winners who were born outside of Canada but settled here after the war ended. Although he eventually returned to his native Ireland, O'Leary considered himself to be a Canadian.

Of the twenty-nine Canadian-born VCs, eleven hailed from Ontario, six from Quebec, six from Manitoba, three from Nova Scotia and three from New Brunswick.

The Canadian VC record in individual battles in World War I is impressive. Four were awarded for bravery in the Second Battle of Ypres, four at Vimy Ridge, six in the struggle for Hill 70 and eight at Passchendaele. During Canada's 100 Days, the final assault of the war, twenty-nine Canadian VCs were awarded.

Twenty of the Canadian VCs in the Great War were killed in action, the first being Frederick William Hall on April 24, 1915, during the Second Battle of Ypres. Five died of wounds the next day and one sixteen days later.

Villagers admiring Michael O'Leary's VC

Chapter Six

"MICK"

... and then one day the world rang with the story of Michael O'Leary's great exploit and we knew that the age of heroes was not yet past.

Deeds that Thrill the Empire

AT the time very few Canadians, if any at all, had even heard of the feat of their first VC in the Great War. In fact no one, save the few who served with him in the NWMP, even knew his name. But in the British Isles, from the moment his award of "the Victoria Cross for conspicuous bravery at Cuinchy on February 1, 1915" appeared in the *London Gazette* two weeks after that action, his fame spread far and wide. The press hailed it as "The greatest deed of the war." Poems were written about him. A song was published, balladeering his glory, and his wax effigy was given a place of stature at Madame Tussaud's.

Few merited the adulation more or were as endowed to accomplish the action that brought it about. Born at Inchigeela near Macroom in County Cork, Southern Ireland on September 29, 1889, Michael John O'Leary was the son of a well-known local athlete who starred at football and won prizes for weightlifting. His father was also admired as a battler for his principles. A fierce nationalist, he was once reported to have beaten off fifty men during a political altercation. The younger O'Leary — "Mick" — joined the Royal Navy at an early age, but was invalided out with rheumatism. However, he recovered sufficiently to be accepted in the Irish Guards.

In August 1913, O'Leary came to Canada and joined the NWMP. On one occasion, he tackled a pair of cutthroat store-robbers in a tussle that lasted two hours before he could subdue them. For his pains, he was presented with a gold ring, a trophy he treasured and wore for the rest of his life.

When the First World War broke out, O'Leary took leave from the NWMP, returned to England, and rejoined the 1st Battalion of the Irish Guards which was immediately sent to France. There, as a lance corporal, O'Leary quickly showed his mettle as a soldier; in November he was Mentioned-in-Dispatches.

After the British and French had stopped the Germans on the Marne in September, both sides began to dig in for a long siege in the trenches that would last for a bitter, bloody four years. By January 1915, the Irish and Coldstream Guard regiments found themselves positioned at Cuinchy, a small village in the dull and dreary countryside which lies south of the Béthune–La Bassée Canal in northeast France. On the last day of the month, in an attempt to force their way through to Calais on the English Channel, the Germans attacked and took possession of the trenches adjacent to the Irish Guards. To stop the enemy from advancing further, and to re-establish the British line, it was critical that those positions be quickly retaken.

In fine, clear weather, early the next morning of February 1, the British opened their assault with a heavy artillery barrage that rained shells and shrapnel on the enemy-held trenches and the area behind them, cutting off all means of escape. Any German who dared show himself above the parapets had his head blown off by the supporting rifle fire. Once the bombardment stopped, the Coldstream Guards swarmed over the top, bayonets fixed, yelling for blood at the top of their voices.

The Germans, virtually trapped, fought back savagely, mowing down many a guardsman with furious fusillades of return fire. When the turn of the Irish came, O'Leary simply ignored the danger. He had decided that the crux of the enemy defense was a machine gun. Because it was not firing, he calculated that it had probably been dismantled during the shelling and was being moved. Having figured out exactly where that spot had to be, his objective was now to neutralize it before it could be put into action and threaten to hold up the Guards' attack.

Charging well ahead of the section he was leading, within seconds he found himself alone in the corner of a trench facing a barricade with five spike-helmeted Germans standing in his way. O'Leary quickly finished them off with five shots from his rifle. A second barricade stood only eighty yards away, but a patch of swampy ground prevented him from assaulting it directly. He had to detour around some railway tracks. Meanwhile, the Germans were feverishly trying to remount their machine gun and put it into action.

O'Leary's attack came just in time. A few yards to the right, he took aim on the officer in charge of the four-man crew. Snapping off three rapid rounds, he dropped him and two others. The remaining pair, thankful still to be alive, threw their hands up in surrender. When he marched his prisoners back to the Irish Guards' trenches, his company quartermaster-sergeant was astounded at how calm he seemed after his exploit. He looked, he said, "As cool as if he had been for a walk in the park."

In the citation, the *London Gazette* applauded the action with the comment: "Thus Lance Corporal O'Leary practically captured the enemy's position by himself." O'Leary's own description was laconic — perhaps modest is a better term — by comparison. "I took some men," he reported, "up to a very important position of theirs [the Huns] and took it from them, capturing their machine gun and killing some of their gunners, and taking a few prisoners. The Huns lost terribly. We had only a few casualties." O'Leary was promoted to sergeant on the spot and that same year was Mentioned-in-Dispatches for a second time. Later, he was commissioned as a 2nd lieutenant in the Connaught Rangers and was awarded the Russian Cross of St. George.

O'Leary received his VC from King George V on December 15, 1917 at Buckingham Palace. Following his investiture he returned home to Macroom where he was greeted with bands — "Bands! I don't want bands" — and fêted with a hero's welcome. When his father Daniel was asked by a reporter if he was surprised at his son's bravery, he responded: "I am surprised he didn't do more. I often laid out twenty men myself with a stick

Canadian troops in the trenches taking their rest before the next assault.

coming from the Macroom Fair, and it is a bad trial of Mick that he could kill only eight, and he having a rifle and bayonet."

Following the war, after being demobilized, O'Leary returned to Canada in 1921. In September, he joined the Ontario Provincial Police and was stationed in Welland, Ont. Shortly afterwards he brought his wife Greta and their twin sons out from England. In 1923, he was appointed sergeant with the Bridgeburg Police (Ont.); a year later, he moved to the United States where he joined the Michigan Railroad Police.

In 1931, he returned to Ireland and afterwards took a job with the Mayfair Hotel in London's West End. In the Second World War he joined up again, serving with the Middlesex Regiment and the Pioneer Corps before being invalided out just prior to the war's end.

In 1945, O'Leary went into the building trade as a contractor in London, retiring in 1954. He wife predeceased him in 1953. On August 2, 1961, Mick O'Leary succumbed to a lengthy illness and died in Whittingdon Hospital at age seventy-two. He was buried at Paddington Cemetery, Mill Hill. His Victoria Cross was presented by the family to the Irish Guards on loan.

Chapter Seven

A MAGNIFICENT DISPLAY

*In spite of the danger to which they were
exposed, the Canadians held their ground
with a magnificent display of
tenacity and courage ...*

Sir John French
Commander
British Expeditionary Force

THE Second Battle of Ypres marked the
first time the First Canadian Division
had been bloodied in battle. In March 1915,
at Neuve Chapelle, Canadian guns had taken
part and the Princess Patricia's Canadian
Light Infantry had gone into action at St.
Eloi. But it was not until April that the
Canadian infantry came to grips with the
enemy, and in an action that set the tone
for the war. In the face of two German poison gas attacks that left the line open for a
possible enemy thrust towards the Channel
ports, the Canadians closed the gap and
held on until reinforcements arrived.

During the five-day encounter between
April 22 and 26, Canadians won four VCs,
two posthumously and two on the same
day. Two of the recipients were Canadian-
born Frederick Fisher and Francis
Alexander Caron Scrimger. The other two,
Edward Donald Bellew and Frederick
William Hall, hailed from Bombay, India
and Kilkenny, Ireland respectively.

This represented as fascinating an
assortment of potential gallantry to be
found anywhere. Fisher and Bellew were
outstanding athletes and both were engi-

neers. Scrimger was a doctor and became the first medical officer to win a VC in the Canadian army. Little is known of Hall's background except that when he moved to Canada before the war he was employed with a firm in Winnipeg. But from all accounts he appears to have been a very determined individual. As an employee with the British Columbia Works Department, Bellew was the only Canadian civil servant ever to fight on the Western Front.

"Hard as nails" is the way the 1909 *Westmount Academy Yearbook* characterized "Bud" Fisher. It applied to his prowess as captain of the school football team, but it could well have described him as a soldier. He proved to be as rugged on the battlefield as he was on the gridiron. Fisher was born in St. Catharines on August 3, 1894, the son of a banker. In 1907, his family moved to Montreal and upon graduating from Westmount Academy, he entered McGill University to study mining engineering. There he starred in athletics and, with the outbreak of war, joined the Royal Highlanders (in 1934 renamed the Black Watch) at Valcartier, Quebec. By December, he held the rank of lance-corporal.

Fred Hall was born in Kilkenny on February 21, 1885. In 1914, he enlisted in the 10th Battalion before transferring to the 8th Battalion (90th Winnipeg Rifles), known as the "Little Black Devils" with which he went to France with the rank of sergeant-major. From all accounts he was a tough nut.

The third generation of his family to serve in the British army, Edward Bellew was born at Malabar Hill in Bombay on October 28, 1882. Educated in England at Blondell's School in Twerton, Clifton College at Bristol, and the Royal Military College, he excelled at sports as a heavyweight boxer and rugby player. In May 1901, he joined the 18th Royal Irish Regiment and he married Charlotte Muriel Rees that same year. Bellew then resigned from the regiment with the rank of lieutenant and moved to British Columbia where he worked as a harbour construction engineer in New Westminster. In 1914, he enlisted in the British Columbia Regiment, 7th Canadian Infantry Battalion, with which he went overseas.

Alex Scrimger was born in Montreal on February 10, 1881, the son of a minister who was the principal of the Presbyterian College. Educated at Montreal High School, he received his M.D. from McGill University in 1905, then took post-graduate studies in

"The Rescue" - Frederick Hall, 8th Battalion

Fred Fisher, 13th Battalion

Europe. Prior to the war, he was medical officer (MO) for the Montreal Heavy Brigade. When hostilities broke out, he joined the 14th Battalion, Royal Montreal Regiment to become its first MO and was rapidly promoted to the rank of captain. Scrimger came from noble stock and wore a noble bearing. He was the only one of his family to bear the ancestral name of Alexander Caron who, under Alexander II of Scotland, in a critical battle during the 13th century, carried the King's Standard across a ford in an action that won the day for his king. His reward for himself and his descendants was the entitlement of the honour and office, in perpetuity, of Standard Bearer of Scotland and bestowal, by Scottish royal assent, of the name Skirmisher (Scrymgeour or Scrimger), meaning "Hardy Fighter." Also awarded was the special privilege of bearing and wearing the Scottish Coat of Arms reversed. At Ypres, in an oblique way, it might be said that, in Scrimger's case, history repeated itself.

When the German attack on the Salient started on April 22, Bud Fisher was fresh out of hospital after recuperating from a wound suffered some days earlier. A member of the 13th Battalion, Royal Highlanders machine-gun section — "The Suicide Club" — he was positioned in reserve at the small Belgian village of St. Julien near battalion headquarters, two miles behind the front lines. His commanding officer wanted him to go easy. That was hardly Fisher's style.

Next day, a battery of two Canadian 18-pounder guns came under heavy assault and was in imminent danger of being overrun. When a covering party was ordered out to protect its withdrawal, Fisher insisted on getting into the act. With six men, he set up his Colt in front of the battery. With the help of some support troops, he held off the Germans with his fire until the battery was withdrawn. But during the encounter, four of Fisher's men were cut down.

Fisher returned to St. Julien where he recruited four more men from the 14th Battalion and went forward again to help secure the unit's position. But en route, the members of his entire troop were either killed or wounded and Fisher reached the front line alone. He set up his machine gun and began spraying the attackers until, with his finger still on the trigger, a bullet struck him in the chest, killing him instantly.

That night, Fred Hall's 8th Battalion, 90th Winnipeg Rifles, was dispatched to the front-line trenches to relieve the 15th which had suffered heavy casualties in the first gas attack. To do so, the relieving troops had to cross a high stretch of ground that the Germans illuminated with flares, exposing them to merciless rifle fire. In the resulting confusion, many Canadians were mowed down, wounded or killed.

After reaching the trenches, Hall discovered that two of the men from his company were missing. Without hesitating, he twice crawled out of the trench under cover of darkness to rescue the wounded men from the bullet-swept crest and carried them to safety. At nine o'clock the following morning, April 24, the sound of groaning could be heard from somewhere over the embankment. Hall quickly organized a rescue and with two others, in broad daylight, climbed over the parados — an earth-packed rear fortification of the trench — instantly drawing heavy enemy fire. Both of his comrades were wounded, but with Hall's help were able to crawl back to the safety of the dugout.

After a few minutes' rest, Hall decided to attempt the rescue again, this time by himself. As he

An illustration of a parados, an elevation of earth behind fortifications to secure them from attack from the rear.

climbed back out of the trench, the German rifle fire had intensified horribly, hellishly low and accurate. Bullets ricocheted off the top of the parados. Nonetheless, Hall miraculously reached the spot on the slope of the hillock where the wounded man lay, so badly crippled he was unable to move. Hall squirmed under the inert body and with Herculean effort managed to hoist the man onto his back.

As he began to crawl towards the trench, he raised his head to check his direction. At that very moment a bullet struck him right between his eyes. Seconds later, the man to whom he had given his life to save was also killed.

That same morning, the Germans launched their second attack on the Allied line, once again using poison gas. During the assault, Edward Bellew, the British Columbia Regiment's 7th Battalion machine-gun officer, had two guns operating on the high ground overlooking Keerdelaere. The battalion was besieged on both its front and right flanks. Exposed by a gap in the line, the gun on the right flank was quickly put out of action. Bellew managed to ward off the assault temporarily until reinforcements arrived, but they were quickly surrounded and killed. With the Germans a mere hundred yards away, Bellew and one other gunner decided to stay and fight it out, and together they kept on firing.

Then his comrade was killed, and Bellew himself was wounded. Bellew kept on firing until his ammunition ran out. With the enemy literally on top of him, he seized a rifle, smashed his machine gun and kept on battling until he was overcome and taken prisoner.

On the following afternoon, a farm-house at Wieltje, two miles north of Ypres, which served as Alex Scrimger's first-aid dressing station, became the target for German artillery and was quickly set on fire. The single road running by the farmhouse was made impassable due to deadly shrapnel from German shelling. The only way the wounded could be moved to safety was by swimming a moat that surrounded the building. With the help of the army medical staff, the patients were helped across a ditch away from the path of the barrage. One soldier, however, Harold McDonald, had been wounded so badly in the head and shoulder he was unable to move. Scrimger had to carry him.

"Captain Scrimger carried me down to a moat fifty feet in front," McDonald later recalled, "where we lay half in the water. Captain Scrimger curled himself round my wounded head and shoulder to protect me from the heavy shell fire, at obvious peril to his own life. He stayed with me all that

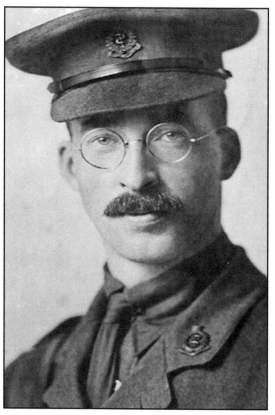

Francis Scrimger, Canadian Army Medical Corps, 14th Battalion

time and by good luck was not hit. At length when the fire slackened, he went after some stretcher-bearers and had me carried to the dressing station. This, however, was only one of many incidents of Captain Scrimger's heroism in those awful three (sic) days. No man better deserves the soldier's highest honour."

CANADA's first posthumous VCs, Bud Fisher and Fred Hall, have no known graves but their names are etched in the Menin Gate Memorial at Ypres. In a letter to Fisher's parents, an officer of the 13th Battalion advised that his body was buried close to what was then the village of Poelcapelle not far from Ypres. He also told them that, had he lived, he would have been commissioned a 2nd lieutenant.

On May 1, 1917, a memorial tablet was unveiled in his honour at the Royal Highlanders of Canada Armouries on Bleury Street in Montreal. Later, on June 12, a memorial service was held at the Church of St. James the Apostle. On June 18, 1970, an Ontario provincial historical plaque was unveiled at Memorial Park in St. Catharines.

Fred Bellew did not learn of his award of the VC until he read an announcement in a Vancouver paper after he had been released as a prisoner of war in 1919. On his return to British Columbia, he became a dredging inspector for the Department of Public Works on the Fraser River before going into semi-retirement on a ranch at Monte Creek, east of Kamloops. In 1974, thirteen years after he died in a Vancouver hospital on February 1, 1961, his Victoria Cross went on the block at Sotheby's in London. The going price at the time was $5,000, but there were no government funds available to put in a bid. However, it was rescued from the hands of collectors by the Ontario mining czar and patriot, Stephen Roman, who bought it and presented it to the Royal Canadian Military Institute in Toronto. It was subsequently stolen and has never been recovered (by no means an isolated case).

In 1975, three VCs were stolen from the Manchester Art Galleries in England. Reginald Geary, an Englishman who won the VC but later came to Canada to live, died in Toronto in 1977. At the time of his funeral, his VC and medals, which had been pinned to a cushion beside his coffin, went missing. His daughter thought that her brother had taken it for safekeeping, and he in turn thought his sister had taken it. They were devastated. The Victoria Cross had simply disappeared.

In October of 1994, when I was in the process of researching the files on Canada's VCs at the Canadian War Museum in Ottawa, a gentleman who was a friend of Dan Glenney, chief of Public Programs for the Canadian War Museum, turned up with the missing Victoria Cross and medals. A friend of his, he said, had had it in his attic all these seventeen years. The only purpose that it had served was when one of his children took it to school to show it off. In appreciation for the Museum's contribution in restoring the Geary VC and medals to the family, a grateful Geary family donated the VC and medals to the Museum. Perhaps the RCMI will be as lucky.

Alex Scrimger was subsequently wounded himself and invalided back to England. After recuperating, he served on the staff of the Canadian Army Hospital at Ramsgate and also worked as a consultant surgeon to several English military hospitals. He received his VC from King George V at Buckingham Palace on July 21, 1915. Promoted to major, he returned to join the staff of the No. 3 Canadian Casualty Station at Boulogne in France. Later, he was promoted to lieutenant-colonel and became chief surgeon of the unit. On September 5, 1918, he married Ellen Emerson Carpenter.

Following the war, Scrimger returned to Montreal as assistant surgeon at the Royal Victoria Hospital. In 1936 he was made surgeon-in-chief. He died the following year on February 13, 1937.

A detail from "The Battle of Second Ypres"

Chapter Eight

ON HIS FORTY-SEVENTH BIRTHDAY

DURING the War of 1812, Frederick William Campbell's great-grandfather had distinguished himself, under Sir Isaac Brock, in helping to repel the American invaders. It followed that his great-grandson came by his military prowess quite honestly. He was destined to live up to that proud family tradition — and then some.

Born in Mount Forest, Wellington County, Ont. on June 15, 1867, Campbell and his parents later that year moved to a farm at Gleneden in Grey County where he was raised. Campbell attended school in Mount Forest and exhibited an interest in the military at an early age. In 1885, when he reached eighteen, he joined the local militia, the 30th Battalion Wellington Rifles.

Fourteen years later, when Britain went to war against the Boers, Campbell enlisted in the South African contingent and went overseas with the Royal Canadian Regiment. There, as a member of a Maxim machine-gun squad, a vocation at which he became expert, he fought in the battles of Johannesburg, Drenfontein, Paardeberg and Cape Colony, and was awarded the Queen's South African Medal with four clasps. He also received special mention for a feat in which he exhibited his extraordinary proclivity for innovation.

At the Modder River, the spokes of one of the wheels of his gun carriage were shot away by a shell. Rather than abandon the carriage, he replaced the damaged spokes with legs from a table that he took from a captured enemy house. That very wheel is presently on exhibit at the Citadel in Quebec City and to all intents stands as a monument to both Campbell and his ingenuity.

In 1900, Campbell returned home with the rank of sergeant, bought a farm next to his father's, and made a specialty of raising horses. In 1902, he married Margaret Annie McGillivray of Mount Forest and they had three children. Campbell became a public school trustee and a director of the Mount Forest Agricultural Society. He also remained a member of the militia, serving with the 30th Wellington Battalion. On August 4, 1914, when Great Britain declared war on Germany, he held the rank of captain. It didn't take the old warhorse long to answer the call to arms.

Campbell immediately went to the Wellington regimental headquarters in Guelph and gained permission to begin recruiting in the Mount Forest area. On April 17, with a dozen other volunteers, he entrained for Valcartier in Quebec where the group was assigned to the 1st Battalion of the 1st Brigade. Because of his record of service, Campbell was given the rank of lieutenant. By the time the first contingent of the Canadian Expeditionary Force sailed for England on September 24, he had been made the battalion's officer-in-command of the machine-gun section and was promoted to the rank of temporary captain. After a miserable winter on Salisbury Plain, in February 1915 the Canadians found themselves in France.

The 1st Battalion received its baptism of fire at the Second Battle of Ypres, although it had been in reserve at the beginning of the gas attack. After that bitter and fearful struggle, the war on the British sector of the Western Front degenerated into a stalemate with sporadic frontal attacks against both sides and no result except appalling casualties.

The British – and the Canadians – suffered more dead and wounded than the Germans, and this was entirely due to lack of sufficient artillery support caused by a shortage of ammunition. Once over the top, without cannon cover and held up by intricate barbed-wire entanglements, the infantry was at the mercy of enemy machine gunners who could cut them down like wheat in a hail storm.

When the press broke this news in England, it precipitated a public outcry that was to have far-reaching ramifications. Already angered by the heavy casualty lists and failure of the spring offensives, Britons demanded an industrial reorganization that would increase the production of guns and munitions. Out of this exigency emerged the British coalition government and the pooling of English and French interests, as well as the placing of the armies under a single supreme command.

All that lay well into the future, but in the meantime on the battlefield in the summer of 1915, the massacre of British and Canadian troops continued. On June 15, the Battle of Givenchy, though an isolated one, was symptomatic of the combat conditions that had brought the crisis about. Fought near the little French town of Givenchy, a few miles west of La Bassée, Canadian losses in that one day amounted to a horrific 400 casualties. In one battalion alone, out of twenty-three officers only three escaped being either killed or injured.

At ten minutes past six in the evening, the Canadian 1st Brigade attacked in support of the British 7th Division. Though the Canadians reached the front-line trench, they were unable to hold their position for long due to their flanks being exposed. In the second wave, Frederick Campbell, who started from the "jumping-off" trench, set out with two machine-gun crews. However, in the dash across No-Man's Land, one crew was wiped out. Only Campbell and Harold Vincent, a sturdy lumberjack from Bracebridge, Ont., reached the captured trench.

Frederick Campbell, 1st Battalion

As an enemy counterattack developed, the survivors of the charge soon ran out of grenades. Campbell ordered them to retire and decided to set up his Colt to cover their retreat. However, the tripod stand had been lost in the race over open ground, and no suitable base could be found, so Vincent offered to support the machine gun on his back.

In this fashion, they were able to hold off the Germans temporarily with Campbell firing off 1,000 rounds of ammunition. Then he took a bullet in his right thigh near the hip joint and could no longer continue. Vincent, badly burned from the heat of the gun, managed to drag the weapon back to his own lines. Campbell crawled back and was rescued by stretcher-bearers. With his irrepressible cheeriness, Frederick Campbell might well have admitted that it had been one hell of a way to celebrate his forty-seventh birthday.

Two days later, they moved Campbell to No. 7 Stationary Hospital at Boulogne. His wound began to heal, but the infection that set in weakened him, and at noon on June 19 he went into a coma from which he never recovered. The doughty old warrior died three hours later of heart failure. He was buried in the Boulogne Easter Cemetery overlooking the English Channel.

Campbell became the first Canadian farmer-to-be to win the VC and the third Canadian to whom it was awarded posthumously. On July 20, 1965 a plaque commemorating Frederick Campbell was unveiled on the grounds of the Royal Canadian Legion Hall in Mount Forest. His daughter, Mrs. V.S. de Vore, did the honours.

Chapter Nine

CANADIAN VCS AT THE SOMME

The Canadians played a part of such distinction that thenceforward they were marked out as storm troops.... Whenever the Germans found the Canadian Corps coming into the line they prepared for the worst.

David Lloyd George, British Prime Minister

BY September 1916, the four Canadian divisions in France were firmly entrenched on the Somme where the British offensive had shifted from the Flanders front. The Corps' first main action was the Battle of Courcelette. In the build-up to it, and during the battle itself, two Canadians fought so spectacularly that they earned the Victoria Cross.

The first was Lionel Beaumaurice Clarke, known to his boyhood friends in Winnipeg, Man. where he went to school as "Nobby." To his comrades-in-arms of the 27th Battalion and later the 2nd — to which he transferred to be near his brother Charlie — he was called "Leo." Clarke won his VC for single-handedly killing eighteen of the enemy and taking one prisoner in an action in which he was wounded.

Clarke was no hero-come-lately; he came from a long line of soldiers and adventurers. His father, Henry Clarke, had travelled to Central Africa to meet with the renowned explorer Henry Stanley on a mission of mercy. His grandfather, Brian Clarke, a chaplain of the East India Company, became known as the "Fighting

Parson" during the Indian Mutiny. His great-grandfather, Alexander Clarke, whose picture hangs in the National Gallery in London, was one of the foremost explorers of his day.

Born in Waterdown, Ont. on December 1, 1892, Leo Clarke spent his early years in England, the homeland of his parents. When he was eleven years old, they returned to Canada to live in Winnipeg. There he attended Argyle and Gladstone schools. After graduation, he worked at a number of jobs and was surveying in northern Canada when war broke out.

The second Canadian VC at Courcelette also won the medal for a single-handed action in which, despite his wounds, he captured sixty-two of the enemy. He was a Nova Scotia lumberman and former Alberta homesteader named John Chipman Kerr, nicknamed "Chip" by members of his company, the 49th Canadian Infantry Battalion.

The objective of the assault was to overcome and occupy the elaborate chain of German redoubts extending from Courcelette to Martinpuich. The attack was planned for September 15. In the meantime, the way had to be paved for the advance.

By September 1, Clarke's 2nd Battalion, part of the Second Canadian Division, which had been moved from the battered Ypres sector, was securely ensconced in the trenches behind Mouquet Farm to the south of Courcelette. On arrival, they got a foretaste of what to expect when they came under heavy enemy artillery fire. Clarke's battalion had been chosen to secure a jutting salient of German trenches some fifty yards long, near the north end of what was called Walker Avenue. The protuberance in the line stabbed forward between the Canadians and Courcelette. Before the village could be attacked, the salient had first to be overcome in order to clear the way to the objective.

The assault began at a quarter to five on the afternoon of September 9. Only the first three companies of the battalion went over the top with fixed bayonets; the fourth was held in reserve. Although the charge had been preceded by the usual heavy artillery barrage, when the Canadians reached the enemy trench they found that the shelling had not reduced German resistance to the extent they had anticipated or hoped. It was still heavily defended.

Acting Corporal Clarke was detailed to take a section forward and clear out the Germans on the left flank. This would allow his

Leo Clarke, 2nd Battalion

company sergeant, Hugh Nichols, to build a "block" — a fortified dugout — that would secure the Canadians' advanced position once the salient was overrun. After Clarke and his men had completed their assignment, they were to join forces with Nichols in the hastily built redoubt.

Clarke reached the trench first, his men close on his heels. They found it so strongly garrisoned that they had to first throw hand grenades, bay by bay, and then force their way ahead by charging with their bayonets and using their rifles like clubs. But in this vicious hand-to-hand fighting they were badly outnumbered and, with their supply of grenades spent, Clarke found himself the only one of his troop who had not been killed or wounded.

Clarke knew it was essential to the success of the overall operation to play for time by holding off the Germans until Nichols, though wounded, could finish building his block. With his only weapon a revolver, as best he could he began erecting a barricade with one hand, his other holding his pistol to fend off the enemy. Meanwhile, a group of Germans including two officers, were cautiously making their way towards him.

When they reached him, the officers ordered their men to attack. But the soldiers, shattered by the Canadians' brazen attack earlier, hesitated. This reluctance was all the time Clarke needed to seize the initiative. He emptied his revolver at them and then picked up a discarded German rifle, exhausted its contents on the enemy, picked up another and continued firing.

Suddenly, in anger and frustration, one of the German officers grabbed a rifle out of the hands of one of his men and lunged forward, stabbing Clarke in the right leg with the bayonet just below the knee. As he did so, Clarke shot his assailant dead.

That left five Germans still standing. By this time, however, they'd become so totally unnerved that they turned tail and ran. In short order Clarke dropped four of them while the fifth shouted for mercy — in perfect English — and surrendered. Then Clarke calmly marched his prisoner over to Nichols who by then had completed building the block.

Altogether, Clarke had killed two enemy officers and sixteen other ranks. In addition to his leg wound, he had also suffered a slight injury to his back in the initial skirmish, though he scarcely noticed it. Although bleeding profusely, Clarke stayed at his post until ordered to a dressing station. At the same time, he was promoted to acting sergeant. Next day, however, he was back with his platoon. His entry in his diary at that time is laconic to say the least:

> Recommended for the Victoria Cross for killing twenty-two (sic) Germans, including two officers. Took the trench fairly easily. Shot and killed every German I saw with my revolver, being bayoneted by one of the officers, who I shot. Up before the Colonel who congratulated me.

Clarke's action had done more than just kill a few Germans. By routing them out he had allowed the permanent block to be built which was essential to securing the position the Canadians had overrun. It prepared the way for the attack on Courcelette a week later in which the second Canadian VC on the Somme was won.

AT 8.40 a.m. on September 15, preceded by a heavy artillery barrage, tanks — the first time these mechanical monsters had been introduced into battle — began rolling into Flers. They were the key factor in the success of the Battle of Courcelette. By nightfall, a sugar refinery, the village and strongholds to the left of the village were in Canadian hands.

The 49th Battalion had arrived at Albert two days earlier and forty hours later had taken up a position before and to the left of Courcelette. On the day of the start of the attack, the battalion, supported by the Princess Patricia's Canadian Light Infantry and the 42nd Battalion, advanced on a line to the left of the town, keeping abreast of the units assaulting and occupying the village. Their assignment was directed entirely to subjugating the trenches and trench machine-gun posts.

By evening, all objectives had been reached and the enemy trenches occupied along the line except for one 250-yard-long dugout. But from this there was no escape. The entrance to the adjoining trench that ran to the rear had been blocked by the shelling. The occupants were trapped. The Canadians decided to deal with it in daylight next day. Except for the occasional exchange of mortar fire, all was quiet overnight.

On the following afternoon Private Chip Kerr, who had been designated first bayonet-man, led a twelve-man hand-grenade attack on the redoubt. Charging well ahead of his party, he leapt into the far end of the trench and began slowly making his way forward. He had advanced about thirty yards when a sentry hurled a hand grenade at him. Kerr saw it coming and instinctively threw up his right hand to shield his face from the blast. That saved his eyesight, but the explosion blew off the upper joint of his forefinger and wounded him slightly in the side.

By this time the other members of his section had joined him in the trench and a free-for-all developed between the Canadians and Germans lobbing grenades at each other sight unseen around and over a corner of the trench. But the situation rapidly reached a stand-off and, with the supply of grenades running low, Kerr decided to take some action to break the stalemate.

Climbing out of the trench, he ran along the parados at the rear until he reached a spot where he could see the enemy below him. Though vulnerable, he was still armed with a rifle and two grenades. He tossed the bombs into the middle of the crowd of Germans, then opened fire on them with his carbine. Then the bolt jammed. Fortunately, his second-bayonet man, Frank Long, had at that moment joined him and Kerr borrowed his rifle and continued firing. At the same time, from his vantage point, he directed the bombing by his men so effectively that the Germans took shelter in the nearest bay.

Despite loss of blood from his wounded finger, Kerr was still very much full of fight. He jumped into the trench followed by the rest of his squad and chased after the enemy and cornered them. Thinking that they had been surrounded, all sixty-two of them threw up their hands in surrender to the twelve Canadians. Kerr and two others escorted the prisoners across open ground under heavy fire to a support trench; then Kerr reported for duty before having his wounds dressed.

LEO Clarke did not survive the war. On October 12, the 2nd Battalion was ordered forward to secure the newly captured Regina trench which was still under heavy enemy artillery fire. Late that morning, Clarke sat crouching in a hole at the rear of the trench when a shell exploded and the back of it caved in, burying him. His brother Charlie immediately went to work, feverishly digging into the pile of earth until he struck Leo's steel helmet with his shovel. He then scooped the dirt away from his brother's face with his bare hands. Leo looked up at him and smiled. It was a brave but futile gesture. He knew he was done for. He was paralyzed; the weight of the earth had crushed his back and injured his spine. Because the trench came under such heavy bombardment, Clarke could not be moved until after dark. At eight o'clock that evening, he was taken to a dressing station, then later was moved to No. 1 Hospital in Étretat, sixteen miles north of Le Havre. He died there on October 19 and was buried in the churchyard.

A letter from Buckingham Palace addressed to Clarke's father, dated February 8, 1917, and signed by King George V, read:

> It is a matter of sincere regret to me that the death of Private (Acting Corporal) Leo Clarke, 2nd Canadian Infantry Battalion, deprived me of the pride of personally conferring upon him the Victoria Cross, the greatest of all rewards for valour and devotion to duty.

In the spring of 1917, Clarke's VC was presented to his father by the Duke of Devonshire at a ceremony in Winnipeg attended by a crowd of 30,000. It marked the first time the medal had been presented in Canada and by the governor general.

In 1925, Pine Street in Winnipeg was renamed Valour Road in honour of the three Canadian VCs who once lived there, making it one of the most uniquely distinguished thoroughfares in the world. A bronze plaque mounted on an ornamental lamp at the intersection of the street and Portage Avenue commemorates the trio of Leo Clarke, Fred Hall and Robert Shankland, the only survivor of World War I of the three, about whose heroism we shall later learn. When in Winnipeg, it's worth a look.

In Leo Clarke's memory and honour, a historical plaque, erected by the Ontario Heritage Foundation, stands on the grounds of the Royal Canadian Legion at Hamilton Street in Waterdown.

ON February 5, 1917, King George V pinned the Victoria Cross to the left breast of Chip Kerr's khaki tunic at an investiture in Buckingham Palace. Although he was born in Fox River, N.S., it was Edmonton, Alta. that gave him a hero's welcome on August 6, 1918 when he returned to Canada from overseas. After attending Fox River School and St. John Commercial School, Kerr had left home in 1906 to work as a lumberjack in the Kootenay area of British Columbia. In 1912, he moved to Spirit River, a little over 300 miles north of Edmonton, where he bought a sixty-five-hectare homestead and farmed with his brother until war broke out. They both decided to join the army. On the door of their shack they left a note: "War is hell, but what is homesteading?"

Together the Kerrs enlisted in the 66th Infantry Battalion which was sent to England to train. In June 1916, Chip Kerr was among those drafted as reinforcements into Edmonton's 49th Canadian Infantry Battalion and sent to France, where it was bloodied in the Ypres sector and then moved to the Somme.

Kerr's homecoming was typical of the manner in which Canadian cities and towns honoured their heroes in those days. Multitudes thronged near the Canadian Pacific Railway depot and the streets were blocked for hours by people waiting for the train to arrive. There to greet him and his English bride, Gertrude, were Mayor Harry Evans and the city aldermen. As bands played, a procession marched past a cheering crowd of 10,000 through streets decorated with flags and bunting to the Legislative Building where the Kerrs were met by Lieutenant-Governor Robert Brett, Premier Charles Stewart, ministers of the cabinet and members of the legislature. "You have brought an honour that could not be bought and it is the highest honour a soldier can win," Brett said.

The Kerrs were then presented with $700 in gold which awed them. "We don't go in for heroics at the front," Kerr responded gratefully. "If a man is chosen for the job, he does it and that is all there is to it unless someone sees him doing his duty and rewards him for it. Nobody thinks of gaining distinction. If a man saves his hide, he thinks himself well off."

Following the war, Kerr and his wife took up residence at his Spirit River homestead, but he soon tired of farming. Six years later he sold the property and worked in the oil fields at Turner Valley near Calgary. He later returned to Spirit River, where he worked as a forest ranger patrolling the Peace River and ran the government ferry at Dunvegan.

When World War II broke out, the fifty-three-year-old war hero re-enlisted in the army. In the hope of going overseas, he transferred to the Royal Canadian Air Force but remained in Canada as a service policeman and sergeant-of-the-guard at Sea Island, B.C.

Following the war, he retired to Port Moody, B.C., where he took up fishing. The hardiness that won him the Commonwealth's highest honour for valour never deserted him. On one occasion in 1955, at age sixty-eight, he braved the icy waters of Burrard Inlet off Loco by swimming 100 metres to refloat his gill-netted fishing boat. Kerr's life came to an end on February 19, 1963 at age seventy-six and he was buried in Mountain View Cemetery, Vancouver, B.C.

In 1951, a mountain in Jasper Park was named after him. In 1975, the Canadian War Museum acquired his VC from his widow. It is currently on loan to the Museum of Alberta in Edmonton. Of interest is the care taken by the conservator to properly clean and protect the Victoria Cross. The metal requires polishing because, unlike silver or gold, brass has a tendency to revert to an oxidation/corrosion state; it develops a protective brown patina.

Polishing compounds are never used to clean it; they contain sharp particles that can scratch and acids that can permanently etch the metal. Skin oils, commonly deposited on the cross in handling, also contain corrosive substances. The VC is cleaned with mineral spirit to degrease it and then it is covered with wax as a anti-corrosive coating.

The great war showed that the pipes still possessed the uncanny power to conjure up and translate into action the spirit which knows no defeat.

Piper Major S. McKinnon in the
Canadian Geographical Journal

THERE was a third Canadian VC of the Somme, a Scot who was a piper with the 16th Canadian Infantry Battalion (the Canadian Scottish). James Cleland Richardson so distinguished himself during the Canadian attack on the Regina trench that he ensured the tradition of bagpipes in the Canadian military forever. On October 8, 1916, he was not included with those pipers of the 16th selected to go over the top the next morning, but Jimmy Richardson pleaded so strongly to be allowed to "go in" that his battalion commander relented.

At 4:50 a.m. on October 9, the artillery barrage thundered down on the enemy position and the attack began. Richardson, his company commander, and the company sergeant-major, Bill Mackie, climbed out of their trench together. Halfway to the enemy trench-line, Mackie wondered why Richardson wasn't playing his pipes. Richardson said that he had been told not to until ordered to do so by the company commander.

When they reached the barbed wire, they were devastated to find that it had not been cut by the artillery fire. Mackie ran ahead to look for an opening but couldn't find one. By the time the rest of the company drew up, the Germans opened up with rifle fire and began lobbing hand grenades at the Canadians. Seeing a large shell hole on his left, Mackie ran over to his company commander and told him to take cover in it while he went in search of some wire-cutters. But at this point, the officer fell with a bullet in his chest.

Richardson leaned over and asked if he could help, but it was too late. Then, sizing up how desperate the situation had become, he asked if he should play his pipes. "Will I gie them wind?" "Aye mon, gie them wind," the sergeant-major replied.

Richardson began coolly playing his pipes, marching slowly and deliberately back and forth along a route 400 yards long in front of the wire, ignoring the bursting gunfire all around him. The high shrill skirl of the Highland airs had a tonic effect on the troops hitherto trapped and grovelling in the mud or taking shelter in the shell holes.

Inspired by the tunes he played and by the brave example he set, they climbed to their feet and charged into the barbed wire, forcing their way through and into the trenches where they quickly overcame all enemy resistance.

Later, after participating in the attack on the trench, Richardson was detailed to take back a wounded comrade and some German prisoners. He had gone about 200 yards when he discovered he had left his pipes behind. Although strongly urged by his comrades not to do so, he insisted on returning to recover his pipes. That was the last that was seen of him. The award of the VC was not gazetted until October 22, 1918.

Jimmy Richardson was born in Bellshill, Lanark, Scotland on November 25, 1895 and was educated at Bellshill Academy, Auchinwraith Public School and John Street School in Glasgow. Prior to World War I, his family moved to Chilliwack, B.C., where his father became chief of police. Richardson took up the trade of electrician, working in Vancouver. There he became known for his skill with the bagpipes, winning many contests. In 1914, he joined the 72nd Seaforth Highlanders and was later attached to the 16th Scottish.

A painting of the action that won him the VC hangs in the main hall of the branch of the Royal Canadian Legion in Chilliwack and a local chapter of the Order of the Imperial Daughters of the Empire was named after him.

Piper James Richardson, 16th Battalion

Chapter Ten

THE CAVALRY CHARGE THAT WON A VC

A N Irish-born Albertan became one of two Canadian cavalrymen in a mounted charge in the First World War to win the Victoria Cross. In March 1917, the Canadian Cavalry Brigade, serving with the 15th Army Corps, was positioned north of Peronne in the Somme. It consisted of the Royal Canadian Dragoons, the Royal Canadian Horse Artillery, the Cavalry Machine Gun Squadron, a field ambulance, the Fort Garry Horse and Lord Strathcona's Horse. It was the latter in which Frederick Maurice Watson Harvey, who was born in Athboy, County Meath, Ireland, on September 1, 1888, enlisted in 1914 and of which he became later known as its "father."

The regiment had been raised for service in South Africa and originally recruited members from the Canadian North-West Mounted Police, one of whom, Arthur Richardson, won the VC at Wolve Spruit in July 1900. Following the Boer War, the regiment became established as part of the rapidly expanding Permanent Canadian Militia. Harvey, the son of a minister who attended Portora Royal School in Enniskiller, came to Canada in 1908 and three years later settled in Fort Macleod where he married Winifred Lillian Patterson in 1914 before joining the Strathconas.

Along with other cavalry regiments, the Canadian Cavalry Brigade fought as infantry in the trenches throughout the fall and winter of 1915-16. Finally, the brigade was withdrawn from the line, remounted and embarked on a period of intense and vigorous retraining.

On the morning of March 24, 1917, the brigade received orders to form up on a twelve-mile front with Nurin as its central focal point and advance beyond the British infantry positions. By evening the Dragoons had overrun several German posts, including the woodland southwest of Lieramount. During the night the Fort Garry's, on the left flank of the advance, captured the villages of Ytres and Etricourt.

Next afternoon, a squadron of the Winnipeggers struck at two enemy-held woods, riding straight into the face of machine-gun and rifle fire, the first cavalry charge of its kind seen in over two years. At six o'clock the following morning, March 26, the Strathconas overran a wood south of Equancourt where they dismounted; then, with the support of the guns from the Horse Artillery, they captured the town itself at bayonet point.

That night and during the early morning of the 27th, the Dragoons occupied the villages of Logasvesnes and Lieramount, turning the defence of the former over to the British infantry, but not before repulsing a strong enemy counterattack. Now came the climax of the entire cavalry operation and the classic individual cavalry action of the war.

The final objective for the Fort Garry's and Strathconas was the high ground around the town of Guyencourt and Grebaussart Wood, where the Germans were firmly and solidly entrenched. A heavy snowstorm delayed the attack until 5:15 that evening. But the moment the storm abated enough to see, a squadron of Fort Garry's galloped up Hill 140 and set up two machine-gun posts. The troops then rode around the hill in the Grebaussart Wood, Jean Copse and Chauffeur Wood, overcoming all resistance, and set up three more machine guns. Then, as the cavalrymen charged into the outskirts of the town of Saulcourt, the Germans bolted and were immediately caught in the machine-gun crossfire of the Machine Gun Squadron. The scene was set for the coup de grâce of the Strathconas.

With Guyencourt now in clear view, the horsemen charged onto a ridge to the left and in front of the town. As they closed in, they found an enemy trench protected by three rows of barbed wire. Then the Germans ran forward and opened fire with rifles and machine guns, inflicting heavy casualties on the Strathconas. Swerving to the northwest corner of the village, they took advantage of its walls for cover.

Fred Harvey, who commanded the leading troop of the charging Strathconas, was riding well ahead of his men when he suddenly found himself the target of an enemy machine gun firing from a trench protected by barbed wire. It threatened his entire company. Jumping from his saddle, he sprinted forward, hurdled the triple-wire entanglement, firing his revolver as he ran, and shot the German gunner dead. As a result of his bold assault, the Strathconas occupied the trench and subsequently captured the town.

The citation for the award of the Victoria Cross to Harvey, "For most conspicuous bravery and devotion to duty," appeared in the *London Gazette* of June 8, 1917. He received the medal from King George V on July 21 at an investiture in Buckingham Palace. The French also awarded him the Croix de Guerre and he was once more decorated, with the Military Cross, for bravery in the Battle of Moreuil Wood on March 30, 1918, during which he was wounded.

Harvey retired to Canada after the war and took up residence in Calgary. In 1938, he was promoted to the rank of lieutenant-colonel and assumed command of Lord Strathcona's Horse (Royal Canadians). During the Second World War, he attained the rank of brigadier and was appointed commander of the 13th Alberta Military District. He retired from the military in 1946 and held the honourary rank of colonel of the Strathconas from 1958 to 1966.

Fred Harvey died on August 22, 1980 and was buried in Fort Macleod. On September 13, his regiment paid him a final tribute with a memorial service at St. Stephens Church in Calgary and a parade.

Frederick Harvey, Lord Strathcona's Horse, at his investiture by King George V

Vimy Ridge Memorial

Chapter Eleven

THE FOUR VCS OF VIMY RIDGE

*Do you know that yesterday was the
anniversary of the most gallant feat
in our military annals? Of course you do;
it was the anniversary of the capture of
Vimy Ridge — that bit of France
(to paraphrase Rupert Brooke) that will be
"forever a little bit of Canada."*

Fred Williams,
Syndicated Newspaper Columnist
April 10, 1933

MACDOWELL-Milne-Sifton-Pattison. Stout-hearted, courageous countrymen, names of soldiers you probably have never heard, but ones that must remain revered and never forgotten in our military history for their part in one of the bravest, and certainly most successful, battles of the entire Great War. In the fall of 1916, the build-up to that monumental epic in which they brought us so much fame and glory began when the four divisions of the Canadian Corps were withdrawn from the bloodsoaked lands of the Somme and moved north to the Arras front in preparation for a spring offensive.

The Canadian objective was the most important of all — the capture of Vimy Ridge, that natural bastion which overlooked and dominated the Artois Plain between Thelus, Arras and the outskirts of Lens, a distance of some five miles. The Germans had held it since the third month of the war and it had formed the backbone of their stance and control of the Western

Front. Their determination to hold it had produced some of the bloodiest fighting yet experienced. In attempting to wrest it from the enemy in 1915, the French had suffered an appalling loss of 130,000 men. In 1916, the British had been repelled time and time again when positions of observation seemed almost within their grasp. But in their stubborn resistance, the Germans had paid a stiff price as well. Their casualties amounted to 60,000. There was no question of its importance to the Allies. It had to be taken at any cost.

The ridge's irregular contours made it a strong defensive bulwark — one seemingly impossible to capture. The Germans had taken full advantage of this by converting it into a virtually impregnable fortress. They laced the slopes with heavy belts of barbed wire protected by countless machine guns housed in concrete emplacements. Deep tunnels connected the reserve depots to the rear with the forward positions where huge dugouts had been built, in some cases large enough to accommodate an entire battalion.

It was in the planning of the assault that Canadian Corps commander, Sir Julian Byng, and the commander of the First Division, General Arthur William Currie, displayed their genius for organization and methodical detail, combining the co-ordinated efforts of the air, the artillery, the cavalry and the infantry. Byng also implemented a period of intense training.

Aerial reconnaissance photographs made it possible to map the German positions on a scale model. To familiarize the troops with the terrain over which they would fight, engineers laid out yards of white tape to indicate the exact layout of the enemy trenches. Coloured flags stuck in the ground showed the position of the German dugouts, machine-gun posts, mined areas and other points. The men spent weeks, day after day, practising the attack until they could almost walk the battlefield in their sleep.

The overall plan for the offensive was to advance four army corps on a front twelve miles wide. An incessant day and night artillery barrage on Vimy Ridge began during the third week of March 1917. The bombardment by 1,000 guns was so heavy and intense that most of the enemy artillery was knocked out and the majority of the workhorses were killed. The Germans called it "the week of suffering." At 5:30 a.m. on Easter Monday, April 9, in driving sleet and snow, the Canadians began their advance. The careful preparation and rehearsal began to pay off quickly. The creeping barrage of shells on one defense line after another allowed the Canadians to advance steadily and quickly. An hour after the attack started, they had overrun the first line of trenches. By mid-afternoon the corps was in complete control of the crest except for two minor positions that fell three days later.

More than 4,000 prisoners had been taken. The swift victory had demonstrated that, with proper planning and preparation, there was no German defense, no matter how complex or large, or seemingly impregnable, that could not be overcome.

Of the four Canadians awarded the Victoria Cross at Vimy, only one survived the war. Two were killed in the attack, the other lost his life in combat eight weeks later.

THE son of a Methodist minister, Thain MacDowell, who was born in Lachute, Que. on September 16, 1890, spent his early days in the Maitland and Brockville areas of Ontario, where he was educated at Maitland Public School and Brockville Collegiate Institute. He later attended Victoria College of the University of Toronto where he was a letter man in football and hockey. In 1914, he received his Bachelor of Arts degree and upon graduating enlisted in the 41st Regiment (Brockville Rifles). He later transferred to the 38th

Canadian Infantry Battalion in which he was commissioned and went overseas. During the Battle of the Somme on November 18, 1916, he was awarded the Distinguished Service Order for his part in the attack on Desire Trench in which he subdued three enemy machine guns and took fifty-three German prisoners. Next day he was wounded and invalided back to England. He recovered quickly, however, and by the beginning of 1917 returned to France with the rank of captain.

A native of Wallacetown, Ont. where he was born on October 12, 1891, Ellis Sifton enlisted in the St. Thomas Regiment in October 1914, then transferred to the 18th Battalion and went overseas the following year. After a stint of front-line duty in France, he served as a transport driver. Although he had a few close calls from enemy shelling, he applied for a transfer to get back into action. As he put it, "I don't want to be thought of as a cream puff." By 1917, he had returned to the trenches with the rank of lance-sergeant.

William Johnstone Milne was born on December 21, 1892 in Cambusnethan, Scotland where he attended Newmains Public School. He emigrated to Canada in 1910 and went to work as a farmhand near Moose Jaw, Sask. which was still enjoying the economic boom that had begun early in the century. Milne enlisted in the army in September 1915 and by June the following year was in France with the 16th Battalion, Manitoba Regiment (Canadian Scottish).

At forty-two years of age, John George Pattison was one of the oldest soldiers on either side to fight at Vimy Ridge. Emigrating to Canada from England in 1906 with his wife and four children, he first lived in Rapid City, Man. before moving to Calgary, Alta. where he worked for the Calgary Gas Company. Born in Woolwich in London's east end on September 8, 1875, he received his education at Clifton School in Deptford. In May 1916, he enlisted in the 137th Infantry Battalion and subsequently transferred to the 50th Battalion.

Thain MacDowell, 38th Battalion

THAIN MacDowell won the Victoria Cross at almost the same moment that the attack on Vimy Ridge started. His battalion's objective was Hill 145, the highest point of the ridge. A methodical planner, he had carefully studied all of the intelligence reports as well as aerial reconnaissance maps. He knew exactly the ground his company had to cover. He had even picked out the dugout where he would establish his headquarters.

MacDowell quickly reached the first enemy trench shortly after dawn, about fifty yards to the right of the point at which he had been aiming.

But most of his men had been separated from their leader; they had reached a point even farther to the right. MacDowell was left with two runners. From his position he could see the dugout in the shell-torn trench he had selected as headquarters, but there was no time to collect a party to capture it. And first, two German machine guns had to be overcome.

One of these MacDowell silenced with several well-aimed hand grenades. The gunner of the second fled in terror into the dugout. MacDowell and his runners gave chase. As they moved through the dugout, it was even more formidable than they had expected, stretching a long way underground.

MacDowell bellowed into the abyss for the Germans to come up and surrender. There was no answer, but there was also no doubt that enemy troops were lurking down there. MacDowell decided to investigate, climbing down fifty-two steps through a narrow passageway. As he turned a corner he suddenly came face to face with a horde of Prussian Guards. In fact, there were seventy-seven.

Thinking on his feet, MacDowell decided on a giant bluff. Looking over his shoulder back up the steps, he shouted orders to an imaginary force giving the impression that the enemy was up against a substantial number. It worked. Up went the hands to cries of "*Kamerarl! Kamerarl!*" He now faced the problem of herding his prisoners to the top of the dugout. And there was still the danger that once the Germans discovered there was only MacDowell and his two runners, they might try to overwhelm the three Canadians.

MacDowell once again demonstrated his ability to come up with an on-the-spot solution. He divided the Germans into groups, sending them up top a dozen at a time. But the Prussians soon realized they had been tricked and the Canadians' worst fear was realized. Furious, one of the Germans seized a discarded rifle and fired at one of the runners. Luckily he missed and the mutiny was quickly quelled. Then, with other men from their company joining them, MacDowell and his runners were left free to explore the massive dugout. MacDowell hastily wrote a report which he dispatched to headquarters. It read:

> While exploring this dugout we discovered a large store of what we believe to be explosives in a room. There is an old sap [extension] leading down in the direction [of a crater]. This was explored. We have cut all the wires for fear of possible destruction posts. The dugout has three entries, and will accommodate easily 250 or 300 men with the sap to spare. Cigars are very choice and my supply of Perrier water is very large.... They are firing at us all the time from the southeast but I have no casualties to report since coming in here, except being scared to death myself by a "big brute." We have taken two machine guns and a third and possibly a fourth will be taken tonight. This post was a machine-gun post and was held by a machine-gun company.... They had plenty of rations.... There is a large number of wounded in front here, as I can see by the rifles stuck in the ground. We are using German rifles, as ours are out of commission.

Though MacDowell was suffering from a hand wound sustained during the attack on the machine-gun posts, he stayed in the line for another five days until relief reinforcements arrived.

MacDowell, to whom capturing Germans appeared to be an obsession (at last count 130), was wounded and invalided back to England on July 15, 1917. Six days later, he received his Victoria Cross from King George V. Granted sick leave, he went home to

Canada but returned to England on March 1, 1918 and from then until the end of the war served at the headquarters for the Overseas Military Force of Canada and at the Canadian Training School.

On Armistice Day, 1918, the University of Toronto conferred upon him an honourary Master of Arts degree. On May 1, 1920, he was appointed Brevet Major of the Ottawa Regiment (The Duke of Cornwall's Own). In 1927, he was transferred to the reserve and six years later was appointed honourary lieutenant-colonel of the Frontenac Regiment.

As a civilian, MacDowell served as private secretary to the Minister of National Defence from 1923 to 1928. He pursued a career in engineering and became director of several mining companies as well as president of Chemical Research Foundation. Thain MacDowell died on March 29, 1960 in Nassau in the Bahamas, and was buried in Oakland Cemetery, Brockville.

On September 20, 1970, a memorial plaque in his honour was unveiled at the intersection of Highway 2 and Maitland Road in Maitland, Ont. His Victoria Cross is on display in the Memorial Tower of the University of Toronto.

IT was early in the attack when "Willie" Milne, a bag of hand grenades slung over his shoulder, found himself in the vanguard of the 16th Battalion's advance through the sea of mud and shell holes filled with water toward its two objectives, the *Zwof Graben* and *Zwischen Stellung* German dugouts. As the Canadians drew within range, they were met by a ferocious fusillade of machine-gun fire causing numerous casualties and driving the men into the shelter of the shell holes. Milne rose out of his hole and spotted the gun; then, crouching on his hands and knees, he cautiously crawled toward it, all the while under fire. Milne kept closing in until he was within bombing distance. Then he leapt to his feet and hurled grenades into the midst of the gun crew, killing some and wounding others. He was finally able to seize the gun.

The Canadians now reformed and proceeded to advance on the *Zwof Graben*, taking prisoners from the dugout and killing the last to resist. They then charged the second objective, the *Zwischen Stellung*. Before reaching it, however, they were held up by a concrete machine-gun emplacement concealed by a haystack. Once again, Milne crouched down on his hands and knees and crawled forward toward the position. He repeated his earlier performance, waiting until he was in range, then rose to his feet fast and hurled grenades, killing the crew and silencing the gun. This time, as he seized the weapon, the entire sub-garrison surrendered to him.

The battalion reached its objective, but Milne did not live long enough to witness it. During the advance, he was last seen falling behind a small knoll after being struck by enemy gunfire. He was never seen again and his body was never found. Milne was one of 3,600 killed in the battle; the list of injured totalled another 7,000.

The Victoria Cross awarded to Willie Milne has been on display at the Canadian War Museum in Ottawa since August 1989. It had been a long — seventy-two years — circuitous journey and a costly, yet rewarding one, to get it there.

The medal was originally presented to Milne's family in Lanarkshire, Scotland. It then passed from his mother to his sister Nellie. Dick Malott, chief curator of collections for the Canadian War Museum, who initiated a search for Canadian VCs in 1967 while still serving in the Royal Canadian Air Force, established that it was still in her possession two years later, but was subsequently acquired by a Scottish collector. In

The field of battle at Vimy Ridge

1979, it was procured by the late Jack Stenabaugh of Huntsville, Ont., also a collector.

In 1989, Stenabaugh had Christie, Mason & Woods Ltd., in London, England put it up for auction. Since it was the last remaining Canadian Vimy Ridge VC available, the Museum felt the time was opportune to acquire it for the people of Canada and prevent it from falling into the hands of other collectors, particularly foreign ones. But it had a high price. Christie's expected it would fetch somewhere between $36,000 and $44,000. As it turned out, that estimate was low. It sold for $94,000 ($79,000 plus taxes and fees). Yet even taking the lowest estimate, such a sum would gobble up a large percentage of the Museum's meagre annual acquisition budget of $115,000. There was only one answer: public subscription.

Malott, a master of public relations and manoeuvre, along with Dan Glenney, the Museum's assistant chief of public programs, went to work. The media was highly sympathetic to the cause. The Toronto *Globe and Mail* gave the quest for funds front-page coverage. The Canadian Press ran with the *Globe and Mail* story. Headlines such as "PRICE OF GLORY MAY BE HIGH FOR MUSEUM" – "MUSEUM SET TO BID ON HISTORY" – "WAR MUSEUM IN FIGHT TO BUY VICTORIA CROSS" appeared in newspapers from coast to coast. Radio and television stations jumped on the bandwagon as well.

Response was instantaneous. Pledges began rolling into Malott's office by mail and telephone from citizens from all walks of life. In Guelph, Ont., factory workers passed the hat and raised $190. A British tourist sent a $20 bill in an envelope before boarding a plane to fly home. Other offers came as high as $50,000 and $75,000.

But Malott's efforts drew flak as well as enthusiasm. The 1989 issue of *Canadian Military Biography* took a shot at him when it carped that "More ink has been spilled in describing how the Canadian War Museum stalked Private Milne's medals than has ever

Ellis Sifton, 18th Battalion

been employed in telling Canadians how he came to sacrifice his life on our behalf."

With up to $200,000 in donations and pledges, the Museum had to lay down strict guidelines as to their sources. There could be no provisos. In one case, an offer had to be politely declined because the benefactor wanted to use the donation to promote self-interests. When it was refused, the Museum received a rebuttal that asked if Malott was running "a museum or a goddamn three-ring circus?"

When the VC finally went on the block on July 25, the auction was carried live on the radio and was featured on the TV national news. When the cross was unveiled at the Museum late in August, Milne's grand-niece, Jean Dobson of Ottawa, was on hand for the ceremony. His VC was the fifteenth of twenty-two acquired by the Museum. Milne has no known grave, but his name is on the Vimy Memorial in France.

THE 18th Battalion, in which Ellis Sifton was serving, quickly overran the first line of defense, but the advance of C Company against the second line of trenches was held up by a hidden machine-gun nest and men were being mowed down mercilessly. Sifton spotted the barrel of the weapon over a parapet. Without hesitation, he ran forward, lobbing hand grenades in the general direction of the enemy, raced through a hole in the barbed wire and attacked the enemy gun crew with his bayonet, killing them all. The gun was silenced and his company charged forward.

Meanwhile, however, a party of Germans had charged down the trench toward him. Sifton fought them off with his bayonet and held them at bay by clubbing them with the butt of his rifle until help arrived. By that time, it was too late. One of the Germans whom he had wounded found enough strength to level his rifle at him and kill him. But by his solo act in the face of danger, Sifton had saved countless Canadian lives and allowed the advance to continue.

Ellis Sifton is buried in Lichfield Crater Cemetery east of Neuville-Saint-Vaast, France and his name is inscribed on the Menen Gate outside Ypres. A provincial plaque erected in his honour in St. Peter's Cemetery at Tyrconnel, southeast of Wallacetown on County Road 15 in western Ontario, was unveiled on May 21, 1961 by his sisters Ella and Lila.

Captain Edward Shuttleworth, president of the 18th Battalion Association and a former captain of Sifton's C Company who presided at the ceremony, recalled the deed that had earned him the VC, and asked, "How many lives did he save? Who knows? Perhaps hundreds, perhaps thousands, perhaps the honour of Canada at Vimy Ridge." Sifton's Victoria Cross was donated to the Regional Museum in St. Thomas, Ont.

ON April 10, the second day of the battle, A Company of the 50th Battalion was another Canadian unit held up by enemy machine guns. The location was a part of the ridge beyond Hill 145. Several times the company had assaulted the position, but each time a German machine-gun nest halted the men in their tracks. Finally, George Pattison decided to take matters in his own hands and do something about it.

Advancing alone into the teeth of the enemy fire, he moved steadily forward in short, quick dashes, taking shelter in any shell hole he could find en route, until he reached one thirty yards from the nest. Pattison stood up, and from that vantage point, in full view of the gunners who fired on him at pointblank range, he threw three hand grenades into the nest so accurately that they knocked all the guns out of action and either killed or wounded the crews.

Pattison took swift advantage of the situation. As his last grenade landed among the Germans, he rushed forward and held off any resistance with his bayonet until his company caught up with him. Twenty minutes later, all of the company's objectives had been reached and consolidated.

John Pattison was killed two months after winning the Victoria Cross in an attack on a generating station at Liéven near Lens, France on June 3, 1917. He is buried in La Chaudière Military Cemetery at Vimy. In his honour and memory, the Geographical Society of the Province of Alberta named a mountain in Jasper National Park after him. His Victoria Cross was donated to the Glenbow Museum in Calgary.

Chapter Twelve

THE HOUR OF THE WOLF

JEAN Combe was the first woman in Canada ever to be invested with the Victoria Cross. In 1919, when the Prince of Wales — later briefly King Edward VIII — visited the Dominion, he presented her with the medal her husband, Robert Grierson Combe, had won at Acheville near Vimy two years earlier.

Bob Combe was born in Aberdeen, Scotland on August 5, 1880 where he attended Aberdeen Grammar School and served his first apprenticeship in pharmacy. He served as an apprentice in London before emigrating to Canada in 1902. Initially, he joined the staff of a drugstore in Moosomin, Sask. where in 1909 he married Jean Donald. Then he opened his own pharmacy in Melville which he managed until he enlisted in the Canadian Expeditionary Force in 1915.

Combe was granted a commission in the 53rd Battalion at Prince Albert. Proceeding overseas, he qualified as a major and was placed on the instructional staff. Later, at his own request, he reverted to the rank of lieutenant so that he could apply for combat duty and was transferred to the 27th Battalion (City of Winnipeg). To be nearer to her husband, his wife Jean had followed him to England and worked in a number of London hospitals as a member of the Voluntary Aid Detachment.

The feat for which Combe was awarded the British Empire's highest honour for valour took place May 3, 1917 between three and four o'clock in the morning, a period of the day known to some North American Indian tribes as the Hour of the Wolf — a time when the zest in the warrior, so they believe, reaches its zenith. This was appropriate for the scenario that was about to unfold.

The Germans had anticipated the Canadian advance, and two hours before the appointed time of attack, 3:15 a.m., they laid down such a heavy artillery barrage that even before the troops were in the jumping-off trench, they had sustained heavy casualties.

Robert Combe, 27th Battalion

As they began their advance in the darkness, the shelling blew sickening gaps in the attacking formations. Men collapsed by the dozens, torn to pieces by shrapnel and crushed by the weight of the earth falling on them from the exploding shells.

By the time they reached a point 500 yards from the enemy lines, Combe was the only officer of his company — by this time a shattered remnant of what had started out — still alive. Even so, he was determined to reach his objective and, with only five men left, he pushed ahead through the frightful shelling. As they drew near to the German position, they now suffered the ironic indignity, not to mention danger, of edging their way through their own artillery barrage. And there was no way of getting word back to the Canadian gunners to ease off.

Miraculously, the small band reached the German trench which they proceeded to bombard with hand grenades. When their own supply ran out, they grabbed some of the enemy's. A fierce and bloody battle ensued. Combe was always in the forefront, fearlessly leading his men around the corners and recesses of the trench. In the end, eighty of the enemy were taken prisoner and 250 yards of trench had been captured. But Combe did not live long to relish his victory. As he rounded a corner, a sniper's bullet killed him. The *London Gazette* read: "His conduct inspired all ranks, and it was entirely due to his magnificent courage that the position was carried, secured and held."

Shortly afterwards, Combe's wife Jean received a letter from one of his fellow officers, Ronald Wheatley:

> France, May 12, 1917
> Dear Mrs Combe, - Your husband lived and died a man. My hope for you is that pride in his heroism may help soften your sorrow at his going forward. As for myself, although I have lost one of my best friends — and he was easily one of the most popular men — in the mess, and was equally so in this battalion — yet all those of us who knew him well are proud of him. That is our greatest feeling. His bravery, coolness and skill were very largely responsible for our success that day. Would that we had more Bob Combes!
>
> It is now possible to piece together from many reports what happened that morning. The battalion went over just before daybreak. The dear old lion-hearted boy got through the enemy's barrage, and arrived at the German's first line of trench with five men only. Undismayed, he bombed his way down the trench, clearing it of the enemy. He collected a few more men who by then had got through, and fighting all the time and encouraging his men by word and deed, he got a block in the trench constructed, and held it against every attack. He was directing the fighting, oblivious of personal danger, when a sniper got him. He was killed instantly and did not know what struck him. Just then another party came up and managed to hold the trench that Bob had so gallantly captured. That that part of the line was taken was due to his heroic leadership.
>
> He was a splendid comrade, a first class officer of infinite charm, whose cheery outlook on life and sense of honour enriched every topic he touched. You would be a prouder woman still if you could have heard what officers and men alike said of him.
>
> I spent the next night going over the place. He was properly buried very near the scene of his great achievement....

Combe's Victoria Cross was donated to the Province of Saskatchewan Archives in Regina.

Chapter Thirteen

MY FATHER'S VC

"Your father was a man among men."

Jimmy Doolittle,
in a letter to the author

MY old man would have liked that. I like it too, just as I took pride on August 12, 1994 in unveiling the Canada Post Corporation commemorative stamp struck in his honour at Air Command Headquarters in Winnipeg, Man. This honour, coupled with Doolittle's remarks, salute the fact that in his day, William Avery Bishop was a living legend whose exploits as the top British Empire Air Ace brought an excitement and glamour to a war bogged down in the appalling massacre of manhood in the muddy, vermin-infested trenches during World War I, and inspired thousands of others to join the Royal Canadian Air Force in World War II. What that Victoria Cross represented was instrumental in helping to build the service, and overall it served as a morale builder.

Billy Bishop was awarded the coveted medal for a solo air raid at dawn on June 2, 1917 on a German aerodrome, in which he shot down three enemy planes in his Nieuport scout that was so riddled with machine-gun bullets that he was lucky to get home without suffering a scratch — an extraordinary feat. Of his distinguished career, The *Toronto Star* once said that he "won the VC many times over."

But before exploring that raid further, let's set one fact about it straight. For many years, I believed the location of his attack to be Estourmel aerodrome southeast of Cambrai. My father recorded it in his combat report as being either Esnes or Awoignt. When I drove through and flew over the area as part of my research to write his biography in 1961, and from sparse information I was able to learn from the German side (most German air force records were lost in the World War II bombing of Dresden), I was led to believe it was Estourmel. However, two noted Canadian air war historians, Arnold Bauer and Stewart Taylor, both close friends, have since that time delved into the question much more thoroughly and have unanimously agreed it was Esnes. So I stand corrected.

Let Taylor tell it in his own words: "Apparently a month or so before Albert

Billy Bishop, Royal Flying Corps

Ball [the then leading British Ace] had suggested to Bishop that they raid a German aerodrome, something that had never been done before — a lone raid on a German aerodrome. Ball never lived to execute that plan. He was killed on the same front early in May. Everybody in Bishop's squadron knew that he wanted to attempt the flight. Bill Fry says in his book *Air of Battle* that Bishop came to him the night before and said he was going to do it, and Fry said that was fine. Bishop arose early that morning about three o'clock and asked if Fry was coming. Fry turned over and went back to sleep, not wanting to have anything to do with it. Likely, most of the other pilots did not want anything to do with it either! So Bishop took off at 4:50 a.m., alone.

"It was very misty, although it turned nice later on. However, the mist was enough to cause him to lose his bearings slightly as he flew southeast over Cambrai, a distance of approximately seventeen miles. There were three German aerodromes there. The one farthest east was Estourmel. At that aerodrome was stationed *Jagdsta V*, an outfit so renowned that it was their job to look after the Cambrai front, which is quite a sizeable territory.

"At Estourmel there were permanent wooden hangars, like the old driving sheds that existed in Canada behind the houses built in 1880. There was no activity at that aerodrome. Again, Bishop had lost his direction. He had never flown over that particular section of the front. The reason he had never flown over that section was that the air activity on his own front — on the Lens front in the Arras area near Vimy Ridge where Canadians made such a name for themselves — had been considerably reduced in May 1917. It had been reduced because the German concentration of air power was then directed to Flanders, where the battle of Ypres was about to commence. All the German outfits, including *Jagdsta XI* and *Jagdsta IV,* were going north. So, to create some interest and look for German machines, Bishop flew south over the Cambrai front.

"After flying over Estourmel, he flew south, almost southwest, and curving back came to a place (though he obviously didn't know it) called Esnes. In a field nearby, he found canvas hangars and seven German Albatros D111's and one LVG two-seater parked on the ground. That is where he shot the squadron up. He came down to 200 feet, 100 feet and fifty feet. The first German machine to take off was hit and it crashed. The pilot was not hurt, but the crash destroyed the machine. Another aircraft took off at 100 feet and spun in. Once again, the pilot would probably not have been hurt. The three machines went in low and the third one crashed into a group of trees at the end of the aerodrome."

That was an experience my father never forgot. Though he rarely talked of his more than 200 fights in the air, he did discuss the VC raid with me on a few — very few — occasions.

When he reached the aerodrome, he saw the seven planes already mentioned and also groups of mechanics standing around them. Flying straight across the field, he opened fire with his Lewis gun. When he reached the edge, he pulled up in a climbing turn. In his words:

> Then I heard the rattle of machine-gun fire. I don't know why, but when I planned the raid, I forgot that the 'drome would be guarded by machine guns. They did a nice job of shredding my wing tips.
> By then one of the Albatrosses began to take off. He was cold meat. He didn't have time to gain enough flying speed. When I got 150 yards or so behind him, I snapped off about thirty rounds. He side-slipped and crashed. Then another machine got off. I swung around and took a shot at it, but I wasn't close enough. So I chased after it, and as I caught up, the pilot turned around in the cockpit and his plane hit a tree.

Just then two more Huns took off. One of them flew away from the field, but the other one came straight at me. I fired at him but missed. But he must have lost control because he spun in. I decided that enough was enough and was bent on getting the hell out of there. But the other fellow who'd taken off and had been hovering about decided to have a go at me. I was in a tricky spot. I'd used up all my ammunition and had to change drums.

I put my nose down and took aim and emptied a whole drum at him. I'm not sure if I hit him or not, but in any case I guess he'd had enough because he broke off giving me a chance to get away.

But I wasn't out of the woods yet. Four enemy scouts suddenly appeared above me. With all my ammunition gone I was in no mood to tangle with them, so I flew directly underneath them hoping they wouldn't spot me. I was in luck. They never noticed me and finally I was able to slip away.

Then the reaction set in. I hadn't eaten any breakfast. I started to feel dizzy and nauseated. I thought I was going to be sick one minute and pass out the next. But when I got back down on the field and climbed out of my machine, the adrenaline returned. My plane was an awful mess, covered with bullet holes. But only the canvas was shot up. Not a single bullet had hit a spar or the engine. I was damned lucky.

His success was confirmed by a member of my father's flight, Spencer Horn, who with two other pilots flew over the field and surveyed the damage. By that time the mist had disappeared, but even at that none of them identified the location properly. It was as my father's combat report had stated: "either Esnes or Awoignt."

On two other occasions I have written at length about my father in my biography of him, *The Courage of the Early Morning*, and in volume one of my Canadian Military Heritage series, *Courage in the Air*. So for the purposes of this compendium, I am content to summarize his life as follows.

He was born in Owen Sound, Ont. on February 8, 1894 where he attended school before entering the Royal Military College in Kingston, Ont. His military career began as cavalry officer before he transferred to the Royal Flying Corps where he first flew as an observer before becoming a pilot. His score of victories was seventy-two, five of them in a single combat. In addition to the VC, the first to be won by a Canadian airman, he was awarded the Distinguished Service Order and bar, the Military Cross, the Distinguished Flying Cross, the Croix de Guerre (Fr.) and Legion of Honour, and was Mentioned-in-Dispatches. In between tours of duty, on October 17, 1917, he married Margaret Burden of Toronto in Timothy Eaton Memorial Church. During World War II, he became director of recruiting for the RCAF with the rank of Air Marshal. He was the author of two books, *Winged Warfare* and *Winged Peace*. He died on September 11, 1956 in Palm Beach, Florida.

He was given a full military funeral, the service being held in the same church in which my mother and father had been married. My father's VC and his other medals and memorabilia have been on display in the Canadian War Museum in Ottawa since I donated them in 1968. Thanks to the energetic efforts of the historian Arnold Bauer (ex-Group Captain, RCAF), whom I have mentioned earlier, the house in Owen Sound where my father was born is now a museum operated by the Billy Bishop Heritage Fund under Bauer's direction. The airport in that city is also named after him.

One other tribute-memorial — John Gray's unforgettable musical parody, *Billy Bishop Goes to War*. Fabulous fun. My old man would have loved that, too.

Chapter Fourteen

THE HELL OF HILL 70

DURING the gory ten-day battle for Hill 70, a hummock at the southeast approaches to the town of Lens, a mining centre on the east side of Vimy, six Canadian VCs were awarded, three of them posthumously. Two of the recipients were over forty years of age, while another was only nineteen.

The fight to take the German position actually began in June 1917 as part of the British summer offensive known as the Third Battle of Ypres. The Allies by then had far larger supplies of munitions than the Germans, and the artillery and barrages were now so heavy and thunderous, it was a wonder that anyone survived them.

Following the capture of Vimy Ridge, the Canadian Corps had been biting its way into Lens. In August, a new attack was ordered to occupy it. But first Hill 70, which gave the Germans an excellent observation post, had to be overrun. Thus began a battle of artillery duels and desperate hand-to-hand fighting that lasted from August 15 to August 25 and in which the Canadian Corps sustained a total of 9,198 casualties.

The limestone knoll was a well-defended position; miners' cottages surrounded it, each one of them a machine-gun nest. At 4:25 a.m. on August 15 the pulverizing artillery assault began and the Canadians of the First and Second Divisions went over the top. Their approach was obscured by black smoke from burning oil storage tanks, but the tons of explosives raining on the Germans from the supporting cannon pummelled their defenses into virtual extinction. The advancing Canadians — some firing their Lewis guns from the hip, others lobbying Mills bombs into the enemy trenches — swept over Hill 70 and across the Lens–La Bassée Road, and captured the suburbs of Cité St. Laurent and Cité St. Emile. To the north they took the Bois Rase and the western half of Bois Hugo. Engineers quickly prepared defenses to ward off an inevitable counterattack by the German reserves.

It started that afternoon and continued throughout the night, the Germans battering the Canadians' freshly won position with relentless machine-gun fire and artillery shelling. By next day the situation had become critical. Three battalions — the 7th, 8th and 10th — were being methodically massacred. All communications with headquarters had been severed. The field telephones had broken down, their lines cut.

In order to break up counterattacks, it was vital to get information back to the gun-line. Flares, early wireless sets, pigeons and ground buzzers were used to convey information, but the most accurate and dangerous way was to send a ground runner. Runners had to get through to the support lines, which could reach headquarters with a message laying out the battalions' position and calling for a counter-cannon barrage.

Private Harry Brown, a stocky nineteen-year-old farm boy from Gananoque, Ont. serving with the 10th Battalion, and a fellow messenger volunteered for the job. When they started out on their arduous journey, a hostile barrage was raking the open ground. They were forced to weave their way through earth being churned up by enemy shelling. They had not gone far when Brown's companion runner was killed. Brown continued on, stumbling through waist-deep craters left by exploding shells. Then a burst of shrapnel struck him in the left arm and shattered it. Stunned, bleeding and in agonizing pain, he sat down to collect himself. Despite his wound, he knew he had to get through or his comrades would be slaughtered to a man.

Aching and weak from loss of blood, Brown determinedly pressed on, alternately staggering and crawling, and occasionally lying down to gather strength. Pale, dirty, haggard, bloodied and helmetless and with his uniform torn to pieces, he finally reached the dugout and stumbled down a small flight of steps into the arms of an officer. Before lapsing into

"The Runner's Last Stride"

unconsciousness from which he never recovered, he managed to hand over the paper he had so bravely carried through the shell-pocked battleground and blurt out the words "important message." He died next day in a field dressing station, but his determination and gallantry saved the three battalions.

MICKEY O'Rourke, a feisty Irish emigrant from Limerick, had already won the Military Medal for bravery at Moquet Farm on September 16, 1916 during the Battle of the Somme, when he wiped out a German position with his rifle and hand grenades. For three days and nights during the fighting around Hill 70, the former British Columbia lumberjack, serving as a stretcher-bearer with the 7th battalion, went without sleep to tend the wounded. Time and again

Michael O'Rourke, 7th Battalion

he left the trenches to venture into No-Man's Land, continually exposed to severe shelling and machine-gun and rifle fire, to bring his injured comrades food and water. Several times he was knocked off his feet and partially buried when shells landed nearby.

On one occasion, seeing a man who had been blinded staggering about in the open, O'Rourke, although in clear view of the enemy, leapt from the trench and guided him back under heavy rifle fire. Another time he ran forward in the face of machine-gun and sniper fire to rescue a wounded man. Later, when the battalion line of advanced posts was retired to the line to be consolidated, O'Rourke again went out to save a badly wounded Canadian soldier who had been left behind. The citation to his award of the VC read: "He showed throughout an absolute disregard for his own safety, going wherever there were wounded to succour."

FREDERICK "Hobbie" Hobson, a veteran of the Boer War where he was Mentioned-in-Dispatches, won the VC for a feat that could be likened to the Roman hero Horatius holding the bridge. Born in London, he had emigrated to Ontario where he enlisted in the Second Canadian Contingent, joining the 20th Battalion in which he was given the rank of sergeant. On April 18, 1917, he and his men were in position in Nabob Valley, a part of a German trench they had captured three days earlier. At twenty minutes to two that morning, the German artillery opened up with an avalanche of shells in preparation for an attack to recapture the trenches they had lost.

Most of the Canadian forward positions were wiped out. Just before daylight, the 20th

Frederick Hobson, 20th Battalion

Battalion headquarters was totally destroyed. All communications had been cut, but in the darkness a runner from the battalion on the right brought a message that the Germans were coming across No-Man's Land. From where he stood in Nabob Valley, Hobson could see them.

Only one Lewis gun was left in the vicinity, and as the men attempted to put it into action a shell burst beside it killing all but one of the gun crew, Arthur Fuller, who was half buried in the mud. Hobson took a shovel and managed to dig him out. Though he was no gunner, he helped Fuller get the weapon in position and began firing. Hobson was hit by an enemy bullet, but continued to operate the gun. The pair were capably keeping their assailants at bay when the gun jammed. By this time the Germans were almost on top of them. Hobson sprang to his feet and ran towards the advancing enemy, shouting to Fuller, "I'll keep them back if you'll fix the gun!"

Hobson now fended off the Germans with his rifle. When he ran out of bullets, he attacked them with his bayonet and clubbed them with his rifle butt. In short order, he killed fourteen of the enemy. By this time Fuller had the Lewis gun working again and kept his finger on the trigger. But when reinforcements arrived to help Hobson, it was too late. He was dead. A stick-bomb had struck him in the stomach, tearing his guts out.

AT the same time that Hobson was performing his gallant deed, Okill Massey Learmonth, a native of Quebec City, was bringing glory upon himself and his battalion, the 2nd. The unit had captured Hugo trench and had occupied it from the Chalk Pit to a point known as Hurray Valley, and for three days, despite the devastating and incessant bombardment, had stoically hung onto it. But by daybreak of August 18, the battalion had been reduced to 614 men. At 4:00 a.m., it was besieged by a barrage that lasted three-quarters of an hour. Then the Germans attacked with flame-throwers. Still, the Canadians held their ground. The enemy now began lobbing stick-bombs into the trench.

Throughout this siege, Learmonth, a major in charge of No. 3 Company, who had earlier in the war won the Military Cross, walked up and down the trench rallying his men from the parapets. When the grenades started falling, Learmonth threw them back and was twice wounded. But he doggedly carried on until he was wounded a third time and his leg broken. He refused to be taken from the field, however, and lying on the floor of the dugout continued to direct the fight until the Germans gave way.

Learmonth turned his command over to a subaltern and was carried by stretcher to a field hospital, but not before stopping at the battalion headquarters on the way to deliver a comprehensive firsthand report of the situation. Later in the day, "the man who would not give in" died in the hospital.

The second phase of the Canadian Corps offensive in the battle for Lens began on the morning of August 21. The jumping-off time was scheduled for 4:35. But twenty-five minutes earlier, the Germans began pouring shells into the parapets of Commotion trench held by the 29th Battalion. This was followed by a deluge of "fish-tail" missiles, among them square-shaped bombs that exploded in flames emitting a dense, suffocating smoke. One company was practically wiped out with every man dead or wounded. At this point, five minutes before the Canadian advance was to begin, a party of Germans attacked the trench but were quickly driven off. Then the Canadian artillery barrage began and the battalion started its advance.

Okill Learmonth, 2nd Battalion

IRISH-born Robert Hanna, who had left his logging job in Vancouver, B.C. to enlist, was in the vanguard of B Company of which he was the sergeant-major. By the time the unit

Robert Hanna (in raincoat), 29th Battalion, shakes hands with fellow VC winner Michael O'Rourke after the investiture.

reached its objective of the German-held Cinnebar trench, it was held up by an enemy strongpoint protected by barbed wire and a machine gun. All the officers were killed, leaving Hanna in charge.

Hanna coolly collected a party of men and led them against the position amid a hail of rifle and machine-gun fire. Forcing his way through the barbed wire, he killed three of the gun crew with his bayonet and brained a fourth with the butt of his rifle.

The group then consolidated their position by hastily building a fortification block. Just in time. The Germans soon attacked in force. Though low on ammunition and out of Mills bombs, Hanna and his party bravely held on time after time until they were relieved later in the day.

BY August 22, the Battle of Hill 70 was winding down. But there was still another Canadian VC to be won. Though the Canadians were in control, it was decided to make one last push to strengthen their positions. The objective was the capture of Green Crassier and other German positions around that point. This called for intense close-in house-to-house and hand-to-hand fighting at which no one was more adept than Filip Konowal, a veteran of five years with the Russian army as a bayonet instructor. In 1913, he had moved to Canada where he worked in the bush near Ottawa. In 1915, he joined the 77th Battalion of the Canadian Expeditionary Force and was transferred overseas to the 47th.

Green Crassier itself consisted of a large expanse of coal-slags thrown up into hillocks by bursting land mines. It was infested with machine-gun nests. To silence them, the German gun crews had to be ferreted out from tunnels, craters, dugouts and cellars. On the first day of the new offensive, Konowal entered a house in search of Germans. Finding none, he dropped down into the cellar, where three men fired at him. In a fierce bayonet and fire duel, with odds of three to one against, Konowal bayoneted the trio to death.

He next led his section along a road towards a crater. From the bodies of dead Canadians around the perimeter of the crater, it was obvious that it had been, or still was, a machine-gun nest. Konowal halted his men and advanced toward it alone. When he reached the lip, he saw seven Germans trying to manoeuvre a machine gun into position. Konowal opened fire, killing three of them. Then he charged forward and finished off the other four with his bayonet. These solo feats resulted in clearing that portion of the line, and Konowal and his men

Filip Konowal, 47th Battalion

were moved to another part of the front which was under incessant enemy counterattack.

Heavy fighting continued throughout the night, and the next morning another battalion requested help from the 47th to subdue a machine-gun nest in a tunnel at a position called Fosse 4. Konowal led his section to the tunnel and threw in two explosive charges of ammonal to demoralize the enemy gun crews. He then led a charge down the dust-filled and darkened tunnel and killed all of the enemy with his bayonet.

In the two days of bitter fighting, Konowal had accounted for sixteen Germans killed. But before the second day was out, he was so severely wounded that he had to be taken out of the line.

PAINTINGS of three of the Hill 40 VC winners — Konowal, Learmonth and O'Rourke — hang in the Canadian War Museum in Ottawa. The Museum has also acquired three of the medals — those of Brown, Hobson and Konowal. Learmonth's VC is on display at the Major Faucet Branch of the Royal Canadian Legion in Portage-la-Prairie, Man. In 1969, Hanna's medal was loaned to the 29th Battalion in Vancouver by his son Frederick. O'Rourke's Victoria Cross can be seen in the officers' mess of the British Columbia Regiment in Vancouver.

Harry Brown, who was born on May 11, 1898, is buried in Noex-les-Mines Communal Cemetery four miles southeast of Bethune in France. After a limited schooling in Peterborough, Ont., at age twelve Brown went to work on his widowed mother's farm in East Emily Township, Victoria County, Ont. Five years later, in 1916, he took a job with a munitions factory in London, Ont. where he lived with his married sister, Mrs. Charles Egelton. Six months later, he joined the Canadian Mounted Rifles.

Brown's VC and his other medals were presented to his sister and passed to his half-brother by his mother's second marriage, Father Lawrence McAuliffe, who died in Haiti in 1962. The medals remained with his order, the Scarboro Foreign Mission Society in Toronto. It took the energetic efforts of Dick Malott of the Canadian War Museum, then still serving in the RCAF, to track them down. In 1970, the society transferred them to the national collection via an unregistered eight-cent Post Office package.

Frederick Hobson has no known grave. His name is etched on the Vimy Memorial in France. Hobson was born in London, England on September 23, 1875. Following the Boer War, he emigrated to Galt, Ont. where he worked for Canadian Canners. He then ran a store before moving to Simcoe, Ont. Meanwhile, he had married and in November 1914 enlisted in the Second Contingent of the CEF.

Hobson's Victoria Cross passed not to his widow but to members of his immediate family and eventually to his married sister, Florence Brown of Toronto. In 1959, along with the 20th Battalion Association, she gave her brother's VC and his other medals to the Fort Malden National Historic Park in Amherstburg, Ont. "for display purposes." In June 1974, Hobson's VC and his World War I service medals were transferred to the national collection at the Canadian War Museum. His Queen's South Africa Medal and King's South Africa Medal were donated at a charity auction held by Eaton's and were untraceable. The British Ministry of Defence issued duplicates to replace them.

Okill Massey Learmonth was born in Quebec City on February 22, 1894. Educated at St. George's School and Quebec High School, on graduation he worked for the Union Bank and later was employed by a private estate on Anticosti Island, Que. At the outbreak of war, he was on the staff of the provincial treasurer's department in Quebec. Like Brown, he is buried in Noex-les-Mines in France.

Robert Hanna, who died on June 15, 1967, was buried in the Masonic Cemetery in Burbank, B.C. Born on August 6, 1887 in Kilkeel, County Down in Ireland, he received his education at local schools and took a job as a farmhand. In 1905, he came to Canada where he worked as a logger in British Columbia. Married in 1914, he and his wife May had one son. On August 21, 1917, he received his Victoria Cross from King George V at an investiture at Buckingham Palace. Following the war, he returned to B.C. where he ran a logging camp at Aldergrove. In 1938, he moved to Mount Lehman, where he took up his original vocation of farming.

Filip Konowal died in the Veterans' Pavilion of the Ottawa Civic Hospital on June 3, 1959. He was born at Kedeski, Podolsky in Russia, on September 25, 1887. The son of a Ukrainian farmer, he emigrated to Canada in 1913 following his five years in the Russian army. After recovering from his wounds sustained at Hill 70, Konowal served with the Canadian Military Attaché at the Russian Embassy in London. He then returned to Canada where in September 1918 he joined the Siberian Expeditionary Force as a sergeant. He returned from Siberia in June 1919, took his discharge and went to live in Hull, Que.

The record of Konowal's life is cloudy and not without a tinge of sadness. He apparently had a very short fuse. That may have been an asset on the Western Front, but on civvie street it proved disastrous. It appears that he killed a man. A newspaper report maintains he had an altercation with an Austrian who had insulted Canada and the flag. In the ensuing scuffle, "the Austrian died." Several authoritative reports claim that Konowal might have caught the man *in flagranté delicto* with his wife. In any event Konowal, who staunchly maintained his innocence, was arrested, tried and sent to a mental institution where the next nine years of his life "passed uselessly." His Victoria Cross was taken away from him.

After his release in 1938, *Liberty Magazine* asserted that Konowal was "turned adrift on the tide of the Depression.... Despondent, despairing, he became a shadow on the streets of Ottawa." Fortuitously, another war veteran took pity on him and took him to see a compatriot VC holder, Milton Gregg, then the sergeant-at-arms in the House of Commons. Gregg found him a job on Parliament Hill scrubbing floors in the Hall of Fame where statues of Canada's VC holders were to have been housed, but the hall never materialized. According to a report, Konowal "scrubbed them, gratefully, thankfully and scrubbed them well."

When Prime Minister Mackenzie King heard of it, he pulled Konowal up off his knees — figuratively and literally. To restore the dignity he so badly needed, King had his Victoria Cross returned to him and put him back in uniform — the uniform of the House of Commons — so that he could wear it. He was next made guardian of Room Sixteen, where the parliamentarians gather.

Konowal was buried in Notre Dame Cemetery in Ottawa. In 1962, three years after his death, the Canadian War Museum made attempts to acquire his Victoria Cross from his relatives who adamantly refused to co-operate. Although details are sketchy, the family apparently loaned it to someone in Toronto, then requested it be returned and sold it to an Ottawa medal collector. In 1969, the VC was offered to the Museum for an undisclosed amount. After four years of negotiations, in 1973, it was finally acquired along with Konowal's

At the time of the German assault through the wood, Bent was commanding officer of the British 9th Battalion Leicestershire Regiment with the rank of lieutenant-colonel. When the Germans attacked, they forced back Bent's right flank. In the resulting confusion, coupled with intense artillery fire, the situation became critical. Bent rallied a platoon held in reserve, along with other troops from various companies and details, and organized a counterattack. Charging forward at the head of his men, he inspired them with the shout, "Come on the Tigers!" His action won the day and secured the position, but during the charge he was cut down by enemy bullets.

Bent was born in Halifax, N.S. on January 3, 1891. Shortly afterwards the family moved to Ashby-de-la-Zouch in Leicestershire, England where Bent attended grammar school. On October 2, 1914, he enlisted in the Royal Scottish Regiment and was granted a temporary commission in the Leicestershire Regiment as 2nd lieutenant the following month. His advancement from that time on was rapid. His permanent commission was granted in June 1915 while he served in the Bedford Regiment, and he was made temporary captain in April 1916. That fall he transferred back to the Leicestershires as acting lieutenant-colonel.

His mother, Sophy Bent, received Bent's VC and DSO from King George V at an investiture in Buckingham Palace. At her request his sword was hung in the parish church at Ashby-de-la-Zouch where he took his first communion. His Victoria Cross is on display at the grammar school. In November 1932, a memorial bedroom at the Leicestershire Regiment headquarters in Nottingham was dedicated in his memory by his fellow officers.

Christopher O'Kelly, 52nd Battalion

Chapter Sixteen

CANADA'S CAVALRY

"That men could survive such an experience and remain sane is, perhaps, even more astonishing than the death toll."

Philip Warren,
Passchendaele, The Tragic Victory of 1917

"A forlorn expenditure of valour and life without equal in futility."

Winston Churchill

ONE of the most murderous battles of all time never should have happened. Nor would it have if General Sir Arthur Currie had been allowed to abort the massacre in which the Canadian Corps suffered 16,000 casualties in only twelve days, from October 26 to November 6, 1917. Instead, what transpired was a senseless sacrifice that yielded a contemptible ground gain of four-and-one-half miles, and one that etched in a blood-sodden battleground a grisly epitaph to the failure of the six-month-long Third Battle of Ypres in an attempt to free the Belgian Channel ports.

On October 18, Currie had taken command of the Ypres sector, and the Canadian Third and Fourth Divisions replaced the Australians and New Zealanders, later to be joined by the First and Second Divisions. After surveying the area, Currie recommended that the proposed assault to capture the Belgian crossroads town of Passchendaele be called off because the battlefield was such a quagmire, a mass of shell holes filled with suffocating ooze, that an advance through all the muck and mire would only get bogged down. Furthermore, the mud and ooze made it impossible to build proper gun emplacements. Currie was convinced that any attack under such conditions would be suicidal — and he was right. Besides, he considered Passchendaele a useless, worthless objective — a wretchedly flat little Flemish burg that offered not a single military vantage point.

However, his vigorous objections were swept aside and overruled by the British commander, Sir Douglas Haig, whose unimaginative military strategy was limited to overwhelming enemy manpower with an expenditure of greater manpower, head to head, no matter what the cost — a ground gain to justify to the British war cabinet his doctrine of victory through sheer brute force. The attack was to proceed as planned. Currie was undeniably the best man for the job, but not even his tactical genius and skill could outweigh or prevent such an unreasoning, pig-headed, callous command to send men to their certain death in the carnage that followed.

At dawn on October 26, 20,000 men began to inch their way forward across No-Man's Land in rain and mist, shell hole by muddy shell hole, struggling up the slippery slopes of the ridge that commanded the battlefield. Adding to their difficulties, during the night German planes had strafed and bombed the supply areas, taking a lot of the artillery out of action. This marked the first time Canadians had been subjected to aerial harassment. Perhaps a saving grace — if it could be called that — lay in the fact that during this Canadian calvary, a total of nine Dominion Victoria Crosses for valour were awarded, four of them on the same day. Two of them had to be made posthumously. Only a trio of the recipients were native Canadians. One VC winner came from the United States, three were from England, and two came from Scotland.

Owing to the difficulty in building deep trenches and dugouts because of the waterlogged ground, the Germans introduced a new type of defence fortification which were called "pillboxes" because of their resemblance — low and round in shape — to the apothecary item. Built of steel and concrete several feet thick, they were heavily armed and surrounded by concentrations of barbed wire, making them formidable bulwarks in the face of a British advance.

By September 1917, at which time the weather had improved, the British had devised a countermeasure. Artillery barrages were directed at each individual pillbox to stun or kill those inside from the concussion of explosions and fumes from the shell bursts. Also, the barrages were extended to clear the ground on either side so that the advancing troops could get around the fortification and attack it from the rear with hand grenades and Mills bombs. The pillboxes were not protected to the rear.

At the outset of the attack, the 4th Royal Canadian Mounted Rifles (RCMRs) on the right flank between Wallemolen and Bellevue were held up by machine-gun and rifle fire from a German pillbox northeast of Wolf Copse. This fortification not only bristled with guns itself, but was augmented by a machine gun on either side of it. The fire from it was so formidable that the regiment's three companies not only sustained heavy casualties but were stopped in their tracks and had to take shelter fifty yards from the pillbox.

At this point, Tommy Holmes, a nineteen-year veteran campaigner from Montreal who had been wounded at Vimy, without any prompting or suggestion decided to take matters into his own hands. Holmes might have looked frail and delicate, but he had the heart of a lion. Holding a grenade in each hand, he suddenly dashed across the battle-

Thomas Holmes, 4th Canadian Mounted Rifles

field towards the closest shell hole. The German machine gunners let fly with such a fusillade that Holmes' comrades looking on were sure that, with the mud splashing up all around him, he would be cut to ribbons. Not Tommy Holmes. On this day, he seemed virtually indestructible. Biding his time, he waited until the enemy gun crews began simultaneously reloading, then raced to another shell hole only fifteen yards away. From there, he began lobbing grenades. This he accomplished with such precision that he knocked out both weapons and killed and wounded the gun crews. He then coolly ran back to where his comrades were sheltered. That was not the end to his venture this day, however, by any means.

Holmes picked up another grenade and raced forward, once again the target of vicious enemy fire, this time from the pillbox itself. And once again he seemed to lead a charmed life. Though bullets whizzed all about him, none of them even grazed him. Running around behind the pillbox, he threw his grenade inside the entrance at the back and waited. There was a loud bang, then nineteen Germans, lucky enough to survive the explosion, streamed out of the small garrison with their hands up to be taken prisoner. Holmes characteristically shucked off his incredible feat with an inimitable grin that was his trademark. His fiery assault, in the face of wicked enemy fire, won his regiment the opportunity to continue its advance.

At 6:30 that morning, to the right of the RCMRs, forty men from D Company of the 43rd Cameron Highlanders Battalion, with Robert Shankland of Winnipeg (born in Ayr, Scotland) in charge, had reached the crest of the hill of the Bellevue Spur, the main German trench line defending Passchendaele. Overrunning it and holding the position was critical to the capture of the town. Unhappily, Shankland and his platoon faced a number of virtually insoluble problems.

On their right the 58th Battalion, under concentrated enemy fire from Snipe Hill, had failed to reach its objective and was forced to withdraw. Some of the men joined with Shankland's group on the hill which was of some help, though it still left that flank naked. For four hours, despite frightful casualties, they nevertheless withstood incessant German artillery shelling, which flung up so much mud it rendered many of the Canadians' weapons temporarily useless. However, they managed to beat off a blistering enemy counterattack all the same.

But by then the 8th Brigade was compelled to withdraw, leaving Shankland's left flank totally exposed. With the right flank already wide open and the Germans approaching in force from Snipe Hill, Shankland and his men were in grave danger of being cut off and the vital position, gained at such heavy cost, lost to the enemy. The situation called for reinforcements, but that measure could only succeed if headquarters had a firsthand, detailed, on-the-spot appraisal of the situation.

Shankland turned over his command to a wounded machine-gun officer who had refused to leave his post, and weaved his way back to battalion headquarters through the shelling to hand in a report giving a clear summary of the critical circumstances into which his platoon had been thrust, along with a recommendation as to how a counter-attack by reinforcements could be achieved — a feat of brilliance and bravery in both assessing the situation and delivering it under fire. With that information, the 52nd and 58th Battalions began driving back the enemy in an assault hitherto considered impossible. And let's not overlook that third credit for Shankland. He returned to his unit through mud and artillery fire to take command of his men in the ensuing attack.

IN the meantime, A company of the 52nd under the command of Winnipegger Christopher O'Kelly was ordered to go to Shankland's assistance. Pressing through an enemy barrage, his troops worked their way toward the crest, where Shankland's men were distracting the Germans with their fire. Sweeping over the hilltop in the teeth of spasmodic fire from enemy pillboxes, O'Kelly's men caught the flank of German troops advancing on Shankland's position and completely routed them.

O'Kelly next led his company against six pillboxes that were holding up the 52nd's advance. Under his combative leadership, they overcame the concrete emplacements and captured 100 Germans. Later that afternoon, his company was forced to entrench to beat off a strong German counterattack. That night, O'Kelly took his men out to capture an enemy raiding party. All in all, within eighteen hours they took 284 prisoners and captured twenty-one machine guns. Quite a performance.

BY October 30, the Canadians were in a position to assault the village of Passchendaele itself. On the Meetcheele Ridge that morning, the 49th Battalion and the Princess Patricia's Canadian Light Infantry (PPCLI) were in the vanguard of the attack. When Hugh McKenzie, who had enlisted in Ottawa and was in charge of four machine guns with the 7th Canadian Machine Gun Company, saw that a company of PPCLI had been all but decimated with most of its officers and non-commissioned officers (NCOs) killed, he put his guns in charge of a corporal and strode out onto the battleground to investigate.

He soon discovered that the culprit inflicting casualties and holding up the advance was a German pillbox on the brow of the hill. McKenzie immediately took charge and detailed a few small parties to circle around the flanks of the concrete stronghold and attack it from the rear. Leading one of them was gunner George Mullin, an American from Portland, Oregon. To draw fire away from the raiders, McKenzie led a frontal assault directly up the slope leading to the fort. As they charged forward, they were met by a deadly fusillade of fire from the pillbox.

Meanwhile, Mullin had decided to rush the stronghold head-on. Blasting it with hand grenades, he ran forward and crawled up on top of the emplacement and, pointing his revolver through the gun aperture, shot the two machine gunners dead. (Ironically, at that very moment McKenzie, charging up the hill, was killed with a bullet through his head.) Mullin forced his way into the pillbox and took its ten surviving occupants prisoner.

SHORTLY after the attack on the Passchendaele Ridge began, the 49th Canadian Infantry Battalion came under intense German artillery shelling. Then machine-gun fire brought the advance to a halt. Cecil "Hoodoo" Kinross, another English emigrant who had taken up farming in Alberta — and didn't give a damn for anybody — made a careful study of the situation and came to the conclusion that the best way to put an end to the machine gun was to take it out straight on.

In his typical, devil-may-care fashion, Kinross stripped off all his gear except his rifle and ammunition belt and started forward. Groping his way up the slope, indifferent to the bullets flying all around him, when he drew within range of the gun pit he leapt into it and killed all six of the gun crew. That action allowed his company to renew their advance for another 300 yards. But for Kinross it was merely a warmup. He continued fighting all day until he was wounded, so severely he had to be taken from the field. This was the second time he had been injured in battle, and he couldn't have cared less. The previous year he had suffered wounds during the Somme fighting.

GEORGE Pearkes, who had joined the Royal North-West Mounted Police before the outbreak of the war, and in command of a company of the 5th Canadian Mounted Rifles, had been ordered to capture Vapour Farm and the outlying defences of Passchendaele. But just before the advance got started, a piece of shrapnel struck him in the left thigh so forcibly that it knocked him down. For an agonizing few moments, his men wondered

An artist's depiction of an attack on a pillbox

whether the advance should be aborted. Pearkes would hear none of it. Struggling to his feet with some difficulty, he assured them he could continue. As he later admitted, "I said to myself, I've got to go on a while, wounded or not." His leg felt stiff but, dragging it, he was able to cope, and his company followed him.

With some fifty troops, Pearkes reached the objective only to find both of his flanks dangerously exposed. The battalion on the left had failed to capture Source Farm, so the RCMRs turned their attention to it and took it by storm. Pearkes then consolidated the position amid a ragged line of shell holes and, reduced to a handful of fewer than twenty men, beat off incessant German counterattacks until after dark, when reinforcements arrived to relieve them. This allowed

George Pearkes, 5th Canadian Mounted Rifles Battalion

Pearkes, by this time in excruciating pain, to be taken to a field hospital to have his wound attended to.

NOVEMBER 6 — a crowning day in the struggle for Passchendaele. On this date, the Canadians captured all that was left of the village by this time: a burned out skeleton of charred buildings and streets of rubble.

The objective of the 3rd Canadian Infantry Battalion was the Goudberg Spur trench line. But the troops were prevented from launching their assault by three German machine guns that guarded one of the last pockets of resistance, a battered house called Vine Cottage that housed a pillbox. The Canadians had tried for a week to take it but were beaten back time and again with heavy losses.

Colin Barron decided to try and break the stalemate by himself. Inching forward on his stomach, when he was close enough he hurled several Mills bombs into the machine-gun nest. Rushing ahead, he found he had killed most of the gun crews. He then turned on the rest with his bayonet and took them prisoner. With the machine guns out of action, his company was free to smash their way into the Vine Cottage and capture the pillbox. The advance towards the Goudberg Spur was able to proceed.

IN another part of the village, a single German machine gun was slowly decimating the 27th Battalion at pointblank range. When a company commander called for volunteers to capture it, James Peter Robertson of Medicine Hat, Alta. was one of the first to step forward and the very first to reach the gun. He crossed into the open in a direct line of fire, and ran around the flank, leapt over the barbed wire and killed four of the enemy gunners with his bayonet. When the rest tried to flee, Robertson had no intention of letting them escape. Seizing the captured gun, he turned it on the Germans.

Next, carrying the machine gun, he led a charge into the village. When the volunteers returned to their own lines, two of their comrades who had been wounded were left in No-Man's Land. Without waiting for orders, Robertson went forward to bring them in. He successfully rescued one of them, but when he went out again to reach the second man he was hit by a bullet and fell. Picking himself up, he continued on, slipping and sliding in the slimy, viscous mud. Although nearly exhausted, he managed to bring the wounded trooper close to his own lines before a shell exploded near him, killing him instantly.

James Robertson, 27th Battalion

IN 1918, all seven surviving Canadian VC winners at Passchendaele were invested with their medals by King George V in parade order as follows: Mullin on March 16, O'Kelly March 23, Barron and Kinross on April 6, Pearkes June 22, and Holmes — the youngest Canadian to receive a VC up to the time — on December 31, all at Buckingham Palace. Shankland received his decoration from the King at Sandringham on October 7.

Of the nine, five of them also earned a string of other decorations for bravery. Hugh McKenzie and Robert Shankland won the Distinguished Conduct Medal as NCOs before earning their commissions as lieutenants. McKenzie also won the Croix de Guerre (Fr.). As corporal of a scout and sniper section, George Harry Mullin won the Military Medal at Vimy Ridge. By the time of the battle of Passchendaele, he had reached the rank of lieutenant. Christopher Patrick John O'Kelly was also decorated for bravery at Vimy Ridge where he won the Military Cross, and eventually held the rank of captain. George Randolph Pearkes won the Military Cross during the battle of the Somme, and in the battle of Amiens in 1918 he was awarded the Distinguished Service Order as well as the Order of Merit (U.S.), the Order of the Knights of St. George and the Croix de Guerre (Fr.). Pearkes was later promoted to major-general.

Three of the VCs won at Passchendaele became the property of the Canadian War Museum in Ottawa. Five of the others are retained by relatives. One was donated to the Owen Sound branch of the Royal Canadian Legion.

Hugh McKenzie's Victoria Cross, along with his service medals, was destroyed when his widow, who had remarried, lost her life in a fire at Amherstburg, Ont. on May 24, 1959. His Distinguished Conduct Medal and Croix de Guerre (Fr.) were in the custody of his family in Scotland. Through the efforts of the Canadian War Museum the destroyed medals were replaced. On March 18, 1979 at a ceremony at the Museum, his daughter, Mrs. Elizabeth McAndrew of Windsor, Ont. presented the complete set to the national collection.

Upon his death, Christopher O'Kelly's VC passed to his family (he was not married). In 1969, Major Dick Malott, later of the Canadian War Museum, traced the set to his two surviving sisters, Margaret Wall and Monica Kiely, both of whom were living in Florida. They willed the medals to the Museum, and in May 1970 the Museum took possession. When they arrived, his service medals were missing but these were soon replaced.

After the death of George Harry Mullin, his VC and service medals were held in trust by the Princess Patricia's Canadian Light Infantry Museum in Calgary, Alta. for his grandson until the death of his widow in 1975. The family then recalled the set from the regiment and put it up for sale. That September, the Canadian War Museum paid an undisclosed amount for the VC, and it has been on loan to the PPCLI ever since. There is a photograph of a drawing of Mullin in the Museum collections.

At the time he won his VC, Colin Fraser Barron held the rank of corporal. Born in Baldavie, Scotland, he moved to Toronto in 1910 where he became a railroad worker. Something of a recluse, nothing is known of his personal life or activity between wars except that he was married and lived in Toronto. In World War II, he re-enlisted and served with the Royal Regiment of Canada in Iceland and Great Britain. Following his discharge with the rank of lieutenant, he was an employee with the Don Street Jail.

Barron died on August 15, 1958 at age sixty-five, and was buried at Prospect Cemetery. No trace has ever been found of his Victoria Cross or his service medals. Presumably they are — or were — in the possession of his widow or other members of his family.

Although Thomas William Holmes was born in Montreal on August 17, 1898, he considered Owen Sound, Ont. his home. His parents had moved to the Georgian Bay port in 1903, and Holmes took his education there at Ryerson School. In December 1915, he enlisted in the 147th Canadian Infantry Battalion, later transferring to the 4th RCMR. Following his discharge with the rank of sergeant, Holmes moved to Toronto, where for fourteen years he worked as a chauffeur with the Toronto Harbour Commission until ill health forced him to retire. He died in Toronto on January 4, 1950 after ten years in hospital. He was buried in the Owen Sound Cemetery.

On January 13, 1959, a plaque erected by the province of Ontario in his memory was unveiled in Queen's Park, Owen Sound. His daughter donated his Victoria Cross and service medals to the Owen Sound Branch of the Legion.

Two hours after Cecil John Kinross received his Victoria Cross from the King on April 6, 1918, as the remaining members of Edmonton's 49th Battalion proudly looked on at attention, he was arrested by the military police while waiting for a train to take him to Scotland and charged with illegally wearing the ribbon. But when he pulled the medal itself from his pocket with his name inscribed on the back to show it to the colonel-in-charge, there were red, shame-faced apologies all round.

On reflection, the incident is not all that surprising. He probably asked for it. In all likelihood his appearance was doubtless so scruffy it would naturally have aroused suspicion. Also, he was not known for his tact. Hoodoo Kinross, who was born in Uxbridge, Middlesex, England and received his education at Birmingham School, was described by one of his officers as a thoroughly unorthodox soldier: "frankly incorrigi-

Cecil Kinross, 49th Battalion, after the investiture

ble. He was strictly a front-line soldier and gloried to be there, but he loathed parades. When he was forced to parade ... his appearance was usually disgraceful. There would be a hard look in his eyes during rebuke — almost but not quite enough to put him on a charge of unspoken insolence."

Kinross's family emigrated to Alberta where they settled on a farm near Lougheed. In October 1915, Kinross enlisted in the 51st Battalion, later transferring to Edmonton's 49th. On January 23, 1919, he was discharged from the army for medical reasons and afterwards returned to the Lougheed farm.

A few days after he arrived home, Edmontonians packed the old Pantages Theatre at 102nd Street and Jasper Avenue to give him a hero's homecoming welcome. In 1929, he returned to England to attend a reception for the VC holders that was hosted by the Prince of Wales.

On civvie street as a farmer, Kinross continued to live up to his unorthodox image. In the summer of 1934, he had to enter University Hospital to have his tonsils removed; he refused to take an anaesthetic. On one occasion when taunted by a friend in the wintertime as to the relative amounts of courage between winning a VC and plunging into icy waters, Kinross stripped off his coat, walked to a hole in the ice and dived in.

In 1956, he attended the 100th anniversary of the founding of the Victoria Cross in London. By this time a confirmed bachelor, he had given up farming and moved into a hotel in Lougheed living on his veteran's pension. There he died on June 21, 1957 in his hotel room.

Kinross was given a funeral with full military honours and an honour guard from Wainwright and was buried in the Soldier's Plot in Lougheed Cemetery. In 1951, one of the most spectacular mountains in Jasper National Park, a 2,731-metre-high peak, was named after him. His Victoria Cross was retained by his sister, last known to be living in Victoria, B.C.

Hugh McKenzie has no known grave, but his name is inscribed on the Menin Gate Memorial at Ypres. Born in Liverpool, England on December 5, 1885, McKenzie received his education in Dundee, Scotland where he worked for the railway. He moved to Canada in 1911 and lived in the Ottawa area where he married the former Marjorie McGuigan and had a son and daughter. In August 1914, he enlisted in the PPCLI. He was promoted in the field to corporal in January 1915 and to sergeant in September of the same year. Towards the end of August 1916, he was transferred to the Canadian Machine Gun Corps in which he was almost immediately promoted to company sergeant-major. He was commissioned on January 28, 1917.

In 1894, when he was two years old (he was born in Oregon on August 15, 1892), George Mullin's parents moved to Moosomin, Sask. where they took up farming. Mullin attended Moosomin Public School and Moosomin Collegiate. Following the war he returned to farming and served with the Assiniboia Militia, attaining the rank of major. In 1934, he was appointed sergeant-at-arms for Saskatchewan and moved to Regina. During the Second World War, he joined the Veterans' Guard as a lieutenant and served for six years. In June 1953, he was among those representing Saskatchewan at the coronation of Queen Elizabeth II. Mullin died ten years later on April 5, 1963 at age eighty. He was laid to rest in the South Cemetery Legion Plot in Moosomin.

Chris O'Kelly was the first man to return to Winnipeg, where he was born on November 18, 1895, wearing the reddish-brown ribbon of the Victoria Cross. On April 14, 1918, his fellow citizens crowded into Columbus Hall to welcome him home at a reception organized by the Catholic Club. Before the war, O'Kelly had attended public schools in Winnipeg. When the war started, he was an undergraduate at St. John's College and was still a student in 1916 when he joined the 144th Battalion, later being transferred to the 52nd. Only two months after winning the VC, he was promoted to captain.

After the war, in 1921, he rejoined the reorganized Winnipeg Rifles with the rank of major. In the fall of the following year, he and an associate travelled north to Lac Seul in northern Ontario to prospect mining sites. The pair were last seen in a canoe powered by an outboard motor. A storm blew up and soon after it abated some equipment from the boat was washed ashore. Very quickly a sharp frost froze over the lake. In the following spring of 1923, when the ice went out, O'Kelly's companion's body was found clinging to the ledge of the shore. O'Kelly's body was never recovered. His regiment erected a wooden cross on nearby Goose Island in his memory.

In 1929, when the Hydro Electric Dam was built at Lower Ear Falls, Lac Seul rose by sixteen feet, submerging the cross. Ten years later, it was found drifting offshore. It was retrieved and given to the Ear Falls Branch of the Royal Canadian Legion, who displayed the upright portion of it. On November 14, 1965, a provincial plaque was unveiled in Chris O'Kelly's memory at the Legion Hall in Red Lake, Ont.

George Pearkes, who was wounded five times, fought in every major battle in which the Canadian Expeditionary Force took part. During his career, he held every major senior army post it was possible to obtain, including that of Minister of Defence. Born in Watford, England on February 26, 1888, he got his early education at Berkhamstead School. Before coming to Canada he joined the Bedfordshire Regiment as a bugle boy.

Around 1911, he arrived at Red Deer, Alta. where he worked on a training farm operated by his old headmaster.

In 1913, he joined the North-West Mounted Police, training in Regina and serving in the Yukon. In 1915, he was able to buy his way out of the Mounties for fifty dollars and enlisted as a trooper in the 2nd Canadian Mounted Rifles which was soon reorganized as an infantry battalion. In France, he was granted a commission and won rapid promotion to lieutenant-colonel.

When the war ended, Pearkes stayed in the army. In 1922, he was made general staff officer at the Royal Military College in Kingston, Ont., a post he held until 1933. He married in 1925, and he and his wife Blytha had a son, John. From 1935 to 1938, Pearkes was director of military training. When the Second World War broke out, he was given command of the First Canadian Division. With the entry of the Japanese into the conflict, he became Commander-in-Chief Pacific Command.

After the war was over, Pearkes retired and was elected Conservative Member of Parliament for Nanaimo, B.C. In 1957, following the Diefenbaker victory, he was appointed minister of Defence. In 1960, he become lieutenant-governor of British Columbia. From 1966 to 1976, Pearkes served as grand president of the Royal Canadian Legion. At the time of his death on May 30, 1984, at ninety-six years of age, he was vice-patron.

Pearkes was accorded a full state and military funeral beginning at Christ Church Cathedral in Victoria. The funeral parade was led by thirty-two Mounties followed by two 100-man units of the PPCLI and a fifty-man guard from the Canadian Scottish. At his burial, he was given a fifteen-gun salute.

In Summerside, P.E.I. and Princeton, B.C., the Legion branches are named after him in his honour. Pearkes's Victoria Cross was donated to the Canadian War Museum in 1994.

Give him full marks for trying, but by 1940 Robert Shankland, who was born in Ayr, Scotland on October 10, 1887, was well into his fifties — too old for combat duty. When the Second World War broke out, he had re-enlisted in his old regiment, by that time renamed the Queen's Own Highlanders of Canada (QOHC), with the rank of major.

The son of a railroad guard, his first job was as a clerk in the station-master's office at the Ayr passenger station. In 1910, he emigrated to Canada where he worked for the Crescent Creamery Company as assistant cashier. In 1914, he enlisted in the 43rd Battalion (Cameron Highlanders of Canada) as a private.

Married with two sons, David and William, during the inter-war years Shankland served as secretary-manager with several Winnipeg firms. In December 1940, he was appointed camp commandant of Canadian Army Headquarters in England with the rank of lieutenant-colonel. In 1946, he left the service to become secretary of a leading securities corporation in Vancouver.

Robert Shankland died on January 20, 1968 in Shaughnessy Hospital in Vancouver and was buried in the Garden of Remembrance at Mountain View Cemetery. His Victoria Cross was willed to his grandson by Shankland's son David who, in October 1973, wrote to Major Dick Malott: "It was my father's expressed wish that I retain possession of the VC so that my son (his only grandson) would grow to know the meaning of it." Hopefully, it may one day find its way into the national collection so that all Canadians can take pride in Robert Shankland's gallantry.

"Singing Pete" Robertson is not only a legend in his own land, but also among the

Brotherhood of Locomotive Engineers the world over. On one occasion, at their international convention in Cleveland, Ohio, 77,000 delegates rose to their feet as a mark of respect to Robertson's bravery and voted unanimously that his photograph and story of his sacrifice be published in *The Locomotive Engineer Journal*. As a further tribute, his picture hangs in the Canadian Pacific Railway station in Montreal, the only person to be so honoured. For "Singing Pete" was a railway engineer before he ever thought of becoming a soldier.

Born in Albion Mines, Pictou, N.S. on October 26, 1883, four years later he moved with his family to Springhill in the same province where he received his early education. In 1899, the Robertsons moved to Medicine Hat, Alta. where "Singing Pete" joined the Canadian Pacific Railway, working his way up to engineer. There he earned his nickname; day or night he could be heard cheerfully singing and whistling whether he was in the cab or the road-house. Early in 1915, he joined the 13th Canadian Mounted Rifles and in England was transferred to the 27th Battalion.

Robertson is buried at Tyne Cot Cemetery at Passchendaele. In April 1918, his mother received his Victoria Cross from Lieutenant-Governor Robert G. Brett of Alberta at a public ceremony in Medicine Hat.

On December 13, 1969, the local branch of the Royal Canadian Legion was named after him, along with a swimming pool and a street — Robertson Way. Robertson's Victoria Cross was last known to be in the possession of his sister, Mrs. C.P Macdonald, who was reported to be living in Long Beach, California. Perhaps it too may one day become part of the Canadian War Museum's collection.

Chapter Seventeen

THE CANADIAN CAVALRY AT CAMBRAI

CAMBRAI is generally remembered as the first successful attack that had the support of tanks. But the Canadian Cavalry Brigade, which the armour was to replace, also played a colourful and valiant part, particularly the Fort Garry Horse. One of its officers, Harcus Strachan, a lieutenant from Alberta, so distinguished himself that his inspired leadership and gallantry earned him the Victoria Cross.

Strachan was born in Burrowstounness, West Lothia, Scotland on November 7, 1883 and received his education at Royal High School and Edinburgh University. He came to Canada in 1908 and lived near Edmonton, Alta. At the outbreak of the war, he tried to enlist in the army but failed to pass an eyesight test. He sailed for England with the intention of joining the London Scottish. However he ended up as a private with the Fort Garry Horse.

On September 1, 1916 Strachan was commissioned as a lieutenant. In May 1917, he was awarded the Military Cross for a courageous action in a raid on enemy outposts at St. Quentin.

With the capture of Passchendaele, the bitter struggle for the Ypres salient came to a close. The Canadian Corps returned to the Lens sector and the stalemate of trench warfare. But Sir Douglas Haig, British commander-in-chief, wanted a breakthrough to satisfy the British war cabinet.

He chose as the battleground the rolling countryside opposite the Hindenburg Line in front of Havricourt Wood, eight miles from the textile town of Cambrai. The objective was the capture of the Bourlon Wood which dominated the German Drocourt-Quéant Switch Line. Tanks were to be the main force of the assault.

As an attack weapon, the tank had been greatly improved since its first appearance at the Somme in 1916 when the vehicles broke down due to mechanical failure or got stuck in the mud. On the morning of November 20, 1917, 380 of these new behemoths rolled across No-Man's Land followed by the army and the cavalry. The elimination of the usual artillery barrage caught the Germans completely by surprise.

The tanks and the infantry advanced an unprecedented four miles to the German trenches between Gonnelieu and Hermies. The advance guard of the cavalry brigade – the Fort Garry Horse – began riding into Masnières and crossed the Sensee River bridge on the main street. But the canal bridge beyond had collapsed from the weight of a tank, which plunged into the water. However, another bridge to the southwest, with some repair work, was sufficiently reinforced to enable B Company of the Fort Garry's to ride across by three o'clock that afternoon and push forward to attack a German stronghold on a ridge beyond it.

Meanwhile, the commanding officer of the regiment had received orders to remain west of the canal, because the infantry and tanks had been brought to a halt. He was also to withdraw all troops that had crossed it, but it was too late. Though messages were dispatched to B Company, they were never received. In any case, the troopers were now in the middle of a pitched battle, coming under heavy enemy machine-gun fire that took the life of their company commander.

Harcus Strachan then took over command of B Company. He led his troopers through a gap that the infantry had cut in the barbed wire ahead of them, and charged towards Rumilly. Riding at a gallop, the troopers assaulted a battery of field guns. Strachan cut down seven of the gunners with his sword. Then a body of enemy infantry appeared. Swinging about, Strachan led his men into the thick of the fight. The Germans fled in disarray.

At this point, under cover of a sunken road, the company halted and waited anxiously for news or the sight of the rest of the regiment. As night began to close in, it became obvious no support would be arriving. By this time, the Germans had surrounded the dismounted cavalrymen.

The enemy made several passes, but each time the Canadians drove them back with their fire. But without relief they could not hold out much longer. Only five horses remained unwounded, the company was reduced to fifty men and ammunition was dwindling. Two of the troopers were dispatched to regimental headquarters in Masnières.

In the meantime, Strachan decided they should make a break for it and fight their way out. First, they cut three German telephone line cables as a distraction and to annoy the enemy. The afternoon light was still strong enough to make out the tower of Rumilly and take a compass bearing from it, so Strachan collected the horses and stampeded them eastwards. The Germans, believing they were under a renewed cavalry attack, machine-gunned the hapless animals.

The diversion allowed Strachan to lead his men away towards the

Harcus Strachan, Fort Garry Horse

British lines. However, the journey back was not exactly a piece of cake. The company was attacked no less than four times, but on each occasion was able to not only fight off the enemy but to take prisoners. When they reached the barbed wire, while searching for a gap the men became separated into two parties. However, both made it back to the British lines.

Under Strachan's leadership, B Company had destroyed an enemy field battery, killed 100 Germans, and captured another fifteen. The citation to his VC in the usual stilted prose read: "The operation ... was only rendered possible by the outstanding gallantry and fearless leading of this officer."

As a breakthrough, the Battle of Cambrai failed although initially it seemed to have succeeded. In Britain, church bells were rung. The German Supreme Command prepared to begin a retreat. Both reactions were premature. The initial gains could not be exploited because the British lacked a reserve of tanks and the infantry wallowed in the Flanders mud. However, while the value of the tank had been proven, the real stars of the show were the cavalry.

Strachan received his VC from King George V on January 6, 1918, by which time he had been promoted to captain. Later that year he was promoted to major. After being demobilized, he returned to Edmonton to farm and later went into the banking business. He also joined the militia as an officer in the 19th Alberta Dragoons. In 1926, he transferred to the 15th Canadian Light Horse and then went on the reserve the following year. When the Second World War started, he re-enlisted in the 15th Alberta Horse and in 1940 was appointed major of the South Alberta Regiment. In July of that same year, he became commanding officer of the Edmonton Fusiliers with the rank of lieutenant-colonel. He returned to the reserve on October 27, 1944 and went on the retired list on July 4, 1946. He later retired from business and lived in Vancouver, B.C., where he died on May 1, 1982. At age ninety-eight, he had been the oldest veteran to have held the Victoria Cross.

There are no details available as to the disposition of his VC, but it is believed to be in the possession of relatives.

Chapter Eighteen

THEIR BACKS TO THE WALL

IN November 1917, the Bolshevik Revolution and the German-Russian truce that followed removed Russia from the war and meant that the Germans could now concentrate all of their strength on a single front. In a desperate attempt to stave off defeat before the full potential of the American entry into the war could be realized, at five o'clock on the morning of March 21, 1918, the Germans launched an attack with sixty-four divisions on a front fifty-nine miles wide between St. Quentin and Arras. The aim was to split the British and French armies and force an armistice. Militarily, it very nearly succeeded. Before the advance was stopped on June 10, the enemy had recovered 230 square miles of lost territory and had reached the Marne, only forty miles from Paris, and at another point had penetrated to a mere twelve miles from Amiens. Politically, however, the offensive was doomed. The Allies were about to be unified under a single French command.

In anticipation of the assault, the British devised an in-depth defence system of three lines of troop emplacements. But when the attack came, with thirty-two divisions in the field (representing only half the German strength), and of those only nineteen in the front line, the Allies were simply overwhelmed.

During the twelve weeks the German advance lasted, four Canadian VCs were awarded, all but one of them posthumously. Ironically, the sole surviving recipient was killed in a freak accident eight years later.

Edmund De Wind, 31st and 15th Battalions

On the first day of the assault, a heavy white blanket of fog prevented the British artillery and machine-gunners from seeing the red emergency flares sent up as a signal that an attack had begun. The Germans quickly penetrated the outer defences and by the end of the day one British army was already in retreat.

Edmund De Wind held his ground for seven hours that day despite being twice wounded. He had come a long way since joining the 31st Canadian Battalion in 1915. He had fought in the battles of St. Eloi, Ypres and the Somme. In September 1917, he qualified for a commission and was transferred to the 17th Battalion Royal Irish Rifles with the rank of lieutenant.

On this, the first day of the "Great Retreat," he was in charge of a machine-gun post at the Race Course Redoubt near Grougie. Though the battalion's casualties were grim, De Wind stayed resolutely to his gun. Twice he also went over the top in the face of fearful German machine-gun and rifle fire to assault and subdue a German trench. In spite of his wounds, he continued to fight on until reinforcements arrived. But by the time they reached him, he was dead.

A keen sportsman, De Wind was born in Comber, County Down, Ireland on December 11, 1883. Educated at Campbell College, he worked as a clerk in the Bank of Ireland until 1911 when he came to Edmonton, where he was employed by the Canadian Bank of Commerce before enlisting. His name and picture appear in the memorial book of the Canadian Imperial Bank of Commerce, and his name is in the memorial of the bank's main branch in Edmonton as well as in the All Saints Cathedral memorial in that city. In addition, a mountain in Jasper Park is named after him.

In Ireland, which also claims him as a VC, his name can be found in the memorial in his native Comber. His Victoria Cross was presented to his mother by King George V at a private investiture in Buckingham Palace. De Wind's brother Norman, who moved to the United States, had possession up until his death sometime in the late 1970s. It is presumably in the hands of a relative.

THE Great Retreat continued. In less than a week the British had been forced back beyond their defence line of 1916, a distance of some forty miles. The rail junction at Chaulnes and the pivotal centre of Roye had been evacuated and the Germans, who had overrun 600 guns and taken 30,000 prisoners, were within twelve miles of Amiens. The critical point of the entire campaign had now been reached. In fact, the situation had become so desperate that Sir Douglas Haig issued his famous order to his troops: "to die where they stood."

On March 30, the Canadian Cavalry Brigade which had been fighting a series of rearguard actions both mounted and on foot since the battle for Amiens began, was ordered to seize a wood known as the Bois de Moreuil, which the Germans had begun to occupy. From the wood, the enemy had a commanding view of the city and the railway to Paris. Wresting the position from the enemy was crucial.

C Squadron of the Lord Strathcona's Horse under Gordon Flowerdew who, since enlisting in the Canadian army in British Columbia in 1914 had risen through the ranks, was ordered to move around the northeastern corner of the wood and seal off the enemy.

Gordon Flowerdew, Lord Strathcona's Horse

On reaching the area, Flowerdew made a careful appraisal of the situation. There were two lines of enemy soldiers, each about sixty strong and 200 yards apart with machine guns on either flank as well as in the centre. He ordered one of his four troops under the command of Fred Harvey, who had won the Victoria Cross with the regiment a year earlier, to dismount and make a diversionary flanking movement to the northeast and position their Hotchkiss guns at the edge of the wood. Meanwhile, Flowerdew decided on a frontal attack with his remaining three troops.

As soon as the Germans saw the Canadian cavalrymen, they opened fire with everything they had: rifles, machine guns, trench mortars and howitzers. As the Strathconas charged forward at full gallop in one of the last cavalry attacks in history, and one reminiscent of the Charge of the Light Brigade, the Germans, throwing hand grenades before them, attacked with their bayonets. The cavalry responded with their swords, hacking, slashing, slicing, piercing, stabbing as they charged through the German lines. Then they wheeled about and attacked again. By this time Flowerdew had lost seventy percent of his men, and he himself had been seriously wounded in both thighs. But the Germans had been badly mauled too, and were forced to regroup. Flowerdew ordered his men to dismount and led a final charge against the Germans, this time in hand-to-hand fighting. The Canadians forced the enemy to break and the brigade captured the wood. The day had been saved by Flowerdew's bold charge. The enemy's advance had been stopped cold and with it the threat to Amiens.

The citation to his Victoria Cross read: "There can be no doubt that this officer's great valour was the prime factor in the capture of the position." Flowerdew died of his wounds

George McKean, 14th Battalion

the next day in hospital. He is buried at Namps-au-Val British Cemetery near the Picardy capital.

Flowerdew's medal was presented to his mother by King George V on June 29, 1918 at Buckingham Palace and for years was framed on a wall in the chapel at Framlingham College in Suffolk where he received his education. It was on loan to the Strathconas Museum, part of the Museum of the Regiments, in Calgary, but it is now back at Framlingham College. At the Canadian War Museum in Ottawa, an oil painting by Sir Alfred Munnings, (a fellow graduate of Framlingham College), titled "Charge of Flowerdew's Squadron" vividly captures, in a somewhat abstract way, the glory, horror, gallantry and grim reality of the epic.

One of a family of ten boys and five girls, Gordon Muriel Flowerdew was born in Billingford, Norfolk on January 2, 1885, where he worked on his father's fruit farm after graduating from school. An ancestor was steward to the Duke of Norfolk. In 1903, he moved to Canada taking up residence in several different towns: Duck Lake, Sask. and Queensbay, Kootenay Lake and Walhachin, B.C. where he enlisted in the 31st British Columbia Horse Regiment, later transferring to the Strathconas.

THOUGH the brunt of the attack on Amiens had been stemmed, to the north the Germans turned their attention to the area around Ypres. Directly to the south around Vimy, between Lens and Arras, the front remained fairly stable though fighting at times was heavy and bitter. One example is the attack on the night of April 27/28 in the Gravelle sector on Hussar trench along the Lys River by the Royal Montreal Regiment of the Canadian 14th Battalion.

To begin with, the redoubt was too close to their own front line for the Canadians to risk shelling it. When E Group led by George McKean, an British-born Montrealer, attacked, it encountered stiff resistance from a fight-to-the-last enemy garrison sheltered in a trench block from which the Germans bombarded McKean's party with grenades and rifle fire. Three times the Montrealers ran out of "Pineapples" — Mills bombs — and three times they sent back to their own line to be rearmed. But all this failed to dislodge the defenders.

McKean knew that the success of his regiment's operation depended on wiping out this stubborn resistance. He also knew that time was running out. He ordered his men to stand aside. Though the trench block was well protected by barbed wire, McKean dived head first over the block and crashed on top of an enemy soldier. When another German lunged forward to attack him with his bayonet, McKean shot him dead with his revolver.

Simultaneously, his men swarmed over the barricade, overcame it, then charged a second block further along the trench. A fierce fight broke out that lasted only a few minutes before the Germans fled into the cover of a dugout. However, the Canadians quickly finished them off with several well-placed Mills bombs and the trench was theirs.

The citation to McKean's Victoria Cross almost did him justice even though the choice of words seems somewhat curious:

> This officer's bravery and dash undoubtedly saved many lives for had not this position been captured the raiding party would have been exposed to dangerous enfilading fire during the withdrawal. His leadership has at all times been beyond praise.

This was the second time McKean had been decorated for bravery in battle, and it would not be the last. In May 1917, he won the Military Medal while leading scouting patrols at Bully-Grenay near Lens and was promoted from NCO to lieutenant. In September 1918, he was awarded the Military Cross for leading an attack on the village of Caigmicourt, an action in which he was wounded. King George V pinned the Victoria Cross and Military Medal to his tunic on July 17, 1918 at an investiture at Buckingham Palace. By this time he had reached the rank of captain.

George Burdon McKean was born in Bishop Auckland, County Durham, England, on July 4, 1888. He emigrated to Canada in 1902 and settled in Edmonton. When the First World War broke out, he was a student at the University of Alberta. He enlisted in the 51st Battalion, later transferring to the 14th. Prior to going overseas he was married to Elizabeth Hall.

After the war, McKean was put in charge of the Bureau of the Khaki University of London, England. He also was the author of two books, *Making Good*, dealing with his coming to and settling in Canada, and *Scouting Thrills*, relating his war experiences. He eventually settled near Brighton where he operated a saw mill. He was accidentally killed on November 28, 1926 when a circular saw broke and pieces of the metal struck him in the head. He was buried in Brighton Extra-Mural Cemetery.

McKean was married twice and it was to his second wife, Constance McKean Raby, that his VC passed after he died. In 1970, the Canadian War Museum traced the VC to her in Gosport Hants where she was living at the time. Nine years later, she put the VC, along with McKean's MM and MC, up for auction with Sothebey Parke Bernet in London where they were sold to the late Jack Stenabaugh, a collector from Huntsville, Ont. Her reasoning was logical. She wanted them to be properly looked after, and the funds she would derive at eighty-one years of age meant that she "didn't have to become a burden on her family." In 1989, the set surfaced again with a British military collector in Colchester, Essex. This time the Museum managed to acquire them for an undisclosed sum, the second time the Museum had purchased a VC since the successful bid for "Willie" Milne's medal earlier that year.

BY the first week of June in 1918, it was clear that the German gamble had failed. And at this time the Allies were getting ready to make a final counter-offensive that would end the war. But the enemy still had a lot of fight left in him.

On the night of June 8, the Germans launched a violent thirty-minute artillery barrage

Joseph Kaeble, 22nd Battalion

in preparation for an attack on the 22nd Canadian Infantry Battalion trench line at Neuville-Vitasse in the Arras sector. Quebecker Joseph Kaeble, a corporal in charge of a machine-gun post, who had earlier been decorated for bravery with the Military Medal and had also been wounded, lost all of his men killed or wounded except one. But Kaeble stayed at his post. He had utter confidence in his Lewis gun and his own ability as a marksman.

As soon as the bombardment stopped, fifty Germans charged the position. Kaeble leapt over the parapet and faced them head-on firing from the hip, emptying one drum after another. Finally, mortally wounded and bleeding profusely, he fell back into the trench firing off a last few rounds over the parapet. Before passing out he exhorted the men around him, "*Tenez bon, mes vieux, ne les laissez passer, il faut les arrêter.*" ("Keep it up boys, don't let them through! We must stop them!") He never learned that his action had won him the VC nor that it had forced the Germans to retreat — in fact he, single-handedly, was responsible for routing three enemy companies — because he succumbed to his wounds shortly afterwards. Kaeble was buried in Wanquetin Communal Cemetery Extension seven miles east of Arras.

No one died more bravely, few so horrifically. No doubt Kaeble would have preferred it that way. For in addition to a lofty sense of duty — "When I get older I will go to France and will be fighting the war" — he was something of a fatalist. "Remember, Adrien, that if I do not come back, you will never abandon dear mother and sister," he told his younger brother before shipping overseas.

Joseph Kaeble was born at St. Moise in Matane County, Quebec on May 5, 1893 and was educated at Les frères de la Croix village school in Sayabec. At the age of seventeen he took a job as a driver-mechanic with a lumber firm in Priceville. On March 21, 1915, he joined 189th Battalion from the lower St. Lawrence, later being posted to the 22nd.

Kaeble had a high sense of duty. From his hospital bed after suffering a shoulder wound he wrote home: "I languish within these walls. I am waiting with eagerness to return to the battlefield." He also had a fierce sense of loyalty, particularly to France. "I am so happy to go to fight for our France," he proudly said to his mother Marie Ducas, whose grandparents had emigrated from Normandy. Paradoxically, on his paternal side an ancestor, Thomas Kebel, had arrived in Canada with the German army in 1776 at the time of the American Revolution. When it was over, he stayed in Canada and married a native Scot.

Succeeding generations changed the name to Keable, confirmed by 20th-century official records, family correspondence and reports, including the authoritative *London Gazette*, which show it as Kaeble. However, there is one notable exception. In a letter from the conservateur of Le Musée, Royal 22e Regiment, Quebec City, dated November 26, 1969, advising the Canadian War Museum that it is in possession of Kaeble's Victoria Cross, the name in question is spelled *Keable*.

Kaeble's mother received the medal from Canada's governor general, the Duke of Devonshire, on December 16, 1918. His name appears in the memorial in the Sayabec parish church, the town where he went to school. A pencil drawing showing Kaeble firing his Lewis gun from the trench parapet is on display at the Canadian War Museum.

Chapter Nineteen

"BUS" MACLEOD AND THE FLYING CIRCUS

That kid has more spirit than all the rest of the pilots and gunners in this squadron.
He's wasted messing around here in England. He ought to be over there at the Front.

Commanding Officer,
51st Royal Flying Corps Home Defense Squadron

WHEN Alan Arnett MacLeod hobbled forward with the aid of a pair of canes to receive his Victoria Cross from King George V, His Majesty's jaw dropped in awe and admiration. He found it hard to believe that the tall youngster with the boyish grin standing to attention before him had actually defied the Richthofen Flying Circus by shooting down three of their planes and surviving five wounds in the process. Just turned nineteen — so young. But preserving royal aplomb, as he pinned the decoration to the Canadian lieutenant's breast under his pilot's wings, the British monarch simply remarked, "I am proud to know you." The king then congratulated him on his "brave deed."

That ceremony took place on September 4, 1918 at Buckingham Palace, a fitting commemoration to the feat for which MacLeod was awarded the VC just over five months earlier on March 27. Ironically and tragically, two months and two days later, the youngest Canadian airman ever to win the coveted medal was dead. On November 6 in a Winnipeg hospital he fell victim, not to enemy gunfire which he had time and time again treated so contemptuously, but to a far more insidious antagonist — that pestilent plague ravaging the Dominion that fall, the Spanish influenza that killed 21 million people worldwide.

"Buster" MacLeod, known as "Bus" to his friends, grew up in the small prairie town of Stonewall, Man., fifteen miles north of the provincial capital of Winnipeg. Born on April 20, 1899, MacLeod (the name has often been misspelled McLeod, even in such official documents as the *London Gazette*) was the son of a doctor whose father came from Scotland as an employee of the Hudson Bay Company. MacLeod's mother was another early Western Canadian Scottish settler, under the aegis of Lord Selkirk. That background possibly explains a restless spirit.

Boyhood chums remember Bus MacLeod as cheerful and active, with lots of get-up-and-go. He liked to drive his father's Ford at the then break-neck speed of thirty miles an hour along the twin ruts of a country road, taking the corners on two wheels. On one occasion, he rode down the school slide on his skates ending up at the bottom in a painful heap. As regular as clockwork he would appear before the board of trustees of the Stonewall Collegiate to explain his caprices. Nonetheless, he was a fair and diligent student who also had his serious side.

He had developed an affinity for the military early on. In June 1913, giving his age as eighteen — he was big for a fourteen-year-old and was allowed to get away with it — he qualified for two weeks of summer training with the Fort Garry Horse at Fort Sewell. Having grown up around horses, he had no trouble with the cavalry curricula. In fact, Trooper MacLeod proved to be one of the unit's most able equestrians.

But when war broke out in 1914, his interest shifted toward flying. It appealed to his sense of adventure and somewhat turbulent nature. At seventeen, he tried to join the cadet wing of the Royal Flying Corps in Toronto. But this time when he lied about his age, he was asked to produce his birth certificate. He was allowed to make application but was told that it would not be processed until he reached eighteen. Next year on his birthday, he was overjoyed when advised he had been accepted and was ordered to report to Long Branch, Desoronto on April 23, 1917 to start pilot training.

Beginning with his first instructional flight on June 4 in a Curtiss JN4, MacLeod took to the air like a nestling takes wing. A natural pilot who learned fast, after only five dual flights he went solo. On June 16, he was sent to Camp Borden and by July 31 had graduated as a pilot.

Following two weeks' leave, which he spent at home in Stonewall, in mid-August with others in his class, he sailed for England. After a short refresher course at Winchester, he was posted to 82 Squadron at Waddington in Lincolnshire which was equipped with the lumbering Armstrong-Whitworth artillery-bomber biplanes that MacLeod described as "having the aerodynamics of a cow." Late in September, the unit received orders to proceed to France. But when the commanding officer checked MacLeod's record, only to discover he was merely eighteen years old, he dropped him from the roster and informed him he would have to wait until he was nineteen to go on active service.

MacLeod was disappointed but accepted the decision philosophically and was subsequently posted to 51 Squadron, a Home Defense unit flying black-painted FE2b fighters — "Fees." For two of the worst months of the year, MacLeod and his mates clawed their way through the murk at night over London in search of German Zeppelin and Gotha bomber-raiders. In addition to enemy fire, there was also the danger of collision. MacLeod was shot down over the British capital on one flight, but managed to land safely. He treated the incident more as a lark than a mishap. In fact, he seemed to enjoy the entire exercise that autumn, moving his commanding officer to remark that here was a youngster who "liked to fly" and prompting him to pull strings to get the eighteen-year old Canadian posted to the Front.

In November, MacLeod was assigned to 2 Squadron, based at Hesdigneul in France, that was equipped with the clumsy Armstrong-Whitworths assigned to night bombing, photographing and artillery co-operation. When the squadron CO first spotted him, he let out a wail of anguish. "What is this, a nursery?" he demanded to know. "This kid can't be more than fifteen. I won't put up with this."

The CO ordered a senior observer to go up with MacLeod to see if the baby-faced youngster could really fly. He was in for a surprise. Few pilots could fly the Armstrong-Whitworth as deftly as MacLeod, both in the air and on take-off and landing (he could put it down in the shortest run of anyone). "He's not bad," the monitor admitted grudgingly.

MacLeod made his first flight across enemy lines on December 2. By the end of the month, despite his CO's early scepticism, he had become recognized as a first-class pilot and an acknowledged all-round expert in gunnery, photographing and counter-battery

Alan MacLeod, Royal Flying Corps

work. On one flight, his aircraft was attacked by a German Albatros. His observer was unable to return the enemy fire because his gun had jammed — or so he thought. However, with a skilful manoeuvre, MacLeod succeeded in eluding the enemy scout and got back to Hesdigneul all in one piece. It turned out that the observer had forgotten to release the safety catch. Any other pilot might have hit the roof over his crewman's ineptitude, but not MacLeod. He laughed it off.

At this point, the former summertime cavalry trooper from Stonewall went seriously on the make, out looking for any trouble wherever he could find it. One of his observers wrote in a letter: "Alan would take on anything, and I was willing to go anywhere with him. I had absolute confidence in him. He was the finest pilot I have ever flown with, and always merry and cheerful as he was determined."

Taking advantage of the first clear day in a week, on January 3, 1918, MacLeod went hunting, starting his personal New Year's offensive. Over the Flanders town of La Bassée where he had spotted a concentration of German troops, he flew back and forth while his observer sprayed the area with machine-gun fire, inflicting heavy casualties. A good start.

Then, on January 14, he and his observer attacked a German observation balloon. This was dangerous work, even for a small fast scout plane. But for a lumbering two-seater bomber to attempt it was virtually suicidal. As they approached the target, the air filled with the ugly grey bursts of exploding anti-aircraft shells and the smell of cordite. Dodging this way and that, MacLeod climbed above the balloon, then put the Armstrong-Whitworth into a dive as if he was flying a fighter.

Finally, he pulled up level with the gas bag, allowing his observer to rake it with his machine gun. The "sausage" suddenly erupted in flames and sagged to earth in a deflated heap. Now, as the bomber turned away, three Albatros scouts attacked. MacLeod twisted and turned to place the observer in a position to get a clear shot at them. With a quick squirt from his Lewis gun, he sent one of the German attackers spiralling down to earth on fire. The other two fled. For the action, MacLeod was Mentioned-in-Dispatches. The stage was now set for the scenario that won him the Victoria Cross.

By March 27, the British army was reeling before the German juggernaut. One of the countermeasures employed was the daylight aerial bombardment of enemy dispositions and installations behind the lines. On this dismal, misty morning, 2 Squadron found itself in just such a role. Flying through thick fog, MacLeod and his observer soon became separated from the rest of their formation. MacLeod turned the Armstrong-Whitworth west until he found a field where they could set down and establish their bearings. More bad news. On landing the airplane's tail skid broke off and they had to wait for a tender to arrive from Hesdigneul with a new one to replace it. Not until well after lunch were they able to take off again. This time, MacLeod steered toward the designated target area around Albert, close to where the Richthofen Flying Circus was stationed at Douai.

At 3,000 feet, just under broken clouds, he and his observer were training on the target — a German gun battery — when one of the Red Baron's Fokker triplanes bounced them from above. MacLeod swung the two-seater around to give his observer a shot at the intruder and with three short bursts he sent the fighter spinning to earth.

But they were far from being out of danger. Through a break in the cumulus they counted seven more triplanes above them, diving in their direction. One of them came so close that MacLeod's observer shot it down at pointblank range. But at that very moment another Fokker swooped down and up from behind and below the Armstrong-Whitworth. Its bullets struck the fuel tank and the fuselage, wounded both the pilot and observer, and set the bomber on fire.

The floor of the observer's seat dropped away so that he was forced to climb up on the gun ring above it. Meanwhile, MacLeod wrestled himself out of the cockpit onto the lower port wing and, by controlling the joy stick with his right hand from a standing position, he put the aircraft into a steep side-slip to blow the flames away from both airmen. One of the triplane pilots, thinking they were done for, made such a close pass that the wounded observer could see his face. Though one of his arms was badly injured, he managed to sight on the enemy plane and shoot it down. But now another Fokker took aim on the observer to put him out of business, its bullets striking the two-seater time and time again while MacLeod manoeuvred his stricken plane down to the ground where he crash-landed in a shell hole.

Both men were luckily thrown clear. Seconds later, the blazing wreckage set off eight bombs and 1,000 rounds of ammunition. Neither were hit by the explosion, but the observer fainted from loss of blood. They went from the frying pan into the fire; they were caught between the lines and in severe danger of becoming targets for German machine-gunners. Though MacLeod had been hit five times, he summoned sufficient strength to drag his partner toward their own lines, but was again struck by an enemy bullet. Finally he collapsed from exhaustion just as members of a South African infantry regiment came to their rescue. MacLeod, though unconscious, was still holding his observer's collar in a vise-like grip.

MacLeod and his father who, because of the critical nature of his son's wounds, had sailed to England to be with him, celebrated the Buckingham Palace investiture with a champagne dinner at the Savoy hosted by Billy Bishop, Canada's first air VC, and Arthur Richardson, first to be awarded the decoration during the Boer War. The Winnipeg and Stonewall communities went all out in welcoming "Bus" home. (Significantly, of the seven Canadian aerial VCs, three — MacLeod, Barker and Mynarski — hailed from Manitoba.) Stonewall declared a civic holiday in MacLeod's honour.

From the speaker's podium, he shyly stuttered, "I am no speaker. I want to thank you very, very much. I only hope I deserve it." Later, in the privacy of his living room, when asked about his exploit he modestly replied: "There is nothing to tell. Whatever I did is in the official report. People will think I'm suffering from a swelled head instead of wounds."

As MacLeod began slowly to recuperate, he looked forward to returning to the Front — and the nineteen-year-old received word that he would be elevated to a captaincy. Then, late in October, he contracted the dreaded influenza. He had not regained sufficient stamina to ward it off. Complications set in and he developed pneumonia. On the evening of November 6, he died in his sleep at Winnipeg General Hospital, only five days before the signing of the Armistice.

Three days later his coffin was borne by six Royal Air Force pall bearers behind a cortège of 200 officers and men from local regiments. Alan Arnett MacLeod was laid to rest in Winnipeg's Kildonan Cemetery. On January 9, 1919, his father received a letter from the Privy Purse Office of Buckingham Palace that read:

> I am commanded by the King and Queen to express their sincere sympathy to you at the loss you have sustained by the death of your gallant son, Lieutenant A.A. McLeod, (sic) VC., who, Their Majesties regret to hear, has succumbed to the illness while in the service of his country.

In January 1924, a tablet placed by the Clan MacLeod Society commemorating Alan MacLeod was unveiled in the Highlanders Memorial Church in Glasgow, Scotland at a ceremony attended by a Royal Air Force detachment and official delegates from Canada.

In 1967, his Victoria Cross, service medals and personal letters sent home, were donated by his sister, Mrs. Helen Annetts, to the Canadian War Museum. In 1992, the VC and his other medals were loaned to the Bishop Building, Air Command Headquarters in Winnipeg.

In September 1918, in welcoming Bus MacLeod home, Mayor David Slattern had told him in front of his townfolk that "Long after you are dead your name will live in history."

Let's hope so! *

Fighting the Flying Circus

Rowland Bourke, Royal Navy Volunteer Reserve

Chapter Twenty

THE RESOLUTE REJECT

"The bravest of all holders of the Victoria Cross."

Admiral Sir Roger Keyes,
Royal Navy Commander of the Dover Patrol

THE Canadian army didn't want him. Our navy turned him down. Bum eyesight, they said. But that didn't stop him — far from it. Rejected by his adopted country, he returned to his native land where he joined the Royal Naval Volunteer Reserve (RNVR). And with that service he took part in the most daring naval raid of the Great War to become the only Canadian sailor to win the Victoria Cross in that conflict.

In World War I, the Royal Navy (RN) was made up of mighty battlewagons designed to slug it out with the enemy's surface fleet. Two cases in point: at Dogger Bank in 1915 and at Jutland a year later it had traded blows with the German Imperial Fleet, and though bloodied and bruised remained unbowed. As a result, the Germans were unable to loosen the grip of the British naval blockade. On the other hand, the RN failed to arrest the German U-boat threat, although it provided convoy escorts to protect merchant shipping across the Atlantic. But that was purely a defensive measure. By April of 1918, the British Admiralty recognized that the only way to destroy this menace was to attack it at the source.

The Germans were operating from the

Belgian port of Bruges, eight miles inland from the coast. Canals opening onto the North Sea at Ostend and Zeebrugge, though shallow, could accommodate the transit of thirty-five destroyers and motor boats and, most important of all, thirty submarines to the inland naval base. In Western Flanders, Sir Douglas Haig's spring offensive aimed at freeing the port had been blunted well short of its objective. The RN decided to take matters into its own hands.

The plan was to render the Bruges base useless by blocking the entrances to the canals with obsolete British cruisers filled with cement and charged with mines to sink them. At Zeebrugge, a fearsome battery of guns protecting the area had first to be overcome. A breakwater one and one-half miles long and eighty feet wide extended out to sea, covered by 229 guns ranging from 15-inch naval guns to $3\frac{1}{2}$-inch cannon as well as innumerable machine guns. Under a heavy smokescreen, Royal Marines were to be put ashore to occupy the pier and create as much damage and confusion as possible to enable the obsolete ships to manoeuvre into position and have the charges set. Also, the crews had to get to awaiting rescue motor launches. The main deterrent at Ostend were batteries on two piers on either side of the canal and it was there — not at the heavily fortified Zeebrugge — that the navy ran into trouble.

The operation was launched on the night of April 22, though it did not quite come off as planned. At Zeebrugge, a southeast wind blew the smokescreen out to sea, exposing the raiders to relentless fire from the defenders on the breakwater. Casualties were heavy. In the face of intense enemy fire, demolition parties scrambled ashore to begin their work of destruction. As the dynamite charges detonated, buildings, store-sheds, hangars and other structures burst into flames, split and crumbled. In addition, the marines blew up a submarine loaded with munitions and fuel that created the largest, loudest seafaring explosion of the war.

By the time it was over, three of the British cruisers lay sunk across the neck of the canal in a V position, effectively blocking it. However, the raid at Ostend did not meet with similar success. The Germans, possibly forewarned, had shifted one of two lighted marker buoys that the British intended to use as navigational guides and had removed the other. In addition, the blockships were blinded by enemy searchlights. As a result, the first one was sunk a mile east of the canal entrance. In the inky darkness, the second obsolete light cruiser rammed into it from astern, driving it further into the sand. Both were well out of harm's way and the canal remained wide open. With the job only half done, this failed attack demanded a second attempt.

At the outset of the operation, Admiral Sir Roger Keyes, commander of the Dover Patrol, had called for 1,600 volunteers (who were told they would probably never be coming back). Rowland Bourke from Crescent Bay, British Columbia was one of the first among them. As commander of the thirty-seven-ton, eighty-foot-long motor launch *ML276*, his job would be to take the crews off the blockship once it had been sunk. But because of his restricted eyesight (he wore glasses), he was not accepted. However, he was able to convince his superiors that he could serve in a stand-by capacity.

In the attack on Ostend, the rescue launch *ML532* was badly damaged. Bourke quickly came to the rescue. Ignoring enemy fire from the piers, he pulled his craft alongside the sunken cruiser *Brilliant*, taking off thirty-eight officers and men. He then towed the crippled *ML532* to within five miles of Dunkirk, where the launch proceeded home under its own power. Bourke received the Distinguished Service Order for his night's work. And he was only getting started.

For a second raid on Ostend scheduled for May 9, Bourke's *ML276* had been so badly damaged during the first sortie that he arranged to act as 1st lieutenant in the rescue launch designated for the operation. He stripped his own ship of its equipment, including the Lewis guns, and fitted them into the other vessel. But just before the raid, Admiral Keyes vetoed the idea of his acting in a subordinate role. However, if he could get his own launch into operational condition in time, he would again be allowed to serve as a back-up. It took some scrounging around, but with the help of his crew, by the night of May 9, Bourke had *ML276* ship-shape again.

Of two cruisers designated as blockships, one had to turn back due to engine trouble. That left *Vindictive*, which had played an instrumental part at Zeebrugge, as the sole means of bottling up the Ostend canal. Again, partial success. In spite of thick fog, the captain managed to steer his ship into the harbour mouth. But as he began to manoeuvre the vessel to a position where it would lie across the channel, a shell landed on the bridge, killing him. His 1st lieutenant immediately took over and tried to swing the stern, but it was too late. The cruiser had run aground. He had no choice but to order the crew to abandon ship.

While following *Vindictive* into the channel, the captain of the rescue launch *ML254*, his second-in-command and a sailor aboard had been wounded. They nevertheless were able to pull alongside and take off forty of the crew. Then, as the launch drew away, the charges set in *Vindictive* blew up and the ship settled on the bottom. Lying at an angle across the canal, it only partly obstructed traffic, but it was considered good enough.

ML254's skipper retained consciousness long enough to back his launch away, then sank exhausted from his wounds. *Vindictive*'s Number One assumed command. As he steered the vessel out of the harbour, he passed Bourke's *ML276* on the way in to check that everyone from *Vindictive* had managed to get away. Bourke cruised around under heavy fire from piers on either side of the canal for about ten minutes and was just leaving when he heard cries for help from the water. Returning, after a prolonged search he found an officer and two sailors clinging desperately to an upturned life-boat. All three were badly wounded.

Despite the relentless fire from the piers being poured into his motor launch, Bourke managed to pick up all three and make for the open sea under reduced power. In the process of the rescue, *ML276* was hit by a 6-inch shell which killed two of her crew. In all, the craft sustained a total of fifty-five strikes to the hull and upper structure.

In its stilted way, the citation to Bourke's Victoria Cross summed up Bourke's feat quite succinctly: "This episode displayed daring and skill of a very high order...." King George V pinned the medal to his tunic on September 11 of that year, during an investiture at Buckingham Palace. The French government also conferred upon him the Chevalier of the Legion of Honour.

Rowland Richard Louis Bourke was born in London on November 28, 1885, the son of a British army surgeon. Before moving to Canada in 1902 at age seventeen, he attended several Roman Catholic Orders in London. At first he tried his hand at gold mining in the Klondike, which he abandoned to take up fruit farming at Crescent Bay near Nelson, B.C. Turned down by both Canadian services, he sailed for England in 1916 where the RNVR accepted him as a lieutenant. Following the Ostend raids he was promoted to the rank of lieutenant-commander.

In 1919, he married Rosalind Barnet of Sydney, Australia. Demobilized the following year, he returned to his fruit farm. By 1931, however, his eyesight had deteriorated so badly that he was afraid he was going blind. He gave up farming and moved to Victoria where he was employed as a supervisor by the Royal Canadian Naval Barracks at Esquimalt and was later appointed to organize the British Columbia Fishermen's Naval Reserve in Vancouver. In World War II, he joined the Royal Canadian Naval Volunteer Reserve and was given administration duties.

After the war ended, he returned to Esquimalt where he worked for the Canadian Civil Service, retiring in 1950. Friends described Bourke as a "very quiet, reserved gentleman who didn't like having a fuss made over him." He went to few of the VC functions and would only allow his picture to be taken under the strongest protest. But he could also display an impish sense of humour. He used to say that he won the VC because he couldn't see well enough to get out of the way.

Rowland Bourke died on August 29, 1958 and was buried at Royal Oak Burial Park. His Victoria Cross is with the National Archives of Canada in Ottawa.

Victoria Cross

Chapter Twenty-One

"I MEAN TO COME BACK WITH THE VC"

ROBERT Edward Cruickshank, a native Manitoban, became the only Canadian in World War I to be awarded the Victoria Cross for valour outside of the European theatre. Before sailing for the Middle East on January 21, 1917, he promised his mother, "I mean to come back with the VC." Cruickshank, who was born in Winnipeg on June 17, 1888, proved as good as his word. But before taking part in the commendable action that won him his VC, he had already had a spectacular military career.

As a private with the London Scottish, he was wounded in the attack on the Lueze Wood on the Somme and invalided back to England. By January of the following year, he had fully recovered and was transferred to the Egyptian Expeditionary Force, taking part in the occupation of Jerusalem and the capture of Jericho from the Turks.

On May 1, 1918, in a bitter desert battle, Cruickshank's platoon came under heavy rifle and machine-gun fire at close range while manoeuvring down a steep bank into a wadi. Most of the men had been hit, and as soon as they reached the bottom the commanding officer was cut down by enemy bullets. The platoon sergeant, who immediately took charge, quickly sent a runner back to company headquarters asking for reinforcements. No sooner had he done so than he too was killed. That left the lance-corporal in command who, sensing that the messenger had also been killed, asked for a volunteer to take back a second message. Cruickshank answered the call without hesitation.

He pushed his way up the slope, but was hit by a bullet and fell back into the *wadi*. Picking himself up, he rushed up the bank again and was again struck down by enemy fire and rolled back down into the stream. After having his wounds dressed, he made another attempt and for a third time was wounded, this time so seriously he couldn't even stand up. He was forced to lie all day exposed to sniper fire until he could be moved under cover of darkness.

Cruickshank's commanding officer wrote his mother: "As you will know by this time your son was wounded on May 1 carrying out dangerous and arduous duties in a most glorious and gallant manner. His work on that day was invaluable to the battalion.... I can assure you that you can pride yourself on having one of the bravest of the many brave sons of Britain."

From a hospital bed in Egypt, Cruickshank himself wrote to a former business colleague in London: "After a long campaign, including many battles, patrol fights, I have at last received my full share of wounds. Altogether I have eight different wounds — three explosive bullets in my left leg, one explosive in the left wrist, one explosive below the muscle on my right arm, one bullet in the right leg, and one in the left thigh." His mother told a reporter, "He never knew when he was beaten."

When he was three years old his father, who was an accountant from Scotland, and his mother, a native of Liverpool, moved from Winnipeg to North London. For the purposes of this compendium, that still qualifies Eddie Cruickshank as a Canadian VC. He was educated in London at Cowper Street Central Foundation School and Bancroft School in Essex. Before joining the Royal Flying Corps in 1915 — from which he transferred to the London Scottish at his own request — he worked for Lever Brothers, Ltd., the soap manufacturers, and took a keen interest in politics as a member of the Liberal Party.

Following the war, in 1919 Cruickshank married Gwendoline May Mansell of Bush Hill Park and they made their home in Leicester. Cruickshank died on September 1, 1961. His Victoria Cross is on display at the London Scottish Museum on Buckingham Palace Road in London.

Chapter Twenty-Two

DAY ONE OF THE 100 DAYS

"Hold fast ... our prospects of victory have never been so bright as they are today."

David Lloyd George,
British Prime Minister commenting on the arrival of 300,000 American troops in France

"August 8 was a black day in the history of the German army."

Erich Ludendorff,
German chief of staff to Paul von Hindenburg, chief commander of the Central Powers

DECEPTION and surprise characterized the launch of the final Allied offensive of the war, in which the Canadian Corps formed the vanguard. Preliminary discussions were never held in the same place. Even divisional commanders were kept in the dark until July 31, 1918, and the troops were not informed until thirty-six hours before the assault was due to start. Troops were moved back and forth from one location to another to confuse enemy reconnaissance. This was particularly true in the case of the Canadians, whose presence anywhere spelled imminent attack to the Germans.

On August 7, the day before the launch, part of the Canadian Corps which had been sent to the Ypres sector as a decoy was moved south to rejoin the rest of the Allied troops situated in the Gentilles Wood near Amiens. At 4:20 a.m., August 8, without warning the enemy with the customary pre-assault artillery barrage, the Canadians, supported by tanks, charged forward on a front 8,500 yards wide.

It was indeed a "black day" for the German army, as Ludendorff noted. By nightfall the "shock troops," as the enemy named the Canadians, had advanced an unprecedented eight miles, captured 8,000 prisoners, 161 guns and countless rounds of ammunition, at a cost of fewer than 4,000 casualties. It was the start of what became known as "Canada's 100 Days," and although many bitter struggles lay ahead, it was also the beginning of the end. Considered to be the most decisive battle of the war, it had so seriously undermined the German Supreme Command that Ludendorff was forced to acknowledge that his war machine was "no longer efficient."

The day's fighting was all the more spectacular for Canada which saw four of her native sons awarded the Victoria Cross: Jean Brillant of the 22nd Canadian Infantry Battalion, John Croak and Herman Good with the 13th and Harry Miner of the 58th. Three of them — Croak, Miner and Brillant — lost their lives and were awarded the decoration posthumously.

Two were Maritimers. John Bernard Croak, who became the first Newfoundlander to win the VC, was born in Little Bay on May 18, 1892. Herman James Good, who hailed from New Brunswick, was born in South Bathurst on November 29, 1887. Jean Brillant was a Quebecker who was born on March 15, 1890 at Assametquaghan. Harry Garnet Bedford Miner came from Raleigh County near Cedar Springs, Ont., where he was born on June 24, 1891.

John Croak, 13th Battalion

When he was four years old, John Croak[1] moved with his parents to Glace Bay's New Aberdeen District in Nova Scotia. That qualifies him as the third Nova Scotian to win the VC as well as being the first from Newfoundland.

Croak attended the New Aberdeen School and St. John's School and afterwards worked as a coal miner. In 1914, he travelled to Western Canada and on his way home volunteered for overseas service in the 55th Battalion then being mobilized in St. John, N.B. After basic training at Sussex, he was transferred to the 13th Battalion (Royal Highlanders of Canada, later the Black Watch). By the time of the Battle of Amiens, he had served two years in the trenches as a private.

Herman Good received his education at Big River School in Gloucester County, N.B. After graduation he went into the lumber business. In 1915, he joined the army and subsequently served with the 55th, 2nd Pioneer and 13th Battalions. Before the launch of the 1918 summer offensive, he had spent three years at the Front, fought at Ypres, the Somme and Vimy Ridge, had been wounded three times and held the rank of corporal.

After graduating from St. Joseph University in New Brunswick, Jean Brillant enlisted in the Canadian Militia, serving with Les Fusiliers de St. Laurent. In 1915, for service at the Front, he joined the 189th Battalion which was later merged with the 22nd in France. Prior to August 8, 1918, Brillant had already been decorated for bravery with the Military Cross and held the rank of lieutenant.

Harry Miner attended Selton Public School near Thamesville, Ont. and Highgate High School. In 1915, he signed on with the 142nd Battalion and then trained with the 161st at Camp Borden. On arriving overseas, he transferred to the 58th (later the Royal Regiment of Canada) which he joined in 1916 in France. During his service at the Front he received two minor wounds and was saved from serious injury when a bullet struck his wristwatch, shattering it.

In December 1917, he distinguished himself by repairing a broken telephone line while under heavy enemy fire for which the French awarded him the Croix de Guerre. Rapid promotion followed in February of 1918, first to lance-corporal and then to full corporal.

---

1 The Newfoundland spelling is Croke and that is what appears on the birth certificate; however in the official records as well as in the *London Gazette*, it is spelled Croak, and that is the way it is entered in the register of the Hangard Wood British Cemetery in France where he was buried.

ON August 8 at first light, drizzle, fog and low scudding clouds covered the battlefield. As the troops began their advance, the artillery opened up, adding smoke to the miasma. The tanks were brought to a halt for fear of running over the infantry ahead of them, now invisible in the smoke-drenched fog. At the same time, the troops behind the tanks were also brought to a halt and forced to wait.

German positions that had not been smashed by the artillery began to fight back. It was one of these that John Croak, who had become separated from his platoon east of Amiens, encountered in the form of a machine-gun nest. Croak hurled several Mills bombs into it and then attacked at bayonet point, putting the weapon out of action and taking its crew prisoner. At that moment an enemy bullet ripped into his right arm. Momentarily stunned, he nonetheless managed to catch up with his unit.

When the platoon ran into another German stronghold, the troops hesitated. But Croak, who had no business being there in the first place — he should have been getting his wound dressed — charged forward on the double. Inspired by his courage, the rest of the unit followed, raining bullets and hand grenades onto the German machine-gun positions. Once again, using his bayonet Croak routed out the enemy, killing many of them and capturing others.

But during the mêlée, Croak was wounded again, this time fatally. As the sun began to set, he knew he did not have long to live. He turned to a comrade and said, "Do you wish to show your gratitude? Kneel down and pray for my soul." With that he died. But his words lived on. They are enshrined on his tombstone in the Hangard Wood Cemetery.

MEANWHILE, another member of the 13th Battalion, Herman Good, made a solo attack on a nest of three German machine guns that were holding up the regiment's advance. With Herculean effort, he killed seven of the enemy crews and took the remainder prisoner. His next exploit he shared with three other Highlanders.

By late afternoon the regiment, which had been in the vanguard of the attack, had penetrated several miles into the enemy lines. Good and his men suddenly encountered an artillery battery of 5.9-inch cannon that was pinning down the Canadian advance and pounding positions to the rear.

At first glance, the idea of four men attacking the battery seemed out of the question — they were badly outnumbered. But Good gambled that the enemy gunners would be inexperienced in hand-to-hand fighting, the métier of the 13th Battalion. Counting on the element of surprise, he led a front-

Herman Good, 13th Battalion

A battle scene typical of World War I

on assault that so unnerved the enemy artillery crews they quickly surrendered, and the Canadians captured three heavy enemy guns to boot without any losses.

EARLY in the day, Jean Brillant's company was held up at Méharicourt by a German machine gun. Frustrated with the halt to the 22nd Battalion's advance, with utter disregard for his own safety Brillant rushed forward and captured the machine gun and killed two of the gunners. Though wounded in the attack, he refused to relinquish his command.

Later in the day, his company was once again stalled by enemy machine-gun fire. Organizing his men into two platoons, he led a charge in which 150 Germans and fifteen of the machine guns were captured. Brillant, who accounted for fifteen Germans killed, was wounded again. But still he refused to leave the field and have his injuries dressed.

Subsequently, he attacked a field gun which was firing at his men at pointblank range. After racing forward for 600 yards, he was wounded for a third time. He continued on for another 200 yards and then collapsed from loss of blood and exhaustion. Before losing consciousness, he said to a subaltern, "*Je suis finis, prends charge de la compagnie, car je sais que ça ne sera pas long.*" ("I am through. Take charge of the company because I know I won't be here long.") He died two days later, on August 10, in hospital.

Jean Brillant is buried in the Villers-Bretonneux Military Cemetery at Fouilloy in France.

AT Demuin east of Amiens, Harry Miner was severely wounded in the head, face and shoulder at the outset of the advance by B Company of the 58th Battalion. However, he stalwartly refused to leave the battlefield and have his injuries attended to. Instead, he led his platoon in an attack on the middle of the German outpost trench line.

Later, when a machine gun held up the advance, Miner single-handedly attacked it, killing the crew and turning the weapon on the enemy. But Miner was still not through for the day, even though by this time he was suffering badly from his wounds.

With two others he overwhelmed a German grenade post, bayoneting two of the enemy and putting the rest to flight. During the action, however, he was again wounded, this time mortally, by a German stick-grenade explosion and died later in the day.

Harry Miner is buried in the Crouy British Cemetery at Crouy-sur-Mer in France some ten miles north of Amiens.

* * *

SHORTLY after his death, John Croak's mother received a letter from his battalion chaplain. It read:

> He was a splendid soldier, had done more than one brave deed in clearing out enemy machine-gun nests, he could not have done more gallantly, and I am stating the truth when I tell you that the Battalion could not honour his action more highly than is done. Death came to him quite instantly, and he is buried with his comrades near the place where he fell.

Among the tributes paid him was the naming of a chapter of the Order of the Imperial Daughters of the Empire after him: "The John Bernard Croak VC Chapter of the IODE of Glace Bay, N.S." In 1976, the New Aberdeen School where he received his education was replaced with a new building and renamed "John Bernard Croak Memorial School."

On May 18, 1992 (his 100th birthday), the John Bernard Croak VC Memorial Park in the Beacon Street Dam area, a stone's throw from where the young coal miner grew up, was dedicated in his honour and a cenotaph built by the Croak Memorial Foundation was unveiled. Three hundred war veterans, six from the First World War, attended the ceremony which was preceded by a church memorial service and a parade.

At noon on June 20, 1920, at Government House in Halifax, Lieutenant-Governor McCallum Grant presented John Croak's Victoria Cross to his mother Cecelia. Following her death in 1928, the medal passed to her son Michael, who lived in New York. In 1971, the VC was traced to Croak's grandson, John Bernard (Bernie), who was living in New Hartford and suffering from ill health. He agreed to place it on loan with the Halifax Army Museum. In 1976, it was purchased by the Canadian War Museum for an undisclosed price, but enough to offset Bernard's anticipated medical expenses.

Herman Good was invested with his Victoria Cross by King George V at Buckingham Palace on March 29, 1919. Shortly afterwards, he returned to the woods of New Brunswick and to his home in Big River on the immediate outskirts of Bathurst. He engaged in both farming and lumbering and served for twenty years as fish, game and fire warden of the district.

In 1927, he joined the New Brunswick Travel Bureau and helped arrange provincial exhibits at sportsmen's shows in Boston and Philadelphia. In 1931, Good was one of a select few taken to the White House where, wearing his uniform, he presented President Herbert Hoover with a hamper of choice moose steaks, venison and Atlantic salmon. Eight years later, in 1939, he was presented to King George VI and Queen Elizabeth when they visited Fredericton on a Royal Tour of Canada.

A lifetime member of the Gloucester Branch Royal Canadian Legion, in 1962 he laid the cornerstone for a new building which in 1966 was named after him: "The Herman J. Good Branch." His wife, Martha Moore, with whom he had three sons, predeceased him in 1941. On April 18, 1969, Good died at eighty years of age after a five-day illness. He was buried in St. Alban's Cemetery. His Victoria Cross is retained by his son Frank who lives in Sudbury, Ont. Hopefully, it may one day find its way into the national collection.

Jean Brillant's Victoria Cross is with the Royal 22nd Regiment Museum at the Citadel in Quebec City. In the same city, a branch of the Royal Canadian Legion is named after him. In Rimouski and Montreal, streets bear his name. In the latter city, at the Jean Brillant Park, a monument which was erected in his memory was unveiled by his brother, Senator Jules Brillant, in the summer of 1971.

On October 6, 1918, the *London Gazette* published the official citation to Harry Miner's Victoria Cross: "For most conspicuous bravery and devotion to duty ..." Five months later, on March 28, 1919, citizens of various local civic groups along with his mother and father, John and Sarah, complete with an honour guard, gathered in the Chatham Armouries in southwestern Ontario to pay tribute to his bravery. At the ceremony an equerry representing the king along with the Duke of Devonshire, the governor general of Canada, and the province's lieutenant-governor presented Miner's parents with his Victoria Cross as well as his Croix de Guerre (Fr.). At the same time, "in recognition of his supreme sacrifice," his mother and father were given the keys to a new house as a gift from the city of Chatham, fully furnished by area chapters of the Imperial Daughters of the British Empire, for the nominal sum of $1.00 for as long as they chose to live there.

On September 22, 1963, a provincial commemorative plaque, located on the grounds of the United Church in Cedar Springs at the intersection of Highway 3 and Country Road 10 southwest of Blenheim, was unveiled in Miner's honour. His Victoria Cross was donated to the Clinton Branch of the Royal Canadian Legion.

Chapter Twenty-Three

COINCIDENCES CANADIAN - VC STYLE

O F the action on the Western Front on August 9, 1918 – the second of Canada's 100 Days – the *London Gazette* read like a page out of *The Boy's Own Annual*:

Sjt. (sic) Zengel's work throughout the attack was excellent, and his utter disregard for personal safety, and the confidence he inspired in all ranks, greatly assisted in bringing the attack to a successful end.

Cpl. Brereton's action was a splendid example of resource and bravery, and not only undoubtedly saved many of his comrades' lives, but also inspired his platoon to charge and capture the remaining posts.

Cpl. Coppins, without hesitation, and on his own initiative, called on four men to follow him and leapt forward in the face of intense machine-gun fire. With his comrades he rushed straight for the machine guns.

The careers of all three of those Canadian VCs were replete with coincidences. For instance, Ralph Louis Zengel and Alexander Picton Brereton were born within two days of each other, November 11 and November 13, two years apart, 1894 and 1892, respectively. By a further coincidence, that was the same date in 1917 on which Zengel won a Military Medal for bravery at Passchendaele. Another coincidence: Brereton also received the MM before being awarded the VC. Also, Brereton and Frederick George Coppins received their Victoria Crosses together from King George V at Buckingham Palace on October 24, 1918. That was fitting. Both were with the same regiment – the 85th Battalion (Winnipeg Rifles), the outfit the Germans tagged the "Little Black Devils." And if their VCs were not won at precisely the same minute, they were awarded for the same action, near the same place, and both involved subduing enemy machine guns.

Zengel and Coppins were American, though in some records Coppins is listed as a native Londoner. Only Brereton was Canadian born. Coincidentally too, all three survived the conflict. And to put a cap on it, Brereton was present when Zengel presented his VC and MM, along with his service medals, to the R.L Zengel Branch of the Royal Canadian Legion at Rocky Mountain House, Alta. in 1972. Both Zengel and Brereton re-enlisted in the Canadian army in World War II.

When the First World War broke out, Zengel was working on a farm near Virden, Man. At an early age he had moved to a homestead in Saskatchewan with his widowed mother from Faribault, Minnesota, where he was born. Enlisting in the 45th Battalion, on arrival

Raphael Zengel, 5th Battalion

in France in 1915 he was drafted to the 5th (North Saskatchewan Regiment).

Alec Brereton was born in Oak River, Man. and went to school in Hamiota. Joining the army in 1916, he was posted to the 8th Battalion.

Fred Coppins was born in London, England on October 25, 1889. Circumstances surrounding his enlistment are fuzzy. He and his family must have emigrated to Canada and lived in Winnipeg, because he ended up as a member of the 8th Battalion.

On August 9, Ray Zengel was leading his platoon in the advance to the east of Warvillers. Suddenly, a wicked volume of machine-gun fire opened up that mowed down the troops on his left flank and left a glaring hole in the line. Zengel charged forward on the double 200 yards ahead of his men, overran the gun, killed one of the gunners as well the officer in charge, and sent the rest of the crew scurrying for cover.

Later in the day, when the entire battalion was held up by vicious enemy machine-gun fire, Zengel took charge directing the return fire so accurately that it knocked out the German crews. Then an enemy shell exploded near Zengel, stunning him. However, he soon came to and continued to direct the battalion's fire against the Germans. His efforts paid off helping to bring the day's action by the Canadians to a victorious conclusion.

Meanwhile, near Aubrecourt, Alec Brereton found his platoon caught in open country exposing the troops to a nest of German machine guns. They had no hope of finding cover. As man after man fell to the gunfire, the unit was in grave danger of being completely wiped out. Brereton knew the situation called for drastic action. He sprang forward and single-handedly attacked the closest enemy gun post, shot the gunner and bayoneted another German trying to man the gun. This quick, startling action so unnerved the enemy that nine of them surrendered to him. It also saved his platoon from total annihilation.

While this took place, near Hackett, with another platoon in the same regiment, Fred Coppins found his unit in the same predicament. They faced such severe enemy machine-gun fire that they could neither advance nor retire. There was no place to hide. Only one answer — the guns had to be silenced. Calling for four volunteers, Coppins rushed forward through a rain of bullets. All four of his men were killed and he was wounded, but he managed to take out a gunner and three of the crew, as well as taking four other German prisoners. His quick, courageous action saved his platoon.

After the war, Ray Zengel took up residence at Rocky Mountain House, Alta. and later moved to Errington, B.C. During World War II, he re-enlisted in the army and held the rank of regimental sergeant-major. He died on February 22, 1977 at age eighty-two.

Following his discharge from the army in 1919, Alec Brereton returned to farming and later acquired 640 acres of land in Elnora, Alta. In World War II, he also re-enlisted and held the rank of quartermaster-sergeant based in Red Deer. He was a lifetime member of the Elnora Branch of the Royal Canadian Legion which was named after him. On July 1, 1976 he died at Golden Hills Lodge in Three Hills, Alta. He was eighty-three. His Victoria Cross is reportedly in the possession of members of the family.

Fred Coppins went to California where he worked for the Pacific Gas and Electric Company as a construction foreman in Oakland. Though details are scarce, it seems that Coppins left his Victoria Cross somewhere in Los Angeles for safekeeping. When he went pick it up some time later, it had disappeared. He had resigned himself to the fact that it was lost when, thirty-eight years later, he received it in the mail in a package from London, England — one that bore no return address or name. Today, it is with the Royal Winnipeg Rifles Museum (Little Black Devils) in Winnipeg.

Coppins died on March 30, 1963 at the U.S. Administration Hospital in Livermore, California. Three days later, a funeral service was held in Oakland attended by members of the Canadian Legion, the Last Post Fund and Canada's consul-general.

A bayonet attack

Chapter Twenty-Four

CONSOLIDATION

B Y August 11, 1918, the Amiens battle had developed into one of consolidation. The Germans had rushed eighteen fresh divisions into the line. The captured trenches had seen better days and field conditions were wet, muggy and deplorable. Ferdinand Foch, the Allied commander, who at first wanted the offensive to continue, finally agreed with Sir Douglas Haig and Sir Arthur Currie that any new thrust should be started elsewhere. The Arras front became the chosen venue. Meanwhile, there was a lot of mopping up to be done to stabilize the line. During this hiatus, three acts of valour were added to the growing Canadian Victoria Cross roster.

One of the VC winners, James Edward Tait, born in Kircudbrightshire, Scotland on May 17, 1886, had received the Military Cross two years earlier for "conspicuous gallantry and devotion to duty." During the storming of Vimy Ridge on Easter Monday, April 9, 1916, early on in the assault he became wounded and all of the other officers in his company had been killed. But that didn't stop him from leading his men forward to overwhelm an enemy position. Although by this time he was unable to walk, he nevertheless directed the consolidation of the captured German post, then crawled to the rear leaving four others to be carried back by stretcher-bearers. For this action he received his medal.

Also, while recuperating from his wounds back in England, he wrote a highly graphic description of the battle which appeared in the periodical CANADA a year later. In it he reminisced about his days as a government surveyor before the war in the Kettle River District of North-West Canada, where he had emigrated from his native Scotland.

> Thoughts of home! Canoes, guns, trail, the camp on the river, the smell of wood smoke at twilight, the sunset on the lake. Oh! sweet memories; the bitter cold, the snow-clad trail, the yelp of the Husky, the howl of the Indian dog, how far away it all seemed, that old world that we left to so long ago and how different to that in which we live now! A world of mud and many-coloured star-shells, of continual thunder and lightning, a world of endless days and restless nights; of "runyars" and "crumps," a world of death and devastation, and unspeakable misery and desolation.

Tait was born in Dumfries, Scotland on May 27, 1886 and attended Laurieknowe School in Maxwelltown, a suburb of Dumfries, as well as the Dumfries Academy. In 1915, he enlisted in the 100th Battalion (Winnipeg Grenadiers) about the same time his brother Robert (who had also emigrated to Canada) joined the 79th Cameron Highlanders in Winnipeg. Tait arrived in England in 1916, where in August he made military application for permission to marry Jessie Biers. In September, he was sent to France to join the 78th Canadian Infantry Battalion. It is likely that his marriage took place while he was recovering from his wounds in 1917.

Between the start of the British offensive on August 8 and August 11, Tait added to his laurels by winning the Victoria Cross. Though the initial attack had been checked with intense machine-gun fire, Tait rallied his company to charge ahead. Then a concealed machine gun started to inflict heavy casualties. Grabbing a rifle with a bayonet mount from one of his troop, Tait dashed forward and killed the German gunner. Inspired by his élan, his men quickly overran the enemy position, captured twelve machine guns and took twenty prisoners. This action allowed Tait's entire battalion to advance. Later, when the Germans counterattacked under an intense artillery barrage, Tait was mortally wounded by an exploding shell. But before he died, he continued to direct and encourage his men.

The location of Tait's interment is uncertain. He is believed to have been buried in the French village of Hallu, then moved to Fouquescourt British Military Cemetery. Tait's name may be found in the Laurieknowe School War Memorial as well as on

James Tait, 78th Battalion

Thomas Dinesen, 42nd Battalion

the Maxwelltown Memorial. His Victoria Cross was last reported, in 1947, to be in the possession of a nephew living in Pennant, Sask.

TOM Dinesen was the only Canadian VC ever to be decorated for the same action twice. On August 12, in ten hours of bloody hand-to-hand fighting, the Danish-born civil engineer won both the VC and the Croix de Guerre (Fr.). He'd almost had to fight as hard to get into battle as he had once he became engaged in it.

Born in Rungsted on August 9, 1892, Dinesen was a graduate of the Copenhagen Polytechnic School. When he tried to enlist in the British and French armies, he was turned down. Then, in 1917, he tried his luck in the United States with the American army, but was again refused. Finally, through the Canadian recruiting office in New York City, he was accepted as a private in the Royal Highland Regiment (Black Watch) and went overseas with the 42nd Canadian Infantry Battalion.

At Parvillers during the Battle of Amiens, Dinesen time and again led assaults on German positions, wielding his bayonet and using his rifle butt as a club. During the day's fighting, he charged the enemy lines no less than five times, putting a host of machine guns out of action and killing twelve of the enemy with his bayonet, rifle and Mills bombs. This resulted in the capture of a mile of strongly garrisoned and stubbornly defended enemy trenches. In addition to being decorated with the VC and the Croix de Guerre (Fr.), Dinesen was also made a knight of the Order of Dennebrog by the king of Denmark. Dinesen would only say, "I wasn't hit at all — it was extraordinary." On November 5, 1918, he received his commission, and on December 13 he was invested with his VC by King George V at Buckingham Palace.

After the war Dinesen moved to Kenya where he took up farming and practised civil engineering until 1925. He looked upon Canada as a second home and helped form the Canadian-Danish Association. He eventually returned to Denmark, combining a literary career with farming and forestry on his 1,400-acre estate at Leerbeck. He wrote a number of books, including *No Man's Land*, a bestseller in Denmark.

Dinesen helped observe the 100th anniversary of the Victoria Cross in London, England in 1956, and was one of the guests at the Canadian Victoria Cross and George Cross holders' reunion in Ottawa during the 1967 Centennial Year. Thomas Dinesen died on March 10, 1974 at his home in Leerbeck at age eighty-five. He was the last surviving VC holder from the Royal Highlanders. Until recently, his Victoria Cross was on display at the Army Museum in Copenhagen.

THE third Canadian VC awarded during this period of consolidation went to "Rob" Spall of Winnipeg, who deliberately sacrificed himself to save his platoon. He was born Robert Spall, in Suffolk County, England on March 5, 1890 and moved to Canada with his parents when he was two years old. He was working in an office in Winnipeg when the war broke out and enlisted in the 90th Winnipeg Rifles, later transferring to the Princess Patricia's Canadian Light Infantry. By 1918, he held the rank of sergeant.

Robert Spall, Princess Patricia's Light Infantry

On the night of August 12/13, his platoon, entrenched near Parvillers, had been cut off and was isolated from the rest of the regiment. It then became the focus of a brutal German counterattack. Spall picked up a drum-fed Lewis machine gun, climbed over the trench parapet and opened fire on the enemy from a mere 200 yards away. After inflicting heavy casualties, he returned to the trench and directed his unit's fire. By this time, the range had closed to seventy-five yards, placing the entire platoon in grave danger.

Once more Spall grabbed the Lewis gun and again climbed out of the trench and levelled the weapon at the onrushing Germans at pointblank range. His fire stopped them in their tracks and saved his platoon from annihilation or capture. But in the action Spall was cut down by enemy bullets and killed.

The brave PPCLI sergeant became the third in his regiment to earn the Victoria Cross. (He was preceded by Hugh MacKenzie and George Mullin at Passchendaele; see Chapter 16, "Canada's Calvary.") Spall has no known grave, but his name is etched on the Vimy Memorial in France. His Victoria Cross was presented to his next-of-kin. On July 24, 1969, the medal was presented to the PPCLI Regimental Museum at Currie Barracks in Calgary, Alta. by his sister, Mrs. Isobel Stoneman.

Chapter Twenty-Five

THE BEMEDALLED VCS OF THE BATTLE OF SCARPE

FIGURATIVELY speaking, as a pair, they virtually won the battle all by themselves. Quite a performance! Only two you ask? Yes — Charles Smith Rutherford and William Hew Clarke-Kennedy — by war's end the most gonged officers in the Canadian army.

Prior to the start of the new offensive, Charlie Rutherford had already been awarded both the Military Medal and the Military Cross before winning the VC. "C.K." Clarke-Kennedy wore the Order of St. Michael and St. George (CMG), the Distinguished Service Order and Bar and the Croix de Guerre with Palm (Fr.) on his chest before adding the red ribbon with the miniature bronze cross to his row. In addition, he had been Mentioned-in-Dispatches four times.

In August 1918, northeast of Arras, familiar territory to the Canadians, General Sir Arthur Currie's Second and Third Divisions were confronted by a formidable array of German fortifications, barriers that had to be overcome to force a breakthrough before the Hindenburg Line, the enemy's final bastion, could be breached. Immediately ahead, between Arras and Cambrai, they faced the trenches dug by the British that were surrendered in March 1918. Two miles east lay the intricate Drocourt-Quéant line, a rugged, deep-seated system of trenches with concrete shelters and heavy wire designed to block any attempt to break out across the Douai plain. Between that emplacement and Cambrai, the hub of the enemy defense system, the Canal du Nord presented an almost impassible barrier.

The Canadian attack began on August 26. Currie placed the Third Division in the centre of the assault directly between the Scarpe River and the road running straight from Arras to Cambrai. The Second Division was on the right and a British division on the left flank. The immediate objective was a north-south line running three miles beyond Monchy-le-Preux. At this point, the Canadians faced only three German divisions and Currie achieved the element of surprise by attacking at three o'clock in the morning. By nightfall, Monchy and the ground 1,000 yards to the rear were in Canadian hands.

Next day, with the goal of breaking the Fresnes-Rouvroy Line, a further advance of five miles, the assault which began at dawn ran into stiff resistance from German reinforcements. By midday, the advance had been brought to a halt in the face of determined enemy machine-gun fire.

On the following day, August 28, with the support of a heavy artillery barrage that smothered the German machine-gun nests, though bitter fighting persisted the Third

Division pierced the Fresnoy-Rouvroy fortification. By August 30, the position had been secured though the cost had been heavy, with 6,000 Canadian casualties. However, 3,000 German prisoners had been taken and the stage had been set for the final campaign that would lead to victory.

CHARLIE Rutherford was born and raised on the family farm near Colborne in Haldimand County, Ont. on January 9, 1892. He received his education at Dudley Public School. In 1916, he joined the Queen's Own Rifles and in June of that year was posted to the 5th Canadian Mounted Rifles Battalion (7th/11th Hussars) as a private and went overseas. He first saw action later that same year on the Somme.

On his first day in the trenches, all the men around him were killed. His second experience was when he carried a dead comrade through a four-foot tunnel that had a foot of water in it — "The hardest thing I had to do," he recalled. In the fight for the Regina trench, Rutherford was wounded. He returned to his regiment in April 1917 in time for the capture of Vimy Ridge, but was wounded again at Avion in June. At the end of October during the battle for Passchendaele, as one of the thirteen survivors of his company who captured the Vapour and Souvre Farms and held them against repeated German counterattacks, Rutherford received his first medal, the Military Medal.

"We started off with two hundred men," he remembered, "and only thirteen of us got to the top of the hill. George [Pearkes] — he was a captain then — was leading us. We were digging in when I looked up. I saw a hundred Germans coming towards us. We were only a handful, but we started shooting and they disappeared. George got the VC for getting us to the top of the ridge. I guess we'd never have got there if he hadn't been along."

Commissioned in April 1918, at the beginning of Canada's 100 Days on August 8, Rutherford won the Military Cross. "We captured two towns," he said afterwards, "first Arvillers, the German division headquarters where I managed to get a paymaster and a lot of German money. The only thing they left behind were a box of pigeons and three hundred new machine guns. Then we captured Bangor and that was as far as we could go." Rutherford and his men managed to hold the position until French troops arrived to relieve them.

Seventeen days later, Rutherford won the Victoria Cross. On August 26, he and his men were in the vanguard of the second "100 Days" attack, in front of Arras. They started forward just before midnight in teeming rain, their objective the vil-

Charles Rutherford, 5th Canadian Mounted Rifles Battalion

lage of Monchy-le-Preux. Rutherford told it in these words. "Three miles up we ran into four field guns. We captured about twenty men who came out of their dugout and surrendered. Then we [got ready to go] into Monchy."

While Canadian artillery was shelling the town, Rutherford went over to another Canadian Mounted Rifles company to see how they were making out. "I was gone about ten minutes," he said. "When I couldn't see my men, I thought they'd gone into the town as the barrage lifted. So I ran as hard as I could to catch up with them." But, in fact, the men had taken shelter in some woods.

"When I was within a hundred yards of the town," Rutherford continued, "all I could see was Germans. So I decided to do the best I could with them. All I had was my loaded revolver. I walked up to the Germans and demanded that they surrender. They were my prisoners. One German who spoke English said 'No prisoner. No, you prisoner.'"

"He went in, and when he came out he gave an order for the others to drop their rifles. They did. Boy, was I in a fix! I didn't know what to do next. Then one of their machine guns opened up on A Company. I said, 'Your machine gun is firing at my men.' I was afraid my men might start firing back. So I said, 'You go stop your machine gun and I'll stop mine.' I ran back. When I was out of sight of the Germans, I took my hat off and waved my men to come on. They were soon there and I sent two men back with forty prisoners. Then we went over to the other machine gun and got thirty prisoners there."

The citation to the VC read: "The bold and gallant action of this officer contributed very materially to the capture of the main objective and was a wonderful inspiration to all ranks in pressing home the attack on a very strong positions." A brother officer put it more memorably: "The newspapers reported that Monchy had fallen to the Third Canadian Division. That morning, Charlie Rutherford was the Third Canadian Division."

"C.K." Kennedy, the other VC winner in the campaign, came from a proud military heritage to which he was to bring further honours. His grandfather had been decorated in the field following the Battle of Waterloo. His father had given his life in the South African War. Born in Dunsky, Ayershire, Scotland, on March 3, 1880, "C.K." attended St. Andrew's College in Southborough, Kent. On graduating in 1896, he went into the life insurance business with a Scottish firm. Three years later, when the Boer War broke out, he joined the British army and served with the Imperial Yeomanry and the Rhodesian Horse.

William Clarke-Kennedy, 24th Battalion

On his return to civilian life, he rejoined the insurance company and in 1903 was transferred to their Canadian office in Montreal, Quebec. There he became very much a part of that city's social scene. He was one of the chief organizers of the fashionable St. Andrew's Ball of 1913 in which the Duke and Duchess of Connaught were guests of honour. Clarke-Kennedy had joined the Canadian militia almost at the time of his arrival, and with the advent of the Great War in 1914 went overseas with the 13th Battalion (Royal Highlanders) holding the rank of captain. While still in training at Valcartier military training camp at Quebec City, he married Kate Redford. He first distinguished himself in battle during the German gas attack at Ypres in April 1915. At one point he was reported killed, but survived to be awarded the Croix de Guerre with Palms by the French. In May he was awarded the DSO for his part in the attack on Festubert. Following the capture of Vimy Ridge in April 1917, by which time he had been promoted to major, he was awarded the CMG.

In February 1918, he took command of the 24th Battalion (Victoria Rifles) and was promoted to the rank of lieutenant-colonel. During the opening round of Canada's 100 Days, he again distinguished himself under fire and was awarded a bar to his DSO. But it was between August 27 and 28 at Wancourt, during the penetration of the German Fresnes-Rouvroy Line, that Clarke-Kennedy won the British Empire's highest honour for valour.

On the second day of the Arras front offensive, August 27, Clarke-Kennedy led his battalion from the Crow and Algrett trenches in front of Wancourt against the German fortification. As the central unit in the attack, it became the focal point of enemy shelling and machine-gun fire that inflicted heavy casualties, particularly to officers and platoon leaders. The battalion momentarily became disorganized and the advance was in danger of slowing to a halt.

Had it not been for Clarke-Kennedy's initiative in rallying and inspiring his troops, the attack might have failed then and there. The German machine guns simply had to be overcome or else. Several times he set an outstanding example by personally leading squads against the nests to put them out of action.

At all times, he somehow also managed to control his entire battalion, in an almost unprecedented test of leadership and skill, to strengthen the line of advance and enable the brigade to keep moving forward as a whole. By mid-afternoon, Clarke-Kennedy's determination and disregard for his personal safety, and his ability to create order out of disorder by reorganizing his battalion from top to bottom, while still leading the advance, enabled the brigade to meet its objectives: reaching the maze of trenches west of Cherisy and Cherisy Village, crossing the Sensee River, and occupying the Occident trench in front of the heavy barbed-wire defences protecting the Fresnes-Rouvroy Line. Under continuous fire, he now marched up and down in front of his battalion's position, constantly encouraging his men well into the night, while at the same time sending concise field situation reports back to brigade and division headquarters.

On the next day, Clarke-Kennedy again demonstrated his leadership and gallantry in the attack on the Fresnes-Rouvroy Line itself and the Upton Wood. Badly wounded in the leg — bleeding profusely and in intense pain — he refused to be evacuated from the battlefield. Using a shell hole as his command post, he continued to direct his battalion. Realizing that his exhausted troops could advance no further, he established a strong defense line to prevent loss to the enemy of important ground gained. Clarke-Kennedy stuck it out for five hours. Then, with a solid defense line established from which it would be possible for relieving troops to advance and break open the Fresnoy-Rouvroy fortification, he allowed stretcher-bearers to carry him from the field to a dressing station in order to have his wounds attended to.

CHARLIE Rutherford and "C.K." Clarke-Kennedy received their Victoria Crosses from King George V at Buckingham Palace on November 23, 1918 and March 1, 1919 respectively.

Rutherford returned to the family farm in Haldimand County after receiving a rousing hero's welcome at Ottawa Central Station. In 1921, he married Helen Hay and they had a son and three daughters. He became a charter member of the Lieutenant Charles Rutherford Branch of the Royal Canadian Legion. In 1939, he was appointed postmaster of Colborne. When World War II broke out, he joined the Veterans Guard of Canada.

One of his assignments was to serve as guard to the Duke of Windsor, the governor of the Bahamas. Another was supervising security of Canadian prisoner-of-war camps. In 1945, he left the service with the rank of captain. After the war he went back to his old job as postmaster of Colborne. He then moved to Keswick, north of Toronto, where he and his wife Helen operated a dry-goods store. At age seventy he retired and returned to the family farm. In 1968, he was among those who attended the reunion of VC holders in London, England. His wife died in 1980. In 1987, his health failing, Charlie Rutherford moved to the Rideau Veterans Home in Ottawa where, two years later he died on June 11, 1989. At the time, at age ninety-seven he was the oldest surviving VC recipient of the First World War. He was buried in Colborne.

After World War I, Clarke-Kennedy returned to the insurance business. In 1940, he was appointed honourary lieutenant-colonel of the 3rd Battalion, Black Watch (Royal Highland Regiment). He retired from business in 1945 and died in Montreal on October 25, 1961 at age eighty-one.

Rutherford's Victoria Cross remained with members of his family. Clarke-Kennedy's family also retained his VC, at Carspairn, Castle Douglas, Scotland.

Chapter Twenty-Six

SEVEN CANADIAN VCS IN ONE DAY IN A SINGLE ACTION

A "red letter day" for Canada that no other nation in the Commonwealth came close to matching! September 2, 1918. Hutcheson, Knight, Metcalf, Nunney, Peck, Rayfield, Young — seven of our bravest and best — all awarded Victoria Crosses in the same battle on the same date. (Significantly, three Canadian Distinguished Service Orders were also awarded for bravery in the action.) That was the day the Canadians captured the vaunted German Drocourt-Quéant Line, a labyrinth of five rows of interlocking trenches with telephones, lighting and storeroom facilities, as well as a mini-rail system to move troops, ammunition and other supplies.

At dawn the infantry, supported by tanks, surged forward toward the fiercely defended redoubt. The plan called for the First Division on the right to overrun the support trenches, then take the connecting system known as the Buissy Switch which encompassed the villages of Buissy and Villers-lez-Cagnicourt. The reserve brigades would explore the natural enemy barrier of the Canal du Nord. In the centre, the Fourth Division was to drive through all five rows of trenches and seize the town of Dury beyond it.

To keep his infantry losses to a minimum, the Canadian Corps commander, General Sir Arthur Currie, brought maximum artillery firepower to bear on the dense German barbed-wire entanglements

119

Claude Nunney, 38th Battalion

— one gun for every twenty-three yards of front. But those defenses were so thick that no cannon barrage could possibly destroy them completely. That was a job for the tanks, which lumbered through them, chopping up the wire like corn fodder, creating wide swaths for the infantry to charge through.

The First Division met little resistance and the Germans surrendered in droves. At Cagnicourt, enough of the enemy were captured to make up an entire battalion. The fiercest resistance took place at the Buissy Switch, but by nightfall it had fizzled out and the situation was well in hand. In the centre, the objectives were attained early in the day; by 7:30 a.m. Dury had fallen. Although not all the distant goals had been achieved, the Drocourt-Quéant Line and most of the Buissy Switch were in Canadian hands. The wedge made into the enemy defenses now threatened to open up a German flank and that forced the enemy to withdraw along the whole of the British 3rd Army front. The British marched into Queant and Pronville without firing a shot.

A memorable day indeed in Canadian military history — the awarding of seven VCs in particular. Collectively, those recipients formed an interesting (not to mention illustrious) composite of four Britons, two Americans and one Canadian.

The sole Dominion native was a burly Maritimer, Cyrus Wesley Peck, descended from New England planters stock, who at forty-seven became the oldest Canadian to win the VC in World War I. And, in addition to the VC, he wore the DSO and Bar and was Mentioned-in-Dispatches five times. Before joining the army, he had been a broker representing salmon canning, saw mill and towing interests in British Columbia.

Peck was one of two members of the Canadian Scottish, 16th Battalion, to win the VC that day. The other was an American from Maine who, as soon as World War I started, without his parents' knowledge left home to join the Canadian army. Bellenden Seymour Hutcheson was a doctor from Illinois who joined the Canadian Army Medical Corps and who also won the Military Cross.

Before the war, of the five British-born Canadian VC winners of September 2, Arthur George Knight chose Regina, Sask. as his home, where he worked as a carpenter. Claude Joseph Nunney, who also won the Distinguished Conduct Medal and Military Medal, moved to Cornwall, Ont. Walter Leigh Rayfield made his home in Vancouver, B.C., where he went into the real estate business. And John Francis Young settled in Montreal, P.Q. and worked for a tobacco company.

AS soldiers go, Claude Nunney was a real tiger. Born in Hastings, England on Christmas Eve, 1892, as a child he was brought to Canada and placed in an orphanage near Ottawa. Later he was "adopted" by a doctor's mother in Pine Hill, Ont., who brought him up. He attended Separate School No. 9 in Lancaster Township before enlisting in the Canadian army. He was posted to the 38th Battalion (Winnipeg Rifles). At Vimy Ridge in April 1917, Nunney, by then a sergeant, was awarded the DCM when, all alone, he stopped an attack by twenty Germans even though he was wounded.

Again, on June 24, he was decorated for bravery in battle, this time with the Military Medal during the capture of an enemy trench near Avion. When his platoon leader was wounded, Nunney took charge and consolidated the position for the next two days. During that time, one of his men was wounded. Unable to find a stretcher-bearer, he proceeded to dress the injury himself.

On September 1, 1918, anticipating a Canadian assault, the Germans launched an attack in the vicinity of Vitry-en-Artois. Laying down a heavy artillery barrage, they charged the 38th Battalion's forward positions. On his own initiative Nunney, who at the time was stationed at company headquarters, left his post and scrambled through the bombardment to lead and encourage the men by his fearless example. As a result, the attack was repulsed and the situation saved.

Early next morning, during the attack on the Drocourt-Quéant Line, Nunney was badly wounded in the arm but refused to leave the field. Instead, he placed himself in the forefront of the advancing infantry, sometimes fifty to seventy-five yards in front of them, single-handedly taking on enemy soldiers. Then he assaulted four machine-gun posts, capturing all of them, and inflicting casualties among the gunners. During the day, he personally accounted for twenty-five Germans killed. In the afternoon, he was wounded again. Once more he refused to go to the rear and kept on fighting. Finally, however, he became so weak from his wounds that he had to be attended to and he was taken by stretcher-bearers to a Casualty Clearing Station where, sixteen days later, he died from his injuries.

WHEN Bill Metcalf's mother learned that her son, who was born in Waite Township in the state of Maine on January 29, 1885, had run off to enlist in Canada, she appealed to Canadian and U.S. government officials to have him sent home. When he arrived in England with the 18th Battalion, Canadian Scottish, he was met by U.S. ambassador to Great Britain, Walter Page, who asked if he was the Metcalf all the letters had been written about. "I told him," Metcalf said many years later, "I wasn't the man and that I was from St. David Ridge, a little mining town outside of St. Stephen. The colonel backed me up and there was nothing he could do about it."

On the morning of the attack on the Drocourt-Quéant Line, the right flank of Lance-Corporal Metcalf's battalion was held up by German machine-gun fire. It was decided to wait for a tank before trying to advance any further. When one finally came along, several men waved their helmets but the tank crew failed to see them. What happened next was recorded by the battalion historian:

> When the tank came within 300 feet of the German wire, a heavy fire was opened upon it. Corporal (sic) Metcalf jumped up from the shell hole where he was, and with his flags pointing towards the enemy's trench, led the tank towards it and then along it. The enemy kept heavy machine-gun fire on the tank and as it got close to the trench commenced to throw at it clusters of bombs tied together. When we afterwards got into the trench, we found seventeen German machine guns, and all of them well used. How Metcalf escaped being shot to pieces has always been a wonder to me.

Later, although wounded, Metcalf continued to advance with his platoon until ordered to get into a shell hole and have the injury dressed. The *London Gazette* praised his action with these words: "His valour throughout was of the highest standard."

"CY" Peck was Metcalf's commanding officer. Peck, who won the VC at almost the same time, was born on April 26, 1871 in Hopewell Hill, N.B., where he took his education. In 1887, the same year the national railway link was completed at Port Moody, he moved with his parents to New Westminster, B.C. He joined the militia and in 1900 volunteered for the Boer War but was refused. Before the First World War, he was elected Unionist Member of Parliament for Skeena. When the war started, he was living in Prince Rupert where he and his wife Katherine were raising their three sons. On November 1, 1914, he was given a captain's commission in the 30th Battalion and sailed for England in February 1915.

In April, he was promoted to the rank of major and transferred to the 16th Battalion and proceeded to France. On May 21, at Festubert, he was wounded in both legs. In January 1916, he was given command of the regiment with the rank of lieutenant-colonel.

Cyrus Peck, 16th Battalion, after the investiture at Buckingham Palace

In April 1917, during the Canadian attack on Vimy Ridge, he won the DSO. He was erroneously reported as having been gassed in the epic encounter, but no gas, other than gas shells, was used at Vimy. The truth is that Peck was invalided back to England with a severe attack of gastritis, an internal stomach inflammatory disorder. He was soon back in action, however, by June of the same year. In the Canadian "Kahki" election of 1917, he was re-elected in absentia as MP for Skeena, the first time a member had been elected while overseas. It was at about this time that he resurrected the ancient tradition of piping the Highlanders into battle to the skirl of bagpipes.

Early on in the Drocourt-Quéant struggle of September 2,

1918, his regiment's advance was blocked by the Germans at Villers-lez-Cagnicourt. Peck personally reconnoitred the area ahead of his troops in the face of relentless machine-gun and sniper fire. Having assessed the situation, he returned to his headquarters, reorganized the battalion so that both flanks were properly covered, and charged forward at the head of his men. Then, under intense artillery shelling, he sought out the tanks. From his own knowledge of the German positions, he was able to direct the tanks to fresh objectives to overcome the enemy resistance and pave the way for another regiment, an infantry battalion, to move forward, with the support of his own battalion.

A month later, Peck was wounded by a gas shell on October 4 and invalided back to England, bringing a distinguished four-year combat career to an end.

ANOTHER Canadian embroiled in the battle at Villers-lez-Cagnicourt was Arthur Knight, a British emigrant who was born in Lewes,

Arthur Knight, 10th Battalion

Sussex on June 26, 1886. A few years later, his parents moved to Mead Vale, Redhill, Surrey, where he attended St. John's School and Redhill Technical School. In December 1914, he joined the 46th Battalion, went overseas the following year, and was sent to the 10th Battalion (Royal Winnipeg Rifles) in France. At Passchendaele in November 1917, Knight, by then a sergeant, so established himself as an aggressive fighter that he was awarded the Croix de Guerre (Bel.).

After an unsuccessful attack by his platoon on the German trench at Cagnicourt, Knight led his men forward under heavy fire in a bombing attack, and engaged the enemy at close quarters. When this failed to dislodge them, he charged forward alone, bayoneted several German machine-gunners and mortar crews and forced the remainder to retreat. He then brought up a Lewis machine gun which he fired at the fleeing enemy.

In the subsequent advance by his platoon, Knight noticed about thirty German infantry trying to escape into a deep tunnel that led off the trench. He again dashed forward by himself and, having killed the officer-in-charge and two NCOs, took twenty soldiers prisoner. Later, once more single-handed, he routed out another enemy party opposing his platoon's

A doctor attends to the wounded in the field

advance. During these encounters, however, Knight was so severely wounded that he had to be carried off the battlefield to a field hospital. He died two days later.

BELLENDEN Hutcheson joined the Canadian Medical Corps in December 1915. Born in Mount Carmel, Illinois on December 16, 1883, he was educated at Mount City High School and graduated from North Western Medical School as a physician and surgeon. Hutcheson went overseas with the 97th Battalion as medical officer with the rank of captain. He was then transferred to the 75th Battalion (Toronto Scottish) in France and became MO of that regiment. He won his first decoration, the Military Medal, in July 1918 for dressing nearly 100 men on the battlefield under heavy enemy fire.

That September, in the attack on the Drocourt-Quéant Line, while under intense German artillery, machine-gun and mortar fire, Hutcheson coolly remained in No-Man's Land to dress the wounded until all of them had been attended to. By this time the stretcher-bearer party had taken its own severe casualties. After bandaging a severely wounded officer, with the help of some German prisoners Hutcheson evacuated him to safety by running the gamut of enemy bullets. Then, immediately afterwards, he rushed back onto the battlefield under a hail of rifle and shell fire to tend to an NCO who had been badly hit.

JOHN Young, who was born in Kidderminister, England on January 14, 1893, was with D Company of the 87th Battalion (Canadian Grenadier Guards), which had penetrated the Drocourt-Quéant Line and was in the process of attacking the German-held ridge at Dury. With a total absence of cover of any kind, the regiment was an open target for enemy gunners and casualties were heavy. As a stretcher-bearer, Young ignored this state of affairs to tend the wounded. When he ran out of bandages and dressings, he braved a storm of bullets to run back to headquarters for fresh supplies and then dashed onto the battlefield once more.

It took him a full hour to apply his ministrations, but in spite of the continuous exposure to enemy fire he stayed with the wounded. Later in the day, when the Canadians had occupied Dury and the German resistance had abated, Young organized rescue parties to bring the men he had attended back to a casualty field dressing station.

WALTER Rayfield, who was born in Richmond-on-Thames in England on October 7, 1881 and went to school in London, won his VC in the battle for the Drocourt-Quéant Line for myriad acts of valour. The wonder is that he was there at all. Twice rejected, he was finally accepted for military enlistment at the British recruiting office in Los Angeles, California in May 1917, and joined the Canadian army in Victoria, B.C. in July. By September 1918, he was a member of the 7th Battalion (British Columbia Regiment) and held the rank of corporal.

Shortly after the attack began, he rushed a heavily occupied German trench, bayoneting two enemy soldiers and taking ten prisoners. On another occasion, under continual rifle fire, he pinpointed an enemy sniper who was inflicting heavy casualties on his company. Rayfield charged that section of the German trench and so demoralized the Germans that thirty surrendered to him. Later, under heavy bombardment by artillery shelling and against relentless machine-gun fire, he rescued a badly wounded comrade from the battlefield.

BOTH posthumous VC winners of the Drocourt-Quéant epic are buried in France, close to where they died of their wounds. Claude Nunney's grave is in the Communal Cemetery Extension at Aubigny-en-Artois. Arthur Knight is buried in the Dominion Cemetery at Hendecourt-lez-Cagnicourt. Nunney's VC, DCM, MM and his campaign medals are on display in the Armoury at Cornwall, Ont. Knight's VC was presented to his parents by King George V at

Stretcher bearers in the field

Walter Rayfield, 7th Battalion

Buckingham Palace on December 19, 1918 and was later donated to the Glenbow Museum in Calgary, where it is on display along with his campaign medals. In his honour, Knight and Sussex Crescents in Coventry Place, Regina, Sask. are named after him.

Both American-Canadians awarded VCs in the battle returned to the United States after the war. Bill Metcalf, who received his VC from King George V at Sandringham on January 26, 1919, and his wife Dorothy lived in Eastport, Maine, where he made his living as a mechanic. In 1956, he was one of the Canadian VC holders who attended the Victoria Cross centennial celebrations in London, England. Metcalf died on August 8, 1968. At his own request he was buried at a spot overlooking the mouth of the St. Croix River. There, crossed American and Canadian flags are placed at his grave. Metcalf's VC is in the possession of his family.

Bellenden Hutcheson received his VC at an investiture at Buckingham Palace by King George V on May 27, 1919 and then took up residence in Cairo, Illinois, where he married Frances Young from Nova Scotia. There he joined the staff of St. Mary's Hospital before setting up his own practice. In 1939, when King George VI and Queen Elizabeth visited Washington, they invited Hutcheson to go with them to Arlington Cemetery to lay a wreath on the Tomb of the Unknown Soldier. Hutcheson died on April 9, 1954 of a lengthy illness and was buried in Mount Carmel Cemetery. His VC is with the Toronto Scottish Regiment Officers Mess at Fort York Armoury in Toronto.

On April 30, 1919, John Young received his Victoria Cross at Buckingham Palace from King George V. After demobilization, he returned to his old job as a tobacco packer in Montreal and married Ida Thatcher. They had one son, John. Sometime later Young contracted tuberculosis and was admitted to a sanatorium at St. Agathe in the Quebec Laurentians. There he died on November 7, 1929 and was buried in Mount Royal Cemetery in Montreal. His VC is in his son's possession.

Cy Peck's and Walter Rayfield's Victoria Crosses are with the Canadian War Museum in Ottawa. Peck was invested with his VC by King George V at Sandringham on January

26, 1919, and Rayfield received his decoration from the monarch at Buckingham Palace on March 8, 1919.

Following the war, Peck took his seat representing the Skeena riding where he became active in veterans' rights affairs. In 1921, he commanded the Canadian Bisley rifle team. After being defeated in the federal election that year, from 1924 to 1933 he represented Saanich and the Islands in the British Columbia Legislature. Between 1936 and 1941, he sat on the Canadian Pensions Commission. Later he served as aide-de-camp to two governors general. Peck died on September 27, 1956 at his home, "Hopewell," named after the city of his birth, only a few weeks after he and his wife attended the VC Centenary celebrations in England. He was cremated and his ashes were interred at the family plot in New Westminster Cemetery. With these words, Sir Arthur Currie may well have written Cy Peck's epitaph: "No braver or kinder heart ever beat in the breast of a man."

At his death, Peck's VC remained the property of his wife and ownership eventually passed to his three sons. For a period of time the VC was placed on loan with the Canadian Scottish Regiment in Victoria, B.C. In 1989, his last surviving son, Edward, and a nephew approached the Canadian War Museum. In September 1993, the medal formally became part of the national collection at a presentation ceremony in Ottawa.

Rayfield's life both before and after the war is somewhat obscure. After being discharged from the army in Vancouver in April 1919 with the rank of corporal, he is reported to have spent some time in the hospital. He then took up farming to improve his health. In 1921 he got married — for the second time. (His son Victor, an Ontario Provincial Police constable, and his daughter only learned of the earlier marriage in 1983, thirty-four years after Rayfield's death on February 19, 1949.)

Rayfield eventually moved to Toronto where for some time he served as sergeant-at-arms at the Ontario Provincial Legislation. Later, he became deputy governor of the Toronto Jail and rose to become governor. He was also an officer of the Queen's Own Rangers. At his own request, he was buried in the Soldier's Plot at Prospect Cemetery in Toronto. His VC and other medals were in his son's possession when Dick Malott of the Canadian War Museum wrote a letter to *Legion Magazine* asking for information as to their whereabouts. Victor Rayfield responded by donating them to the Museum.

Chapter Twenty-Seven

BREAKTHROUGH— THE LAST MAJOR BATTLE OF THE WAR

THIS was the most complex, complicated and difficult operation of the entire war. The strategy of Marshal Ferdinand Foch, commander of the Allied armies, called for a four-pronged mass attack by the British, French, U.S. and Belgian armies on a front stretching from Bruges in the north to St. Mihiel in the south. The Canadian Corps' role was the key one: capture the textile town of Cambrai that lay due southeast from Arras, a vital lateral communications and rail link on a north-south axis. The capture of Cambrai meant crossing the Canal du Nord and taking the Bourlon Wood, a high ground in front of the town. Between that barrier and the town stood the Marcoing defence system, a honeycomb of machine-gun nests.

Once again, General Sir Arthur Currie demonstrated his genius for surprise and for minimizing casualties. He knew that a frontal attack would be costly in men and equipment. The canal was only 100 feet wide, but the Germans had flooded the marshes on either side, broadening the obstacle. To get across would require building and crossing bridges and these would present highly vulnerable targets. However, to the south, a 4,000-yard stretch of the waterway was dry and its bed ran between higher and firmer ground. It was here that the Canadian Corps would begin its advance.

In the dusk of the cold, damp evening of

September 26, 1918, the assaulting troops tumbled out of their dugouts in the captured Drocourt-Quéant Line and began moving towards the canal. Then at dawn in a slight drizzle, behind an intense artillery barrage, 50,000 men, guns and transport supported by fifteen tanks were funnelled through a corridor one and a half miles wide. As they reached the other side they fanned out in a 10,000-yard-wide arc to the north and east, enveloping the German defenses as they went.

By 9:15 a.m., the Canal du Nord had been cleared, and by the end of the day a number of villages had fallen and the Bourlon Wood was in Canadian hands. But the Germans were determined to defend Cambrai. Between September 27 and October 1, enemy strength in the town grew from four divisions to ten, as well as thirteen Marksmen Machine Gun Companies. On September 28, the Canadians overran the Marcoing Line, but progress for the next few days was confined to probing and fending off enemy counterattacks. Casualties were heavy and by the night of October 1, due to the exhausted state of his troops, Currie broke off the action.

In five days of continuous fighting, the last organized enemy resistance on the Canadian front had been broken. More than 7,000 German prisoners had been taken and 250 guns captured. The Canadian flanking movement had allowed two British armies to breach the Hindenberg line south of Cambrai. The entire offensive had so consumed the German reserves that they were incapable of any further major resistance.

In the brief battle, six Canadian VCs were won: George Fraser "Bobbie" Kerr from Deseronto, Ont.; Graham Thomas Lyall, a Canadian transplant from Manchester, England; Samuel Lewis Honey, a former school teacher from Conn, Ont.; another school teacher, Milton Fowler Gregg, born in Mountain Dale, N.B.; Scottish-born John MacGregor, a contractor from Powell River, B.C.; and William Merrifield from Sault Ste. Marie, Ont., who had been born in Brentwood, England.

"BOBBIE" Kerr, who was born on June 8, 1894, had just completed school in Toronto and was working for a bank when the war broke out. On September 22, 1914, he enlisted as a private with the 3rd Battalion at Valcartier, Que., and two weeks later embarked for Britain. After a period of intense training, he arrived in France in February 1915. His initiative and leadership qualities soon earned him his first promotion to the rank of corporal. In June 1916, at Mount Sorrel in the Ypres Salient, he won the Military Medal.

In that action, after his platoon leader had been killed and the sergeant wounded, Kerr led the unit forward to secure a bombing post and held it throughout the day. The following September he was wounded but soon returned to duty, by which time he had been commissioned a lieutenant. In August 1918, during the Battle of Amiens, he discovered a gap in the advancing Canadian line which he quickly filled with his own platoon and put several enemy machine-gun nests out of action. Though wounded, he continued fighting, capturing a machine-gun nest as well as two field guns. He soldiered on, serving in the line for the next two days. For his actions, he was awarded the Military Cross and was promoted to captain.

A month later he received a bar to the medal when, between September 2 and 3, in the attack on the Drocourt-Quéant Line, he overcame a German machine-gun crew and personally accounted for several of the enemy killed. He was once again wounded, this time in the arm. But the greater expression of valour was yet to come.

George Kerr, 3rd Battalion, centre

On September 26, Kerr was still recuperating in hospital when he learned that his battalion was one of those picked to be in the vanguard of the Canal du Nord crossing and the attack on the Bourlon Wood. He left his sick bed to rejoin his company. Next morning, at the outskirts of the hamlet of Raillencourt, close to the Arras-Cambrai road, a series of German machine-gun posts were putting up such stiff resistance that they threatened to hold up the advance. With total disregard for his own safety, Kerr rushed the position, captured four machine guns and took thirty-one prisoners. As the Toronto *Globe and Mail* would later write of him: "Here was heroism of the highest order. And the hero was little more than a boy, but stout of heart and active of brain. He appeared to have been born with military genius; fine courage was interwoven in his make-up."

Kerr received his Victoria Cross from King George V at Buckingham Palace on May 22, 1919. Two months later, on July 16, he was declared medically unfit for further duty and was struck off strength. He returned to Toronto, married, had a daughter and became manager of a major metal supply firm, Lewis Lazarus and Sons. He was active in the militia and in 1921 was promoted captain of the Toronto Regiment.

On December 8, 1929 Kerr died from a freak accident when he was asphyxiated by carbon monoxide fumes while sitting in his car in his garage waiting for it to warm up. He was buried with military honours at Mount Pleasant Cemetery. Six other VC holders acted as honourary pall bearers: Colin Barron, Benjamin Geary, Tommy Holmes, Henry Robson, Charles Rutherford and Robert Shankland.

On Memorial Day, November 11, 1973, a plaque in his commemoration was unveiled by his three grandchildren. It is located between Main Street and the waterfront in Deseronto, Ont. Kerr's Victoria Cross is held in safe-keeping in a bank vault in Oakville, Ont., the property of his daughter, Mrs. Janet Ross.

DURING the attack on the Bourlon Wood and later on the advance on the Marcoing

defense system, Graham Thomson Lyall set an all-time record for number of enemy soldiers and equipment captured. The son of a minister from Darwen, Lancashire, he was
born in Manchester on March 8, 1892 and was educated at Nelson Municipal Secondary
School. Later, after graduating as a mechanical engineer, he emigrated to Welland, Ont.
and worked for Canadian Steel Foundries and the Niagara Power Company. In September
1914, he enlisted in the Canadian army at St. Catharines, Ont. as a private. In 1915, he
arrived in France with the 4th Canadian Mounted Rifles. Later, after a short course at
the Canadian Officers' Training School at Bexhill-on-Sea in England, Lyall was granted
an officer's commission as a lieutenant and subsequently joined the 102nd Battalion.

It was on September 27, 1918, in the battle for the Bourlon Wood, and on October
1, in the neighbourhood of Blécourt, that he made military history. On the first day of
the assault, while leading his platoon, he and his men overran a German strongpoint
with a flanking movement that netted thirteen prisoners, four machine guns and a field
gun. Afterwards, although the unit was considerably weakened by heavy casualties, Lyall
led what remained of his platoon up to an enemy redoubt. He charged forward and
single-handedly killed the officer in charge, took another forty-five prisoners and captured four more machine guns.

On October 1, he overran another German defence post near Blécourt that yielded
eighty prisoners and seventeen machine guns. Altogether, his total bag for the two occasions numbered two officers and 182 other ranks taken prisoner and twenty-six machine
guns and a field gun captured. The *London Gazette* citation for the VC read: "He showed
the utmost valour and high power of command."

Lyall was decorated by King George V on March 13, 1918 at Buckingham Palace and
the citizens of Darwen, Lancashire (his father's birthplace) presented him with an orna-

Graham Lyall, 102nd Battalion, pictured with relatives after the investiture

mented French bronze clock in appreciation of his valour. On April 24 he married Elizabeth Moffatt Frew, daughter of the Provost of Airdrie. Lyall's father, the Reverend Robert Henry Lyall, performed the ceremony.

Lyall became manager of Drumbathie Brickworks (Alexander Frew & Co.) and took up residence at Forrest Park in Airdrie. When World War II began, he joined the British army and was attached to the Royal Army Ordnance Corps. He was killed in action on November 18, 1941 in Egypt at Mersa Matruh. At the time he held the rank of colonel. He is buried in the Halfaya Sollum War Cemetery, eleven miles from the Libyan border. His Victoria Cross is in the possession of a nephew living in Framingham, Massachusetts.

BEFORE he enlisted in the 34th Canadian Battalion at Walkerton, Ont., "Lew" Honey had already carved out a career as a school teacher. Born in the village of Conn in Wellington County on February 9, 1894, he attended the Continuation Schools of Drayton and Princeton and at the age of sixteen took charge of a school on the Six Nations Indian Reserve near Brantford, Ont. Two years later, he taught school at Drumbo, Ont. With this experience, though he was under age, he was allowed to enter the Normal School in London, Ont.

After a year of teaching at Landsborough School in Huron County, he spent the next year studying at Walkerton High School. In June 1914, he passed the Honours Matriculation examination with first-class honours in English and French and second-class honours in Latin and German. He also received the Cartier Scholarship and sixty dollars awarded by the department of education. That fall he returned to teaching, at Bloomington School in Whitechurch Township, York County. But with the declaration of war, he found it hard to keep his mind on his work. In January 1915, he joined the army as a private and went overseas in October with the rank of sergeant.

On arrival in Great Britain, Honey was selected for special training at Aldershot in bayonet fighting and physical fitness. From January to August 1916, he instructed in both these fields at Bramshott camp before going to France with the 78th Battalion. There he soon demonstrated his mettle as a fighting man.

In January 1917, Honey won the first of three decorations he would earn when he was awarded the Military Medal for bravery during a pair of raids on German trenches. The value of these sorties was gathering intelligence and capturing prisoners for interrogation — the forerunners of World War II's commando raids. Honey wrote home:

> I took part in two raids in three days, both completely successful, and that's what I'm being decorated for. When all is said and done, what I did, didn't amount to much, but our party was lucky.... The biggest part of my job was leading the party across and it really isn't as easy as it sounds.... Some day, perhaps, I'll try to tell you what it feels like to go "over the top,' as the boys say, but ... I'm due to go out on a working party tonight.

In April that year at Vimy Ridge, Honey again distinguished himself in battle for which he received the Distinguished Conduct Medal. When his platoon commander was wounded, he assumed command leading his men forward in the face of fierce enemy fire until forced by casualties to dig in, a position he held for three days until relieved. "I guess I was a lucky guy," he commented afterwards. One of the battalion's officers put it less modestly when, in a letter to Honey's parents, he stated: "Lew had a great faith. He realized the dangers fully and went on just the same setting a good example to others not fortunate to have such good faith and strong will."

Honey was immediately recommended for a commission and returned to England to attend the Canadian Officers' Training School at Bexhill. He rejoined his regiment in October, then during the following spring took a Lewis gun course for which he was characteristically praised for his "exceptional good work."

At the outset of the assault on the Bourlon Wood on the morning of September 27, Honey's company commander and all of the other officers in the unit became casualties, either killed or wounded. Honey took command and continued the advance. Then, when German machine-gun fire began cutting down his men, he charged the post all by himself, capturing the guns and taking ten prisoners. Later, he fought off four successive enemy counterattacks. That night he went out alone and located a

Samuel Honey, 78th Battalion

German outpost. Gathering a squad of his men together, he led an attack on the position, captured it and seized three machine guns. Two days later, while again leading his company against another enemy stronghold, he was severely wounded and had to be taken to hospital. He died of his injuries two days later on September 30.

In a letter to his parents, commenting on Honey's action that won him the VC, the battalion commanding officer wrote:

> ... never have I seen such gallant work as this boy of yours displayed.... He was the first to reach the final objective during the first day, and throughout the days that followed he was an example of grit and determination that was the talk of the whole company. The men idolized him, and as they bore him by me that morning there was a tenderness in their care that only strong men can show.

Honey was buried in Quéant Cemetery, in a district wrenched from the Germans a few weeks earlier. On July 26, 1964, a provincial plaque dedicated to his memory, located on the grounds of Westcott United Church in the village of Conn on Highway 89 east of Mount Forest, was unveiled by his sister, Isabel Honey. His Victoria Cross was sent to the family and in due course was left to his sister. In 1975 she turned it, along with his other decorations and service medals, over to the Canadian War Museum with the proviso that they not be loaned to any other private or public institution.

OF winning the Victoria Cross, Milton Gregg once said: "When you are looked upon with favour, you wonder whether it was anything of intrinsic value in yourself or whether it was because you happened to have a special decoration."

The citation published in the *London Gazette* reflects a comfortable blend of both and requires no embellishment. It read:

> For most conspicuous bravery and initiative during operations near Cambrai, 27th September to 1st October, 1918.
>
> On 28th September, when the advance of the brigade was held up by fire from both flanks and by thick uncut wire, he [Lieutenant Gregg] crawled forward alone and explored the wire until he found a small gap through which he subsequently led his men and forced an entry into the enemy trench. The enemy counterattacked in force, and through lack of bombs the situation became critical. Although wounded, Lieutenant Gregg returned alone under terrific fire and collected a further supply. Then, rejoining his party, which by this time was much reduced in numbers, and in spite of a second wound, he re-organized his men and led them against the enemy with the greatest determination against the enemy trenches, which he finally cleared.
>
> He personally killed or wounded 11 of the enemy and took 25 prisoners, in addition to 12 machine guns captured in this trench. Remaining with his company in spite of his wounds, he again, on the 30th September, led his men in an attack until severely wounded. The outstanding valour of this officer saved many casualties and enabled the advance to continue.

Soldier, statesman, cabinet minister, university chancellor, teacher, salesman and entrepreneur, Milton Gregg, who was born at Mountain Dale (changed to Snider Mountain) in Kings County, southern New Brunswick, led one of the most heroic, productive and versatile lives of almost any Canadian.

The son of a successful farmer, he was educated at the local school and also attended the Provincial Normal School in Fredericton. After graduating from Acadian and Dalhousie universities, he taught school for a short period in Carleton Country. His military career began in 1910 when he joined the 8th New Brunswick Hussars militia regiment.

When war broke out in 1914, Gregg enlisted that September in the 13th Canadian Infantry Battalion (Black Watch) as a private and proceeded overseas. In May 1915, he received the first of his many wounds at Festubert. The following year he attended the Imperial Officers' Training School at Cambridge in England, received his commission and joined the Royal Canadian Regiment in France as a lieutenant. On June 9, 1917 at Lens, he received the Military Cross for leading a bombing attack with egg-shaped Mills bombs on a German machine-gun post. Though wounded himself, he helped carry an injured comrade to safety.

On August 26, 1918, Gregg received a bar to his MC at Monchy-le-Preux during an attack on the Bois de Sart. In the teeth of devastating enemy fire, he led a bombing party against two machine-gun crews, killing them all. Later, he was instrumental in staving off a German counterattack.

Gregg recovered sufficiently from wounds sustained in the action that earned him the VC to rejoin his regiment in time to take part in the final Canadian advance during November that led to Mons. On February 26, 1919, he received the decoration from King George V at Buckingham Palace. Returning to Canada that spring, he accepted a position with the government in the department of soldiers' civil re-establishment, the predecessor of the Department of Veterans Affairs of which he later became minister. He then joined the Soldiers' Settlement Board before entering civilian life, working first as an advertising salesman, then for a mining company and, for a time, as an automobile dealer in Halifax. In 1934, he was made sergeant-at-arms of the House of Commons in Ottawa. During World War II, he put on the uniform again and sailed overseas with his old regiment, the RCRs. Within a year he was promoted to lieutenant-colonel and made commanding officer of the West Nova Scotia Regiment.

In 1941, he was given command of the Canadian Officers' Training Unit in England, and then in 1942 he returned to Canada as a full colonel to take over the Canadian Officers' Training Camp at Brockville, Ont. A year later he was promoted to the rank of brigadier and was appointed chairman of the Officers' Selection Board. He served another stint overseas before becoming commander of the Canadian Battle School in Vernon, B.C.

In the summer of 1944, Gregg was offered the presidency of the University of New Brunswick. To this position he brought the same leadership qualities that had served him so well during his military career: decisiveness, a sense of purpose, and a tolerance for those serving under him. For the next three years, the "Brigadier," as he became known familiarly, presided over the exploding enrolment that included more than 1,000 veterans.

In 1947, Prime Minister Mackenzie King persuaded Gregg to join the Canadian cabinet. Handily elected Member of Parliament for York-Sunbury, he became successively Minister of Fisheries, Department of Veterans Affairs, and Labour. In the latter capacity, in the midst of the bitter railway strike in August 1950 in which 125,000 workers threatened to walk off the job and create a national crisis, Gregg settled the dispute in nine days.

With the defeat of the Liberals in 1957, Gregg's political career came to an abrupt halt. He then embarked on an equally spectacular one as a diplomat. Within nine months, he was in Iraq as represen-

Milton Gregg, The Royal Canadian Regiment

tative of the United Nations Technical Assistance Board. Between 1960 and 1963, he served in Indonesia for the United Nations International Children's Emergency Fund. In 1963 and 1964, he was made Canadian Representative to the UN. Then at age seventy-one, in 1964 he became Canadian high commissioner in Guyana.

Three years later Gregg retired to Fredericton — officially. But he still retained many interests. As a board member for the New Brunswick League for Urban Renewal, he was instrumental in launching the "New Horizons" program for the preservation of the province's covered bridges. He also served on the board of Katimavik, the government-sponsored youth program to promote physical and mental health in young Canadians. In 1968, he was made president of the Canadian Council for International Co-operation. In 1975, he was named the first Grand Patron of the New Brunswick Command of the Royal Canadian Legion. He also received the Order of Canada.

Milton Gregg died at home on March 31, 1978. The funeral was held at Christ Church Cathedral in Fredericton. Participating were 200 members of his old unit, the Royal Canadian Regiment, along with members of the Legion. He was buried at the nearby Snider Mountain Baptist Cemetery. No eulogies were said for Milton Gregg, but the then defence minister, Barney Danson, one of the honourary pall bearers, later wrote this tribute:

> The most unlikely hero one could imagine. An outstanding soldier who looked like someone's older uncle, yet won the nation's highest award for bravery. A far from accomplished speaker who could inspire the best in each of us. An indifferent administrator who built some of the most efficient organizations which served this nation.

Gregg was survived by his second wife, the former Erica Deichman of Fredericton. His first wife, the former Amy Dorothy Alward of Havelock, predeceased him in 1958. A daughter, Mrs. Eleanor Grant of Upper Cape, also survived him. His VC was donated by the family to the Royal Canadian Regiment of Canada in London, Ont. in 1978. On Christmas Eve, 1978, it was stolen from the RCR Museum and to date has not been recovered.

GENERAL Currie once said of John MacGregor: "[He] combines good judgment with sound military knowledge and wide experience. Good power of command and leadership; he inspires men. Excellent character, good appearance, strong personality; tactful, resourceful and co-operative."

Small wonder this man was decorated for bravery four times. Born in Cawdor, Nairnshire, in Scotland on February 11, 1888, he came to Canada in 1909 and went into the contracting business in British Columbia. In March 1915, after snowshoeing across country for 120 miles to Prince Rupert, he enlisted in the 11th Canadian Mounted Rifles as a private. In September, in France, he was promoted to sergeant and about that time won his first decoration, the Distinguished Conduct Medal. He single-handedly captured a German machine gun after killing the gun crew.

On May 12, 1917, MacGregor was commissioned a lieutenant. On January 12, 1918 he won his second medal, the Military Cross. On this occasion he led his men in an assault on a German trench, wiping out the enemy garrison along with three pillboxes, killing eight of the enemy and taking one prisoner. When the signal to retire was given, assisted by his sergeant, MacGregor skilfully withdrew his men and his prisoner into his own line without any casualties. Sometime later he was awarded a bar to the MC although according to Dick Malott, former chief curator of collections for the Canadian War Museum, no citation was ever published.

The action that won MacGregor the Victoria Cross took place between September 29 and October 3. This was another case of a wounded man carrying on despite his injuries. When the Canadian advance was checked by German machine-gun nests, MacGregor dashed forward ahead of his men, located the machine guns and put them out of action. With his rifle fire and bayonet, he killed four Germans and took eight prisoners, and was wounded in that action.

Later, with the enemy putting up stubborn resistance, MacGregor reorganized his company and despite his wounds took charge of the leading wave and continued the advance. Finally, he was able to establish his company in the village of Neuville St. Remy, which allowed other Canadian troops to capture Tilloy to the north of Cambrai.

MacGregor received his VC from King George V at a Buckingham Palace investiture on February 26, 1919 and returned to Canada where he was discharged from the army at Vancouver on April 9. Little is known of his activities between wars other than that he lived in Powell River where he probably returned to the contracting business, was married and raised a family.

When World War II began, MacGregor quietly enlisted in the Canadian Scottish Regiment as a private. He was quickly promoted, however, and was destined to go to Hong Kong with the 2nd Battalion when plans were changed. He was then placed in command of the Canadian Army Training Centre at Wainwright, Alta. with the rank of lieutenant-colonel. When the war ended, he was awarded the Efficiency Decoration.

MacGregor returned to Powell River where he established a concrete plant at Cranberry

John MacGregor, 2nd Canadian Mounted Rifles, after the investiture

Lake. He died on June 9, 1952 in Powell River Hospital after a lengthy illness and was buried in Cranberry Lake Cemetery. Attending his funeral were three Victoria Cross holders: George Pearkes, Cy Peck and Charles Train of England, a resident of Canada for thirty-nine years.

MacGregor's Victoria Cross is retained by members of his family.

AN aura of mystery surrounds the early life of William Merrifield, but it has been established that he was born on October 9, 1890 in Brentwood, Sussex, England. His son Verne, one of three children, said that he seldom talked about himself so that little is known of his youth. But Verne believes that his father emigrated to Aylmer, Que. with an uncle when he was ten years old. He then apparently went back to England only to later return to Sudbury, Ont. where he took a job as a

William Merrifield, 4th Battalion

fireman for the Canadian Pacific Railway before enlisting in the Canadian army in 1914.

If Merrifield's childhood presents a bit of an enigma, his military record is real enough, and an admirable and gallant one it is. As a member of the 4th Canadian Infantry Battalion, on November 6 and 7, 1917 he was decorated with the Military Medal for bravery at Passchendaele. On October 1, 1918, by which time he had reached the rank of sergeant, his regiment was being pinned down by two German machine-gun emplacements near Abancourt. Merrifield attacked them both. Dashing from shell hole to shell hole, he killed the occupants of the first post but was wounded in the process. However, that didn't stop him from attacking the second position. Lobbying a Mills bomb into it, he killed the gun crew. Though bleeding profusely, he refused to be taken from the battlefield and continued to lead his men until he was so severely weakened he had to be carried to hospital.

Following the war, Merrifield settled in Sault Ste. Marie, Ont. where he took a job with the Algoma Central Railroad. In 1921, he married Maude Bovington of the Soo. In 1939, he suffered a stroke from which he never recovered. Merrifield died in Christie Street Military Hospital in Toronto on August 8, 1943 and was buried in West Korah Cemetery in Sault Ste. Marie. His Victoria Cross is held by his son.

Coulson Norman Mitchell, 4th Battalion

Chapter Twenty-Eight

CAPTURE AND PREVENTION AT CAMBRAI

AFTER a week's rest, the Canadian Corps returned to battle on the night of October 8/9, 1918. Objective: the capture of Cambrai. The plan called for seizing the bridges over the Canal de l'Escaudoeuvres at the eastern approaches to the town and then, to avoid house-to-house fighting, cutting it off from the north. The attack, made in the middle of a dark, inky, gusty night, caught the Germans in the act of preparing to evacuate. By dawn, patrols pushing their way into the centre of Cambrai found it deserted except for a few enemy demolition squads. By 8:30 a.m., the town was in Canadian hands.

It had all gone according to plan. Still, it was not without its heroic moments as the story of Norman Mitchell from Winnipeg, an explosives expert and captain with the 4th Battalion, Canadian Engineers, reveals. Leading a small sapper party ahead of the first wave of infantry, Mitchell's assignment was to prevent the Germans from blowing up the main Pont d'Aire bridge across l'Escaudoeuvres. There were three altogether. The first, a twenty-five-foot brick arch across a spillway some 300 yards short of the canal, had already been blown. The second, also a brick arch, was intact and no charges were detected. Ahead lay the main bridge. Mitchell, with a sergeant and two sappers, crossed quickly and quietly, two on each side. Handles of German stick-grenades warned them of the danger and the job ahead. There was no time to waste. The bridge could blow at any moment. The electrical leads had to be located — and located fast.

Mitchell posted the two sappers as sentries on either side of the bridge while he and his sergeant slid down under the bank which consisted of two seventy-five-foot steel girder spans on stone abutments and a centre pier, with a concrete block about fifteen feet above the tow-path. The beam of a searchlight showed a large boxed-charge in the nearest girder, an indicator that the other girders would be similarly mined. Fortunately, the Germans, in their haste, had not had time to remove the scaffold and ladder. They came in handy. The electrical circuit was immediately cut and Mitchell and the sergeant began dealing with the leads and charges when suddenly they heard shouting and rifle fire. The German bridge guard had come to life.

One of the sappers killed two of the enemy before Mitchell and the sergeant reached the top of the bank. Mitchell killed a third with his revolver. That checked the attackers, but only momentarily. They charged again, but Mitchell and his men mowed them down. Mitchell sent one of the sentries back to get help while they stood guard. When an infantry-covering party arrived, equipped with a Lewis machine gun, Mitchell and the sergeant returned to the explosives and removed six charges amounting to 500 pounds from the girders. The grey light of dawn revealed the survivors of the German bridge guard huddled on the tow-path, docile, ready to surrender. They had had enough.

The *London Gazette* citation to the Victoria Cross, the only one awarded to a Canadian Engineer, read: "It was entirely due to his valour and decisive action that this important bridge across the canal was saved from destruction."

This was the second time Mitchell had been decorated for bravery. At Ypres in the spring of 1916, as an officer with the 1st Tunnelling Company of the Canadian Engineers, while laying mines he was cut off from his own lines for twelve hours. For this action he received the Military Cross.

Coulson Norman Mitchell was born in Winnipeg on December 11, 1889. Graduating from the University of Manitoba as an engineer, he was engaged in several projects in British Columbia and Manitoba when war broke out. In January 1915, he enlisted in the army and served as a signaller in an engineer field troop before sailing to England with a railway construction unit. On April 16, he received his commission as a lieutenant, and in September 17, in France, was promoted to captain. The tunnelling companies were subsequently absorbed by engineer battalions of which there were three to each division. In July 1918, Mitchell was posted to the 4th Battalion (Second Division).

After receiving his VC from King George V at Buckingham Palace on April 3, 1919, Mitchell returned to Winnipeg to practice civil engineering. He also served in the militia between September 1930 and March 1933 with the rank of captain. Early in World War II, Mitchell signed up for active service and was given the rank of major. He was assigned to a pioneer battalion of the Royal Canadian Engineers at Camp Borden in July 1940 and sailed for England in August. In July 1941, he was appointed to command a field company and in February 1942 was promoted to the rank of lieutenant-colonel and put in charge of replacement training. Transferred back to Canada in September 1943, he was first attached to National Defence Headquarters in Ottawa for special duties, then joined the staff of the RCE Training Centre at Petawawa. In August

1944, he was given command of the Royal School of Military Engineers in Chilliwack, B.C.

Following his discharge from the army in October 1946, Mitchell made his home in Montreal where he joined an engineering firm in an executive capacity. In 1965, the Montreal Branch of the Royal Canadian Legion was renamed the Norman Mitchell VC Branch, with which he became very active. Married with two daughters, he died on November 17, 1978. His VC and MC along with his service medals are on display at the Royal Canadian Engineers Museum in Chilliwack. A street in the town of Mount Royal is named after him.

Chapter Twenty-Nine

THE ELEVENTH HOUR

OCTOBER 11 to November 11, 1918. During those remaining days of the Great War, the Canadian Corps spearheaded the attack on an uninterrupted advance through Mount Huoy and Valenciennes to Mons on the day the Armistice was signed. From the date the counterattack began on August 4, the Dominion's forces had taken 18,585 prisoners and had captured 371 heavy guns along with 1,923 machine guns and trench mortars. Over 116 square miles had been overrun and fifty-four towns and villages liberated. A commendable, heroic effort. And in those last gallant thirty-two days, Canada added four more of it sons to its growing roll of VCs, one of them for an aerial combat that has been described as "the greatest in the annals of war in the air."

An illustrious quartet indeed. Wallace Lloyd Algie of the 20th Canadian Infantry Battalion, who led the capture of Iwuy on October 11. Thomas Ricketts, Canada's youngest VC, who lied about his age to get into the army. William George Barker, the fighter ace who, on the morning of October 27, took on what amounted to an entire *Jagdgeschwader* of over eighty German fighters, was wounded three times, crashed into the ground and yet survived, having accounted for six enemy planes. Hugh Cairns of the 46th Infantry Battalion, who died of his wounds ten days before the war ended after a German officer he had taken prisoner shot him in the stomach.

Wallace Algie, from Alton, Ont., left the

banking business in Toronto to join the army. He was a lieutenant with the 20th Battalion during the attack on Iwuy, northeast of Cambrai on the morning of October 11. The Canadians faced a formidable barrier of piles of lumber and masses of wire from which the Germans were laying down a steady curtain of fire at the entrance to the village, causing heavy casualties to the battalion. While reorganizing, they observed the Germans bringing up additional machine guns on small handcarts. Once these were in position, the entire 4th Brigade would be threatened.

Quickly assessing the situation, Algie called for volunteers to form a small party to thwart the enemy's intentions. His plan was to move to the left, well outside the battalion's "boundary," and deny the east end of the village to the Germans. In its first onrush, the group captured two machine guns and killed the gun crews. Using the German guns and their own Lewis gun, the Canadians opened fire, two of them using headstones in the town's cemetery as mounts.

After a brief struggle, the German defenders were quickly overcome and taken prisoner. This cleared the east end of the town, making its capture possible. Algie returned to his battalion for reinforcements. Then, while leading them forward, he was cut down by enemy fire and killed. He was buried in the Niagara Cemetery five miles north of Cambrai. His Victoria Cross was presented to his family and remained in their possession until recently. It was sold at an auction at Christies in London, England, late 1994.

ON January 19, 1919, when King George V pinned the Victoria Cross to Private

Thomas Ricketts, 1st Battalion

Tommy Ricketts' khaki tunic at a private investiture at York House, he turned to Princess Mary with a smile and said proudly, "This is the youngest VC in my army!" At the time Ricketts was still only seventeen years old and was the youngest Canadian ever to win the award. By a happy coincidence, General Sir Dighton Probyn, at eighty-five, then the oldest living VC — won in the Indian Mutiny — was also on hand for the ceremony.

When he joined the army in September 1916, Ricketts was under sixteen years of age. His birth certificate indeed shows he was born in Middle Arm, White Bay, Nfld. on April 15, 1901, the son of a fisherman. Ricketts went overseas in June 1917, as a member of the 1st Battalion, Royal Newfoundland Regiment, reaching the front in France in June of the same year where he first saw action at Steebeek. In September 1918, he was wounded in the fighting at Marcoing but was back in action by October 14 at Ledeghem in Belgium for the action that won him the VC.

The Royal Newfoundland Regiment had successfully beaten back the enemy, though not without heavy losses, when Ricketts' B Company became pinned down by German field guns. A counter-barrage would have been the logical solution, but the Newfoundlanders had outrun their own artillery cover.

Ricketts volunteered to go forward with his platoon leader, armed with a Lewis gun, to try and outflank the enemy position. Advancing in stages under heavy fire — "every yard a death-trap of hissing bullets and screaming shell splinters" — they soon ran out of ammunition and were still 300 yards from the German battery. Seeing their predicament, the Germans began bringing up extra guns in teams. Ricketts dashed back to his own lines, picked up fresh ammunition and returned to the attack, all the while dodging bullets and shrapnel. But with their accurate fire, he and his platoon leader successfully drove the enemy into farm buildings for refuge. As a result, the platoon was able to advance without casualties, capturing four machine guns, one field gun, and taking eight German prisoners.

In addition to winning the VC for his exploit, Ricketts was also awarded the Croix de Guerre (Fr.) with Gold Star and was promoted to sergeant. Ten days after the investiture, he was back in Newfoundland. Before he disembarked, *The Evening Telegram* sent out a young reporter to interview him on his troopship in St. John's Harbour, another Newfoundlander who would make quite a name for himself — Joey Smallwood.

Ricketts took up residence in St. John's and became a druggist. He died on February 10, 1967 and was give a state funeral. Buried in the Anglican Cemetery, Forest Road in St. John's, his Victoria Cross and Croix de Guerre along with his service medals were on display in the Newfoundland Naval and Military Museum in the Confederation Building until recently. They are now in the custody of his family.

ON October 26, Billy Barker who, since September had been temporarily attached to 201 Squadron of the Royal Air Force to test the combat qualities of the new Sopwith Snipe scout plane — Britain's answer to the Fokker-DV11 — received orders to return to England with his plane the next day. Over the last two months, he

William Barker, Royal Air Force

Barker beside his Sopwith Snipe

had boosted his score to forty-seven enemy planes shot down and nine observation balloons destroyed with the stubby fighter (it was less than twenty feet in length) that could fly 135 miles an hour and reach a height of 24,700 feet.

Barker had won the Distinguished Service Order twice, the Military Cross three times, along with the Croix de Guerre (Fr.) and the Italian Silver Medal for Military Valour, and had been Mentioned-in-Dispatches three times. But he was far from through. Next morning over the Morinal Forest, he staged the epic individual air battle of all time.

Barker, known variously as Bill, Billy, George, Will or Willy, was born on November 3, 1894 in Dauphin, Man. where he attended Russell High School and Dauphin Collegiate. He was brought up on a farm, an environment which prepared him for the role of a fighter pilot. His father was a blacksmith who owned a saw mill and was one of the first to apply the steam engine to farming. It was no surprise that young Barker developed an early appreciation of things mechanical. He was also a splendid horseman which honed his reflexes, and because game abounded in that part of the country, he quickly became a crack shot with a rifle. By the time the war came along, Barker had established a successful automobile livery in his home town.

In August 1914, he enlisted in the Canadian Mounted Rifles at Brandon as a private and proceeded to France in 1915. In December he obtained a transfer to the Royal Flying Corps, and after training as an observer he was commissioned as a 2nd lieutenant in 1916 and returned to France where he engaged in artillery spotting. He was slightly wounded and he also received his first medal, the MC. Later in the year, he was posted to England for pilot training, then rejoined the squadron in France as a flight commander. In September 1917, he was sent to England as an instructor, which hardly suited his aggressive, ebullient temperament. He made such a nuisance of himself that he was finally sent off to France to join 28 Squadron.

In the fall of that year, following the Italian defeat at Caporetto, his squadron, of which he was now commanding officer, was posted to the Italian Front. Then, in 1918, Barker was recalled to France to test the Snipe in battle. On the morning of October 27 he climbed to 15,000 feet, crossing enemy lines over the Morinal Forest. He shot down a German Rumpler two-seater. Meanwhile, however, a Fokker triplane snuck up behind him and snapped off a burst of machine-gun fire, shattering Barker's right leg with an explosive shell. Fainting from pain, he temporarily lost control and spun down, hotly pursued by the enemy pilot. After plunging for 2,000 feet, he regained consciousness and broke in to meet his attacker whom he demolished with a short, close burst of fire. Then, as he headed for his own lines, twenty Fokkers bounced him from above. Fighting nausea, he wheeled into the attack once again, his one good leg taking the full load on the rudder bar. Incredibly, he shot down three of them in succession. But in that exchange, an enemy bullet struck his left leg. Now both legs were virtually useless. Barker passed out again, and the Snipe barrelled down, rudderless once more. Fortunately a burst of fresh air revived him and he levelled out only to find himself in the middle of a gaggle of at least sixty German fighters. Pulling into a tight turn, he fired at anything that crossed his sights. Another triplane fell to his guns. Then a bullet struck his left elbow and his arm went limp. He passed out again and lost another 5,000 feet before coming to. Bullets whizzed all around him and Barker, figuring he had nothing to lose, decided to take an enemy plane with him. He aimed his machine at the nearest Fokker, intending to ram it and opened fire. To his utter surprise, it disintegrated and he flew through the debris.

Meanwhile, incendiaries ripped into the Snipe's gas tank, which miraculously failed to catch fire. Semi-conscious, Barker piled up the battered machine in a shell hole just inside the British lines where Scottish troops pulled him from the wreckage.

Barker recovered from his wounds, though the damage to the elbow socket in his left arm was irreparable. However, though crippled, he still managed to cope with one arm. In 1919, he ventured into commercial aviation with Billy Bishop, operating a flying boat passenger service between Toronto and the Muskoka Lakes. In 1920, he married Bishop's second cousin, Jean Kilbourne Smith of Toronto, daughter of an industrial tycoon. In 1922 their daughter Antoinette was born, and Barker rejoined the Canadian Air Force and eventually becoming commanding officer of Camp Borden. In 1924, he was made acting director of the RCAF as well as honourary aide-de-camp to the governor general, and went to England to take the RAF staff course. In 1926, he returned to Canada and resigned his commission. He later became general manager of Fairchild Aviation Company of Canada. On March 1, 1930, while he was demonstrating a new type of two-seater for the Department of National Defence at Rockliffe, the aircraft's engine failed and Barker crashed into the Ottawa River and was drowned.

A small private funeral service was held at the Smith residence in Toronto on St. Clair Avenue West, but he was buried with full military honours in Mount Pleasant Cemetery. His Victoria Cross and his other medals were donated to the Canadian War Museum in 1983 by his widow, Jean Greene, who had remarried. On display at the Museum are the remnants of the Sopwith Snipe in which he fought his notorious battle.

HUGH Cairns became the last Canadian to win the VC in World War I, for what General Sir Arthur Currie termed a "superhuman deed." Born in Ashington, Northumberland, England, on December 4, 1896, he moved to North Saskatoon, Sask. with his family in 1911. When the war started, Cairns left his plumbing apprenticeship to join the 65th Battalion with which he went overseas. He transferred to the 46th Battalion (Saskatchewan Dragoons). At Vimy Ridge in April 1917, he was awarded the Distinguished Conduct Medal for an action in which he led a party forward to provide covering fire for the flank of his regiment. Recovering two machine guns that had been left behind in the advance, he set up posts and repelled three different German counterattacks. Though wounded, he held on until his ammunition was spent.

On November 1, 1918, ten days before the signing of the armistice, the Saskatchewans found themselves in the thick of the fighting around the town of Valenciennes, only twenty miles from Mons where the Canadian advance would end the war. In the battle, a German machine gun opened up on the platoon being led by Hugh Cairns, by this time promoted to

Hugh Cairns, 46th Battalion

sergeant. Unhesitatingly, Cairns picked up a Lewis gun and in the face of withering enemy fire charged the position, killing all five of the crew and taking the gun as a prize.

A little later his unit was again stopped in its tracks by machine-gun fire. Cairns rushed forward, killed twelve of the enemy and took eighteen prisoners along with their guns. But during the action he was wounded in the shoulder. Cairns ignored the pain. When the advance bogged down once more, this time by field gun as well as machine-gun fire, Cairns led his party in an outflanking movement, killing many of the enemy and forcing fifty of them to surrender.

After consolidating their position, the party, consisting of an officer in charge, Cairns carrying his Lewis gun, and two others, moved forward to reconnoitre the hamlet of Marly, where they found a yard filled with enemy soldiers. Breaking down the barnyard door, they forced all sixty of them to throw down their arms and put up their hands. But when the German officer in charge passed in front of the Canadians and got close enough to Cairns, he shot him in the stomach with his revolver. His knees buckling from pain, Cairns nevertheless shot back with a burst from his Lewis. Then a mêlée broke out; the Germans picked up their rifles and Cairns was again wounded, this time in the wrist. A moment later the butt of his machine gun was shattered and he collapsed from loss of blood. While a Canadian officer and soldier held the Germans at bay, others who had arrived on the scene removed Cairns from the yard.

Using a door as a stretcher, two of them began carrying him from the field. But the Germans were still inflicting casualties. They killed one of the bearers and wounded Cairns again. Finally more reinforcements arrived, forcing the Germans to surrender again. Next day, Cairns died of his wounds in hospital.

Cairns is buried in Auberchicourt British Cemetery, east of Douai, in France. On the afternoon of July 25, 1936, the day preceding the unveiling of the Vimy Memorial, a street in Valenciennes commemorating the heroism of Cairns was rechristened "L'avenue du Sergent Hugh Cairns." A special medallion struck in his honour, inscribed with the arms of the town, was presented to his parents, Mr. and Mrs. George Cairns, who attended the ceremony. At the same time, the French Republic announced it had conferred the Legion of Honour upon him.

In the City Park in Saskatoon, a statue was erected by his comrades and the citizens of the community in his memory. Cairns' VC, DCM and service medals are in the Canadian War Museum, acquired from a nephew, William Milne.

Chapter Thirty

THE CANADIAN VCs OF WORLD WAR II

THE median age of the sixteen Canadian Victoria Cross recipients in World War II was thirty-three, the oldest being fifty-two and the youngest twenty-four. Two were Great War veterans. One VC was awarded for action at Hong Kong, one in Japan, one in Burma, one in North Africa, two in Italy, eight in Europe, and one in the North Atlantic. Four VC winners were airmen, one with the Royal Air Force, two with the Royal Canadian Air Force, and the other as a member of the Fleet Air Arm. One VC winner was with the Royal Navy, one with the British army and nine with the Canadian army, one as an airborne parachuter.

Seven of the VCs were killed in action and one accidentally. One recipient lost both legs. Two became prisoners of war. Five hailed from Ontario, five from British Columbia and two from Manitoba, one Manitoban having emigrated from England. One came from Alberta, Saskatchewan, Quebec and Prince Edward Island, respectively.

Chapter Thirty-One

"DUCK LADS!"

"No troops ever fought more bravely or with greater skill against more hopeless odds."

Jean Chretien, Canadian Prime Minister

IT was at Hong Kong in December 1941 that units of the Canadian army went into battle for the first time in World War II, an action in which the first Canadian VC was won. On October 27, 1941, the Royal Rifles of Canada and the Winnipeg Grenadiers sailed from Vancouver, B.C. They had received no training; in fact, some of the men had only been in the army for sixteen weeks. However, their role as an armed force was figurative in any case. It was believed that reinforcing the British garrison would deter Japan from making war against the British and Americans. But the battle-hardened Japanese army's plans of conquest were not about to be upset by the addition of fewer than 2,000 unskilled Canadian troops whose 212 vehicles never reached them.

Anyhow, it was generally conceded that if an attack occurred, defence of the island was hopeless. There was no air or sea cover and the British, Canadian and Indian defenders faced a numerically superior foe. The battalions were simply a presence – almost a pretense – nothing more.

On the morning of December 7, with the attack on Pearl Harbor the entire garrison went on alert. At 8:00 a.m., the Japanese bombed Kai Tak airfield and put what few obsolete aircraft the Royal Air Force had out of business. Because the garrison commander feared an invasion from the sea, the Canadians were assigned the job of defending Hong Kong's south shore, while two British Battalions manned the mainland defences. It took three Japanese regiments less than a week to overrun them. By December 13, the mainland was completely abandoned.

Between 8:30 and 9:00 p.m. on December 18, in driving rain, the Japanese began landing on the northeast shore of the island. The defenders would fight on bravely for a week but with the U.S. Fleet decimated at Pearl Harbor and the two British capital ships sunk off Singapore, there was no hope of relief. Next morning, during an assault on the steep slopes of Mount Butler, a navy veteran from Norfolk, Virginia who moved to Western Canada between the wars, where he joined the Winnipeg Grenadiers in 1933, sacrificed his life to save those of his comrades with a deed that won the Victoria Cross.

John Robert Osborn was born on January 2, 1899 and during World War I served with the Royal Naval Volunteer Reserve as a seaman and saw action at the Battle of Jutland in May 1916. Following the war, he moved to Saskatchewan where he took up farming, then worked for the maintenance division of the Canadian Pacific Railway in Winnipeg, where he married. He and Margaret Elizabeth had five children. On

September 3, 1939, he was called to active duty with his regiment, holding the rank of company sergeant-major. The day before he shipped out, his youngest daughter Patricia was badly burned in a fire. It was a sad departure for Osborn because she was not expected to live (she survived, however). Before he left, Osborn donated blood for her at the hospital.

On the morning of December 19, 1941, one company of the Winnipeg Grenadiers was deployed to seize the hills known as Jardine's Lookout and Mount Butler. It soon became divided. The group led by Johnny Osborn captured Butler at bayonet point and held on for three hours, but owing to the Japanese superiority of numbers and an exposed flank that attracted intense enemy fire, the position quickly became untenable. Osborn and a small party of men covered the withdrawal. When they in turn were forced to fall back, Osborn single-handedly fought off the attacking Japanese, all the while dodging machine-gun and rifle fire, allowing his men to get away.

That afternoon, the company became separated from the rest of the battalion. Completely surrounded, they found themselves within grenade-throwing range of the enemy. When the Japanese began lobbing the missiles into the slight depression in which the Winnipeggers had positioned themselves, Osborn picked up the live missiles with his bare hands and hurled them back. But one landed in a spot where it was impossible to pick up before it exploded. Shouting "Duck Lads!", Osborn threw himself on top of the grenade. That action, for which he received the Victoria Cross, killed him instantly.

Ironically, the first Canadian VC earned in World War II was the last to be gazetted (*London Gazette*, April 2, 1946). The deed went unknown until after the Japanese surrender in 1945 when it was related by witnesses who had been captured, among them

The Canadian Contingent, C Force, in Hong Kong

John Osborn, The Winnipeg Grenadiers

Harry Atkinson who was only fifty metres away from where the action took place. In 1956, Osborn's widow Margaret received the medal from Queen Elizabeth in London, England.

Osborn has no known grave, but his name appears on the Hong Kong Memorial and the British Army Victoria Barracks was renamed after him. In 1970, in Winnipeg, Margaret Osborn and her son, Warrant Officer Gerald Osborn, received a plaque commemorating that honour at a ceremony attended by former members of his regiment, Hong Kong veterans and the Winnipeg Grenadiers Cadet Corps.

At forty-two years of age, Osborn was the second-oldest Canadian VC recipient in World War II. Company Sergeant Major Osborn's VC and medal were presented to the Canadian War Museum in August 1995.

Chapter Thirty-Two

FOOTE AND MERRITT AT DIEPPE

THE raid on Dieppe marked the second time the Canadian army had gone into action in World War II, and the Victoria Cross was awarded to two Canadians in that raid. Like the initial baptism of fire for the army at Hong Kong, it was a fiasco.

Beginning at 4:50 a.m. on August 19, 1942, six infantry battalions of the Second Canadian Division, along with the 14th Calgary Tank regiment, 1,075 British commandoes and fifty American Rangers, made five landings on a front ten miles wide upon the pebble beaches and surrounding flanks of the French coastal resort. It was doomed from the start. The landings were made without preliminary aerial bombing or naval bombardment, and only four destroyers supported the force. The Germans were prepared and in complete control, and from their vantage point high on the cliffs overlooking the beach they could sweep it with withering gunfire. Canadians were cut down as they came ashore, though some managed to reach the sea wall. The tanks and armoured cars were useless — they got bogged down on the beach.

The raid was supposed to last a day, but the order to evacuate what was left of the force came as early as 9:00 a.m. By 1:00 p.m., it was all over. Of the 4,963 Canadians who embarked on the venture, only 2,210 were evacuated, many of them wounded, 907 had been killed, and 1,964 were taken prisoner.

Charles Cecil Ingersoll Merritt, a Vancouver lawyer, and John Weir Foote, a Presbyterian clergy from Madoc, Ont., were both awarded the Victoria Cross for their part in the debacle. Foote was the only member of the Canadian Chaplain Services ever to be awarded the medal. Both he and Merritt spent the rest of the war in prison camps.

John Foote was born on May 5, 1904 and took his education at the University of Western Ontario and Queen's University, and graduated in Theology from the Montreal Presbyterian College at McGill. He was ordained a minister at Bristol, Que. and later went to Fort Coulogne in 1933 where he had his first parish. Remaining there for two years, he next became minister of St. Paul's Presbyterian Church in Port Hope, Ont. In December 1939, he joined the Canadian Army Chaplain Service and went overseas with the Royal Hamilton Light Infantry (Wentworth Regiment).

"Cec" (pronounced Sess) Merritt was born on November 10, 1908, the son of a First World War hero who was killed in action at Ypres and Mentioned-in-Dispatches for bravery. Merritt was educated at Lord Roberts School in Vancouver and University School in Victoria, B.C. He graduated from the Royal Military College in Kingston, Ont. He then became a lawyer and, prior to the outbreak of World War II, was an officer with the Seaforth Highlanders. In 1942, prior to the Dieppe raid, he was transferred to the South

John Foote (right), Canadian Chaplain Services, Royal
Hamilton Light Infantry

Saskatchewan Regiment as commanding officer with the rank of lieutenant-colonel.

On the Dieppe beach, firing a Bren gun at the Germans, as a clergyman — ecclesiastically speaking — John Foote was definitely out of character. But then he never was exactly one of your run-of-the-mill padres. Earlier, when he had learned that a military manoeuvre was in the offing, he asked to be included. The request was summarily denied by the regiment's commanding officer. Foote told him he was going to go along anyway and that the best his commander could do was arrest him afterwards for disobeying orders. The colonel finally relented and assigned Foote to the regimental aid post as a stretcher-bearer.

The RHLI was one of two battalions that carried out the main assault on the beach. Touching down on White Beach, the centre of the right flank at 5:20 a.m., one company was all but wiped out by German machine-gun fire. Those fortunate enough to survive made for the protection of the sea wall. But even there, fire rained down on them from the West Headland.

While the battle raged, Foote assisted the medical officer in administering to the wounded. This he carried out for the next six hours, carrying more than thirty wounded back to the aid post, all the while under relentless enemy fire.

When the time came to evacuate, he helped carry the wounded into the landing craft. Because his sodden boots slowed him down he took them off, a measure he was later to regret. Finally, he boarded one of the last boats to leave the beach and, seizing a Bren gun, he fired in frustration as a rear-guard action against the Germans. Then, suddenly, he changed his mind. Seeing that there were many Canadians still left on the beach, he coolly jumped overboard and swam ashore to surrender to the Germans. He decided that those of his regiment who were about to become prisoners of war and face long years of captivity would need his services — comfort and above all, hope — more than those returning to England.

In describing the action that won Cec Merritt his VC, the noted Canadian war correspondent Wally Rayburn wrote: "As I watched him lead his men through that thundering barrage, I felt a quiver run up and down my spine. I had never seen anything like it."

At 5:05 a.m., the South Saskatchewan Regiment landed on Green Beach, near Pourville, and blew holes in the barbed-wire defenses. The objective was for two companies east of the Scie River to advance along the high ground to a radar station on the cliff edge, and another to attack Quatre Vents Farm. But before this could be achieved, they first had to cross a bridge spanning the Scie. Wide and exposed, it was 200 feet long and the Germans were sweeping it with mortar, machine-gun and artillery fire. The first group that tried to get across was mowed down.

Cec Merritt took his helmet off and asked, "What's the hold-up?" "It's a hotspot. We can't get across," was the reply. Merritt dashed ahead, waving his helmet. "Follow me," he shouted, "we're going across. There's nothing to stop us here."

He subsequently led four parties across the bridge and then headed up an advance which was held up by enemy pillboxes. Merritt promptly launched an attack, destroying one himself by throwing hand grenades into it. Although twice wounded, he continued to direct his regiment's operations and, while organizing the withdrawal, he felled a German sniper with his Bren gun. Merritt then took up a position to cover the evacuation before being forced to surrender — but only after the last boats had left the beach. As he said afterwards, "My war lasted six hours."

When landing at Dieppe, John Foote's regiment had a strength of 582 men. That day 480 were lost: killed, wounded or taken prisoner. The night after the raid, Foote and his fellow officers (he held the rank of captain) were taken to a church at Envermeu outside the town and locked up. "I spent the night lying on the church's stone floor, and although I was worn out, I rolled a lot on the floor," he later recalled.

The next two days were spent on a forced march to imprisonment, a particularly gruelling one for Foote who had to walk barefoot along the cinders of railway tracks and over rugged country to prison camp Oglag VIIB. But Foote did not remain there for long. He arranged a transfer to a camp for other ranks in the regiment. Among them he provided such comfort and hope that he became a legend, known only as Padre X until 1943 when his wife — the former Edith Sheridan of Brockville, Ont. — identified him as her husband.

Foote kept his "congregation" busy. As an example, he organized three camp bands with instruments received from Canada and an accordion given him by a German guard. Of the guards Foote said: "They put up with an awful lot from us — more than we would have put up with from them if the situation had been reversed." The exception was the day of the capture. "The Germans had their losses too, and they weren't in the mood for kidding. There was no horseplay on that day."

Foote and his comrades were released from captivity by the British Grenadier Guards after a nightmarish thirty-seven-day trek across Germany toward Bremen, as the Nazis sought to prevent their release by the Russians.

When Cec Merritt was captured, he was taken to a prisoner-of-war

Charles Cecil Merritt, The South Saskatchewan Regiment

camp at Eichstatt in Bavaria where he became the senior officer of the Escaping Committee. He actually managed to escape himself. However, his freedom was short-lived because he was recaptured and remained a prisoner until he was liberated in the spring of 1945. Later he said of his time spent in the prison camp: "It was an enforced idleness. It cannot be escalated into virtue."

John Foote did not learn that he had won the VC until he returned to Canada. After the war, he remained with the Army Chaplain Service until 1948. He became Member of Provincial Parliament for Durham County, Ont., and made his home in Cobourg. He was later given the post of Minister of Reform Institutions for Ontario.

He died on May 2, 1988 at age eighty-four after a bout of flu that aggravated heart problems. A funeral service was held in St. Andrew's Presbyterian Church in Cobourg and he was buried in Union Cemetery. Attending the funeral was Charles Rutherford from nearby Colbourne, the then oldest VC holder from the First World War. Foote had donated his VC and medals to his old regiment the RHLI some years earlier, his wife having predeceased him by two years.

Immediately following the war, in 1945 Merritt was elected Member of Parliament for Vancouver-Burrard, a seat he held until 1949 when he lost out in that year's general election. He then returned to his law practice in Vancouver where he and his wife Grace Graham took up residence. In 1951, he was appointed commanding officer of his old reserve unit, the Seaforth Highlanders, which post he held for three years. At the time of writing this book, he is one of two Canadian VC holders still living, the other being Ernest Avia "Smokey" Smith.

A disabled scout car on the pebble beach at Dieppe

Frederick Thornton Peters, Royal Navy

Chapter Thirty-Three

ORDEAL AT ORAN

*"The finest British naval engagement
since Trafalgar."*

Winston Churchill,
British Prime Minister

*"The enterprise was one of desperate
hazard. Courage and leadership achieved
all that could be done against odds that
proved overwhelming."*

Sir Andrew Cunningham,
Admiral of the Fleet

OPERATION Torch, the landings in
North Africa on November 8, 1942,
marked a turning point for the Allies. It
was the first joint American-British military undertaking and apart from some tactical setbacks (the German Ardennes
offensive late in 1944), from that point on
the Allies moved to offensive.

The capture of Oran Harbour and the
town itself was vital to landing the United
States 6th Armoured Corps. It wasn't going
to be easy. Fourteen well-armed Vichy-
French warships, ranging from a heavy
cruiser to a submarine had to be taken out
of action. There were heavily imbedded
shore batteries to be faced as well.

Allied intelligence had built their hopes
on shaky German-Vichy relations. That
was wishful thinking. The French fleet at
Oran was still smarting over the sinking
by the British of its major battleships after
Dunkirk to prevent them falling into
German hands. That action scuppered
Anglo-French relations for over a decade.

157

So if the Allies were counting on the same passive French resistance in their attack on Oran Harbour — the key axis port in Western North Africa — they were mistaken. And there was another factor that was hard to puzzle out. Why had Tom Troubridge, the task force commander, been ordered to launch the assault two hours after the American and British troops had landed elsewhere, thereby eliminating the element of surprise?

There was a saving grace to this scenario, however, and that emerged in the shape of the man who would lead the attack — Frederick Thornton "Fritz" Peters. If anyone could carve his way through a jungle of muddled thinking and poor planning, as well as face fierce enemy opposition, he was the one.

The son of the attorney general and first Liberal premier of Prince Edward Island, and the grandson of John Hamilton Grey, one of the founders of Confederation, Peters was born on September 17, 1889 and was educated at St. Peter's Private School in P.E.I. Later, when his family moved to British Columbia, Peters went to school in Victoria. From an early age, the navy fascinated him to the extent that, in 1905, when he reached the age of sixteen, his parents allowed him to travel to England to join the Royal Navy as a cadet — the start of a truly remarkable career at sea. A year later he graduated from the Royal Naval College as a midshipman. Three years later he received his commission as a sub-lieutenant. During the pre-World War I years, he spent most of his time aboard gunboats patrolling the Orient to protect British interests. His mettle was first recognized by the Italians, who decorated him for leading rescue parties to evacuate the populace threatened by the eruption of the Mount Messina volcano a year before the start of the Great War.

Peters won his first medal for bravery in battle while serving as a 1st lieutenant aboard HMS Meteor during a naval engagement off Dogger Bank in January 1915. *Meteor* was disabled by German naval guns and several of the crew were killed. For his part in the battle, Peters received the Distinguished Service Order, the first ever given to a Canadian and a rare award for a junior officer. Peters won his second decoration for bravery a year later — the Distinguished Service Cross — "for good service" while serving aboard destroyers.

Following the armistice, in 1919 Peters retired from the Royal Navy with the rank of lieutenant-commander after turning down a staff appointment. He returned to British Columbia and became somewhat of a drifter, going from one job to another, finally finding work on the African Gold Coast. A fresh outbreak of war in 1939 rescued him from an aimless life. Working his way back to England aboard a tramp steamer, he re-enlisted in the British navy.

Peters was commissioned and placed in charge of a flotilla of small ships, whalers and trawlers operating against German submarines from bases in the Orkneys and Shetland Islands off the coast of Scotland. Between October 1939 and June 1940, Peters sank two enemy U-boats in the North Atlantic and was rewarded with a bar to his DSC "for good service since the outbreak of war." He was then posted to the Directorate of Naval Intelligence where he came to know two of the most famous traitors in British history — Gary Burgess and Kim Philby. The two double agents were working for British Intelligence at the time, operating a school for spies at Hertfordshire. Fritz Peters, now a commander, was seconded to the pair as commandant of the training school.

The job bored Peters. He had no affinity for paperwork and was in the process of submitting his resignation when he was advised that he had been selected for a special assignment called "Operation Reservist," in support of the North African landings. The plan called for several motor launches to lay down a smoke screen while two former U.S. Coast Guard cutters, Walney and Hartland, acquired by the RN under the lease-lend agreement, would ram a boom lying across the 200-foot mouth of Oran Harbour and smash it.

Both vessels were slow, lightly armoured and had only two 4-inch guns apiece, but the authorities considered them to be up to the task. Once inside the 3,000-yard-long breakwaters, with *Hartland* drawing fire, *Walney*, captained by Peters, would steam up the quay and unload four canoe teams equipped with self-propelled mines. These teams would take the French warships by surprise. Then, American troops would go aboard and commandeer them. Meanwhile, *Hartland* was to secure the jetties and ships at the entrance to the harbour. Then, with the port and vessels in Allied hands, the surrender of the town would be a mere formality. Jim Dandy! At least that's the way it looked on the plotting table. It was also the stuff of which dreams are made.

Because there was no element of surprise, at 2:45 a.m. on the morning of November 8, as the two boats approached in the darkness backed by the British light cruiser *Aurora* and a flotilla of destroyers, the French gunners were ready and waiting. Searchlights pinpointed the two cutters and gunners opened up with small-arms fire. Ignoring the fusillade, Peters bellowed in French over the ship's hailer (bullhorn) demanding a surrender.

This enraged the French. Their shore batteries and warships opened up with a fearful barrage at pointblank range. Nevertheless, at 3:10 a.m. *Walney*, partly screened by smoke and with major launch outriders on either side, broke through the boom. But now she came face to face with the French destroyer *La Surprise*. Peters tried to ram, but missed. The French ship responded with a concentration of fire that damaged both engines and caused casualties in killed and wounded. *Walney* managed to limp further into the harbour towards *Epervier*, a French destroyer which Peters intended to board and use as a base for embarking his canoe teams.

But his ship was forced to run a relentless gauntlet of fire and steel — submarines berthed to the north, *Epervier* on the south. *Walney*'s boiler took a direct hit and exploded. Another shell struck the bridge which burst into flames. Peters was one of only seventeen to survive the blast when, wounded in the shoulder and blinded in one eye, he was blown clear of the bridge. By this time, the cutter was nothing more than a blazing wreck; most of her crew and the landing troops were dead or wounded. Some of the soldiers managed to find their way above decks to lob hand grenades at the submarines and spray them with rifle and machine-gun fire. The injured were carried below to the wardroom, but a shell exploded in the confined space and killed them all.

To help put mooring lines ashore, Peters moved forward, then aft. He then realized he could never get his ship berthed, so he gave orders to abandon ship. *Walney* drifted away from the pier, explosions from the hold rocking her. Finally, with all hands overboard, Peters himself jumped into the water and swam for shore. Somewhere between nine and ten o'clock that morning, the cutter rolled slowly onto her side and sank, part of her hull protruding above the shallow water, a stricken monument to a heroic battle lost.

Hartland suffered a similar fate. Groping her way through the harbour entrance after *Walney* had shattered the boom, she immediately came under intense shell fire. A brief broadside brought her to a standstill. Attempts to berth alongside a trawler failed and

Sailors' Memorial, Halifax, N. S.

now, ablaze from stem to stern, the battered vessel drifted into the centre of the enclosure. She had no alternative but to anchor, absorbing shell fire from both sides of the inlet. By 4:00 a.m., most of the crew board had either been killed or wounded. The survivors abandoned ship as best they could. At dawn *Hartland* blew up and sank.

It had been carnage. The casualties had been horrendous. Between the two ships, 270 men were killed and another 157 wounded; seventy-seven survived and were taken prisoner, Peters among them. Two days after his capture, Peters was freed from a French prison in Oran by Allied troops who liberated the town. In the parade that followed, he was borne through the streets on the shoulders of its citizens and hailed with flowers from a grateful populace.

In addition to the Victoria Cross awarded for his feat, making him the first Canadian naval officer to win the medal in World War II, Peters was also cited for the award of the American Distinguished Service Cross, the highest decoration awarded to a foreigner. But he never received either medal. Five days after the battle at Oran, he and four other naval officers climbed aboard a Sunderland flying boat to take them back to England. The weather forecast called for calm and clear conditions.

Just before take-off Peters told the flight engineer who was taking the passengers' names for the manifest: "You know, we navy men are a bit superstitious ... we shouldn't be taking off on Friday the thirteenth." Perhaps he had a premonition. Not long into the flight, conditions quickly worsened. The Sunderland's crew had to fight head winds of over forty knots, accompanied by hail, sleet and lightning. But by this time, they had passed the point of no return. With insufficient fuel for a diversion, they were forced to press on. Then they ran into fog and pitch-black darkness. By the time they reached

Plymouth Harbour, they only had fifteen minutes of fuel left. The pilot took the only course open to him; he tried to land the Sunderland on the water by instruments. But his dials failed him. The altimeter read 600 feet when the flying boat suddenly crashed into the sea and turned turtle. The pilot and crew made their way safely out of the aircraft. The others drowned. Peters, who lost his life at age fifty-three, has no known grave but his name appears in the Naval Memorial at Plymouth.

Peters' Victoria Cross, the only one awarded to a Prince Edward Islander, was never presented ceremoniously. His family received the Commonwealth's highest decoration for valour through His Majesty's mail, accompanied by a standard letter of acknowledgement. By contrast, General Dwight Eisenhower, later to become the Supreme Allied Commander in Europe, dispatched two of his senior officers to Nelson, B.C. to formally present Peters' American DSC to his mother in a private ceremony at her residence.

There was one more irony to the affair. Within the British Admiralty there was intense concern over whether or not Fritz Peters' bravery at Oran Harbour should be recognized for fear of offending the French. Finally, after much humming and hawing, they decided to announce the award posthumously. The Americans had no such qualms; they went right ahead and made their award. Until recently, Peters' medals were held in safekeeping by a family member.

Despite a determined effort to raise funds to purchase the Peters' VC and the American DSC for the province of Prince Edward Island, the plan fell short of its required $100,000 in 1994. In late 1994, the Peters' VC and two other medals were sold at Christie's auction to an English collector.

Chapter Thirty-Four

"ILS NE PASSERONT PAS"

"I have seen the ground on which Major Triquet fought this action.
In view of the difficult conditions then prevailing
and the strength of the enemy position,
I consider it an outstanding deed of heroism."

Major-General Christopher Vokes,
Commander, First Canadian Division

THE name Casa Berardi conjures up a vision of a romantic Italian holiday villa on the shores of the Adriatic. In truth, it is anything but. It simply means "Berardi's House," a modest, rather weathered, three-storey farm dwelling not far from the outskirts of Ortona on the eastern coast of southern Italy. But to this day, for the Berardi family and the men of the Royal 22nd Regiment (the Van Doos), both past and present, it will always hold a special meaning. A plaque affixed to the side of the structure commemorates the heroic five-day action in which the Canadians lost all but nine of their original strength of eighty-three in securing the vital road junction between Orsogna and Ortona. It reads:

Casa Berardi
Medaglio D'Oro
Capt. Paul Triquet
Royal 22nd Regiment
Canadian
Ortona 1943

As a result of the Allied conquest of Sicily in July and August 1943, Benito Mussolini was overthrown and the Germans took control of Italy. As part of the British 8th Army, the First Canadian Division invaded the mainland at the beginning of September and began advancing northward along the Adriatic coast. At the end of November a stalemate developed and the British-Canadians struck hard along the Sangro River to relieve pressure on the Americans who were driving towards Rome in the west.

On the night of December 5/6, the Canadians crossed the Moro River with the objective of capturing the port of Ortona, perched high on a ledge of the Adriatic coast. Now began the bitterest fighting the Canadians encountered during the entire Italian campaign. Along the two-mile advance through the Vino "gully," the capture of the "Cider" junction of the highway leading from Orsogna to Ortona was vital. This meant seizing

Paul Triquet, Royal 22nd Regiment

the Casa Berardi from the 90th German Panzer Division, comprised of infantry and tanks. A gully in front of the casa presented a formidable barrier. Paul Triquet's company of the Royal 22nd Regiment, with the support of the Canadian Armoured Division, was ordered to cross the gully and secure the position. No better choice could have been made to tackle such an onerous assignment than that of Paul Triquet.

Born in Cabano, Que. near Rimouski on April 2, 1910, he attended Cabano Academy where he became a member of the Cabano Cadet Corps which his father, who had fought with the French army in the Great War before coming to Canada, had organized. After attending night school in Quebec City for six years, Triquet enlisted in the Royal 22nd in November 1927 as a private. Although promotions were slow in the permanent force during peacetime, by the time the Second World War broke out he had attained the rank of sergeant-major. He briefly flirted with the idea of joining the French army because, as the son of a former Poilu, he qualified. But his father quickly nixed the notion. "If you're going to play soldier," he said, "play it in Canada."

Triquet went overseas with the first Canadian contingent in 1939, but returned to Canada the following year to apply for his commission. In March 1941, he was promoted to lieutenant and proceeded overseas again. Landing with his unit in Sicily on July 10, 1943, he was promoted to captain during that campaign.

On December 14, Triquet led his company in a head-on attack against the 90th German Panzers which immediately returned fire. All of the company's officers except Triquet were killed, and half of his men were either killed or wounded. Triquet urged on the remainder shouting, "Don't mind the Germans — they can't shoot straight." By this time they were within hearing distance of the casa, and it became clear that they were completely surrounded. The Germans called out from the building for them to surrender, whereupon the Canadians replied in no uncertain terms. (On one of the four visits he and an honour guard made to the site after the war, Triquet related the incident in polite language. "When we got to the house, we could hear the Germans talking and they called to us to surrender. I won't tell you what we said, but it's the same thing that you'd say today.")

Behind Casa Berardi was a well, long since abandoned, but at the time it created problems. "You might say it was a trap," Triquet later recalled. "It was exposed and right in the line of fire. I tried to keep the men away from it, but they were thirsty. Those that went near it got killed."

Over the noise of shell fire, Triquet exhorted his men, "The safest place is ahead," he cried and charged forward. That broke the deadlock. The Canadians put four enemy tanks out of action as well as silencing a nest of machine guns. By this time the company had been reduced to Triquet himself, two sergeants and fifteen men. Expecting a counterattack, he organized his troops in a defensive perimeter and told them, "*Ils ne passeront pas,*" a phrase borrowed from Generalissimo Robert Georges Nivelle's words at Verdun in 1916: "They shall not pass."

Neither did they. When the Germans attacked, Triquet, at the head of his men, personally accounted for several of the enemy killed. For four more days they beat off one attack after the other against overwhelming odds, inflicting heavy enemy casualties, until the remainder of the Van Doos relieved them on December 8. There was only Triquet, a sergeant and nine men left. During the fighting, Triquet learned he had been promoted to major; he heard it over the radio from one of his own tanks.

For his "magnificent courage ... tactical skill and leadership," Triquet received the Victoria Cross, the third member of the Royal 22nd Regiment to win the decoration. He was also awarded the Legion of Honour by the French and the Gold Medal by the Italians, that country's highest honour. During the five days Triquet lost twenty-two pounds. It probably much affected his health which deteriorated in his later years.

Triquet was wounded on January 8, 1944 but remained on active duty until February 18, when a recurrence of the injury forced him to retire from further combat for treatment. On March 27, he received his VC from King George VI at an investiture at Buckingham Palace. In 1947, he retired from the Royal 22nd after twenty years of service and became district sales manager of MacMillan, Bloedel and Powell River Ltd., the forest products company with headquarters in Quebec City. In 1951, he joined the reserve as CO of the Regiment de Lévis, then commanded the 8th Militia Group. He was also aide-de-camp to the governor general. He eventually left the reserve with the rank of brigadier and retired to Florida. His health steadily declined. He lost one eye and began losing the sight of the other. He also had arthritis, gout and diabetes, and suffered three heart attacks.

Paul Triquet died on August 8, 1980 and was buried with full military honours in Quebec City. Attending the funeral were Governor General Edward Schreyer and Lieutenant-Governor Jean-Pierre Côté of Quebec. His Victoria Cross and other medals are housed in the Royal 22nd Regiment Museum at the Quebec Citadel.

Chapter Thirty-Five

LIFTING THE SEIGE OF ARAKAN

C HARLES Ferguson Hoey was one of two Canadians awarded the Victoria Cross in the war against Japan. When World War II began, he had already served for two years on the northern frontier of India with the Lincolnshire Regiment of the British army.

By February of 1944, the British advance in Burma had come to a grinding halt as a result of the Japanese increasing their strength from five army divisions to eight. The enemy's objective was to invade East India and create a rebellion against the British. The initial attack came from the Arakan Hills to capture the port of Chittagong and draw the British forces to that area. In the fighting, two Indian divisions were cut off from the British 7th Division. It now became the task of that division to relieve them. For days the British troops worked their way through jungles and swamps and over mountains, skirmishing occasionally with enemy patrols. By February 15, they had reached the enemy force. The Lincolnshire Regiment was ordered to break through to one of the Arakan peaks near the Ngakyedauk Pass, which would give them command of the situation and force a Japanese withdrawal. Charles Hoey's company was to act as advance guard.

The commanding officer could hardly have made a better choice. Hoey was well trained and had the experience for such an assignment.

Born in Duncan on Vancouver Island, B.C. on March 29, 1914, he attended both Duncan Grammar and High Schools. On graduation he had his heart set on a military career and in 1933 travelled to England where he enlisted in the West Kent Regiment. In 1935, he was accepted for training by the Royal Military College at Sandhurst, graduating in December 1936. After a brief visit home, he returned to England where he joined the 2nd Battalion of the Lincolnshire Regiment. Then, in September 1937, he was transferred to the 1st Battalion of the Lincolnshires which, at that time, was stationed in India.

Hoey was successively promoted from lieutenant to captain to major and in the spring of 1943 he was Mentioned-in-Dispatches. During the summer of that same year, he won the Military Cross for "gallant and distinguished service" in leading a commando raid against the Japanese at Maunglaw.

On February 15, 1944, the Lincolnshires began their operation to relieve the Indian divisions at Arakan, Charles Hoey in the lead. It meant initially advancing up a valley between hills on either side infested with Japanese machine-gun nests until they reached the advanced enemy post before going on to their objective, a salient peak among the mountains. Hoey led his men over a field and across a river swept by enemy fire until they reached the base of the hill. There they ran into a Japanese post manned by more than forty of the enemy. Hoey grabbed a Bren gun from one of his troops and shouted: "Follow me — we've got to take this objective!" Firing from the hip, he led the attack on the enemy position, accounting for all of the enemy casualties. But in the process his own company had suffered heavy losses, too.

As he raced ahead, what was left of his force did their best to keep up with him. By this time Hoey himself had been wounded in the left leg and in the head, which was covered with blood. He arrived just short of the objective, the top of the peak, with only five men.

Hoey charged the position on his own and jumped into the enemy trenches. He inflicted heavy enemy casualties but was wounded again, this time fatally. He was buried that very day on the hill he had captured almost single-handedly, while those conducting the service were still under enemy fire. His body was later moved to the Taukkyan Cemetery in Rangoon, Burma. The capture of this vital peak caused the enemy to withdraw and take 5,000 casualties.

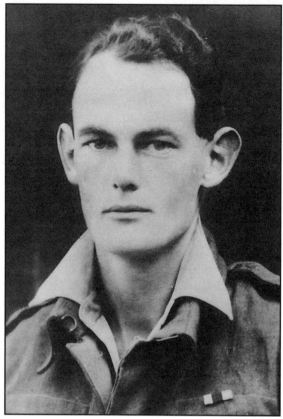

Charles Hoey, The Lincolnshire Regiment

Hoey's Victoria Cross was sent to his mother, Mary Hoey, who at her bequest donated it to the Regimental Museum of the Lincolnshire Regiment, where it is on display at the Sabraon Barracks in Lincoln. The citation to the award of Hoey's VC hangs in a place of honour in Duncan City Hall. In the late 1960s, a primary school in Duncan was opened and named in his honour: Charles Hoey VC Primary School.

Chapter Thirty-Six

STUBBORN RESISTANCE ON THE MELFA BRIDGEHEAD

THE Battle of the Liri Valley in Italy, from May 11 to June 3, 1943, embodied the breaking of the vaunted Gustav and Hitler Lines, and ended with the march on Rome. It was the first offensive undertaken by a complete Canadian Corps since Canada's 100 Days that ended the Great War in 1918. One of the keys was to cross the Melfa River. The date set for the assault was May 24. The German 10th Army fought bitterly to avoid being cut off, but the Canadian bridgehead was able to hold on. John Keefer Mahony, a former newspaperman from Vancouver, B.C., won the Victoria Cross in that action.

Born on June 30, 1911 in New Westminster, B.C., he received his education at Duke of Connaught High School, following which he took a job as a reporter with the *Vancouver Province*. He joined the militia as an officer with the Westminster Regiment and was one of the first to enlist when the war began. By 1944, he held the rank of major.

At three minutes after eight that Wednesday morning, tanks of the Fifth Armoured Division began the assault. John Mahony's A Company of the motorized Westminster Regiment had been ordered to establish the initial bridgehead across the fifty-yard-wide river. It was a challenging assignment to say the least. Although he led the crossing in full view of the enemy under heavy machine-gun fire, he did succeed in establishing a foothold. However, because of the terrain, it was only possible to dig shallow weapons pits. Next came the real test.

The Germans had ringed the bridgehead on all three sides: one 88-mm self-propelled gun 450 yards to the right and four anti-aircraft guns 100 yards to the left of that position. On the left flank, the Canadians faced a heavy Spandau gun, a second 88-mm weapon, and an infantry company armed with an arsenal of mortars and machine guns. As the Westminsters began digging in, Mahony prepared himself for the inevitable enemy counterattack.

The expected onslaught against the New Westminsters' Melfa River bridgehead came on with a vengeance, with the Germans throwing everything they had at the Canadians. But the defences held and beat off the attack with PIAT[1] guns, 2-inch mortars and hand grenades. Mahony was wounded three times, once in the head and twice in the leg, but refused medical aid. In agony, he continued to direct the defences. By this time his company had been reduced to sixty men.

---

1 Projector, Infantry, Anti-Tank gun.

An hour later, German tanks formed up 500 yards ahead of the defenders, with a company of infantry in support, to make a second counterattack. Four of the Westminsters tried to hide behind a mound of hay but the Germans caught them in the act and their machine-gunners opened fire. Mahony tossed out some smoke-grenades to screen his men. "I ran to help them," he recalled. "I saw a bright light and heard a swishing sound. The bullet's air pressure just about knocked my helmet off my head."

The assault was finally warded off with the Canadians destroying three enemy self-propelled guns, a Panther tank and inflicting heavy German casualties.

During the incessant enemy harassment that followed, the Germans realized that Mahony was the moving spirit behind the stubborn defence and made him their target as he conspicuously moved from one position to another, exhorting his men. By the time the remaining companies of the battalion were able to cross the river to reinforce the bridgehead, Mahony's unit had held off the Germans for a solid five hours. His defence of the perimeter against overwhelming odds and under the severest battle conditions had been crucial to the outcome of the Battle of the Liri Valley. With reinforcements present, Mahony allowed his wounds to be dressed.

Mahony received his Victoria Cross from King George VI — twice. The first time took place on July 31 in the field when His Majesty, travelling incognito in Italy as a "General Collingwood," reviewed Canadian troops on an airfield near Raviscanina in the Volturno Valley. Still recuperating from his wounds and racked by fatigue and dysentery, he wobbled so unsteadily the king had difficulty pinning the ribbon to his tunic. Many months later at the Buckingham Palace investiture Mahony apologized for the incident. The monarch, who had never really wanted to be king but who had seen action in the Battle of Jutland in 1916, reassured him: "I know what it means to be nervous, Mahony."

After the war Mahony remained in the army until 1962, serving successively as commandant cadet officer of Western Command, director of publications for the Canadian army, and assistant adjutant and quartermaster-general of the Western

John Mahony, The Westminster Regiment

Ontario Area. In 1954, he was posted to Washington as Canadian liaison officer. He retired to London, Ont. where he engaged in youth work as executive director of the local branch of the Junior Achievement organization.

On a pilgrimage back to the battlefield along with the other veterans of the Italian campaign some years after he retired, Mahony had difficulty tracing the Melfa crossing action. The scene of his gallantry has yielded to peacetime punishment. The banks of the river were green and wild with growth, respectful to the memory, but the river had become a giant gravel pit while overhead a bridge carried trucks over the expressway to Rome. Both the quarry and the autostrada have erased the bridgehead Mahony and his company defended so bravely for those five valiant hours.

In later years, those who knew him well would find it hard to picture John Mahony in the midst of the fierce fire-fight that ensued. Quiet and gentle, he was known for his modesty.

Mahony died in London on December 16, 1990 in St. Mary's Hospital, at seventy-nine years of age, after a long battle with Parkinson's disease. At his own request, he was buried without a military funeral.

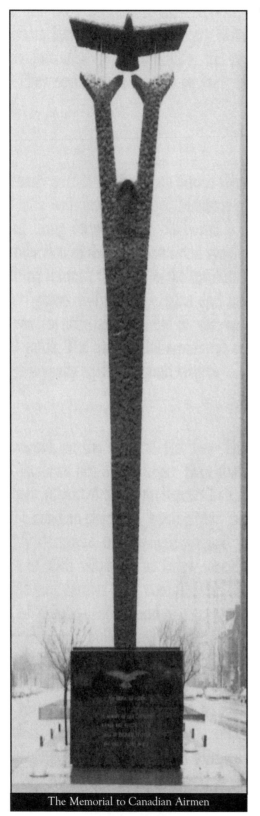

The Memorial to Canadian Airmen

Chapter Thirty-Seven

THE SUPREME SACRIFICE OF THREE AIR FORCE VCS

THEY paid the full price. All three Victoria Crosses awarded to Canadian airmen of the Commonwealth air forces in the Second World War were made posthumously and all resulted from actions that occurred in less than a two-month period during the summer of 1944. Count them: Andrew Charles Mynarski of Winnipeg, Man. on June 12; David Ernest "Bud" Hornell of Mimico, Ont. on June 25; and Ian Willoughby Bazalgette of Calgary, Alta. on August 4. Both Mynarski and Hornell served with the Royal Canadian Air Force. Hornell joined up on June 8, 1941 and Mynarski on September 23 of that same year. Bazalgette enlisted in the Royal Artillery in England on July 16, 1939, and in September 1940 transferred to the Royal Air Force Volunteer Reserve.

Bazalgette and Hornell were pilots. Bazalgette flew a four-engine Lancaster with 635 Pathfinder Squadron, RAF Bomber Command from Downham Market, Norfolk; Hornell piloted a twin-engine Canso flying-boat with 162 Squadron Coastal Command out of Wick in northern Scotland. Mynarski was a mid-upper air gunner of a Lancaster with 419 Squadron, 6 Group RCAF Bomber Command, stationed at Middleton St. George in Durham.

Bazalgette and Mynarski both won their VCs for actions in bombing raids on targets in German-occupied France, and Hornell in an attack against a German U-boat over the North Sea.

Andy Mynarski, the son of Polish immigrants, was born on October 14, 1916 in Winnipeg, where he took his education at King Edward and Isaac Newton Elementary Schools. He then attended St. John's Technical School. Before he joined the air force, he took a job as a leather worker, a trade he plied for three years to help support his family after his father died. On December 18, 1942, he received his Air Gunner's badge at a Wings Parade at No. 3 Bombing/Gunnery School in MacDonald, Man. where he had taken his training. He then proceeded overseas. After operational instruction in England and a stint with 9 Squadron RAF, he joined 419 Squadron RCAF on April 10, 1944.

Bud Hornell was born in Mimico on January 26, 1910 and was educated at John English Public High School, Mimico High School and Western Technical School. Upon graduation he went to work with the Goodyear Tire and Rubber Company. Married, he made his home in Mimico where he became highly respected for his community work with boys. Hornell received his pilot's wings on September 25, 1941 at Brantford Service Flying Training School and was selected for Coastal Command duties. After further instruction at the General Reconnaissance School in Charlottetown, P.E.I., he was posted to the RCAF station at Coal Lake on northern Vancouver Island. In 1943, he joined 162 Squadron RCAF Coastal Command, which in January 1944 was sent to Reykjavik, Iceland for anti-submarine patrol duty. That spring, with heavy U-boat activity off the north coast of Scotland, a detachment from the squadron was posted to Wick. Hornell and his crew arrived there on June 3.

Ian "Baz" Bazalgette was born in Calgary on October 19, 1918, the son of an army pensioner who had been gassed at Ypres in World War I with the 44th Winnipeg Battalion. In 1923, the family moved to Toronto and there, at Balmy Beach School, he received his initial education. When the family moved again, this time to England, Bazalgette completed his schooling at Rokeby, the Downs, Wimbledon as well as taking private tuition. When war broke out he was serving with the Searchlight section of the Royal Artillery as an officer. After completing his flying training with the RAF, to which he had transferred, he joined 115 Squadron on September 15, 1942, flying twin-engine Wellington bombers and made thirty-three operational sorties. During that tour, he was awarded the Distinguished Flying Cross for a low-level night attack on Milan, Italy in April 1943. In September, he was taken off operations for a stint as an operational training instructor. Then, on April 20, 1944, he joined 635 Pathfinder Squadron as a flight commander with the rank of squadron leader.

ANDY Mynarski and his crewmate, tail-gunner Pat Brophy, were the closest of buddies. Up until June 11, 1944, at which time Mynarski was commissioned and made gunnery officer, because Brophy was an officer and Mynarski a sergeant their ranks had kept them apart — although only figuratively. They had to live in different quarters, but they made a joke of it. Bidding each other good night, Brophy would clap Mynarski on the back and say, "Good night, Irish," to which Mynarski, with an exaggerated mock salute would reply, with just a hint of a Polish accent, "Good night, *Sir*."

On the evening of June 12, a week after D-Day, at Middleton St. George, Mynarski and Brophy and the rest of their crew were idling the time away sprawled on the grass by

Andrew Mynarski, Royal Canadian Air Force

their Lancaster bomber, waiting to take off. A few hours earlier they had been briefed for a raid on the railway yards at Cambrai in northern France. Apprehension seemed somewhat heavier than normal. This was their thirteenth mission and they would be over the target shortly after midnight on June 13. Emphasis: unlucky 13. As if to allay superstitions, Mynarski plucked a four-leaf clover and twirled it between his thumb and forefinger. Turning to Brophy, he said: "Here Pat, you take it." The tail-gunner stuck it under his leather flying helmet for good luck.

German air defences were busy that night as more than 200 Lancasters from 6 Group RCAF set out to prowl the darkness over France in search of their targets. As "A" for "Able" — the bomber carrying Mynarski and his mates — crossed the coast near the Pas de Calais, ugly orange flak bursts exploded above, below and around them, none of them, thankfully, very close.

Over the intercom Art de Breyne, the pilot, calmly announced, "Eighty minutes to target."

"Thanks," Mynarski replied from the mid-upper gun turret. "No rush."

Searchlights meandered across the sky, eagerly seeking out raiders to pinpoint for the lurking Luftwaffe night-fighters. Suddenly one of the light beams caught "A" for "Able" cold. "Hang on," de Breyne called out, "we're coned," and climbed the Lancaster to escape the searchlight's glare. Then he began a slow descent; to ensure accuracy, the railway yards at Cambrai were to be bombed at 2,000 feet.

They had reached 5,000 feet when Brophy, who was in the tail turret, spotted a twin-engine German Junkers 88. "Bogie astern!" he shouted into the intercom. "Six o'clock!"

De Breyne immediately put the aircraft into a corkscrew pattern to evade. Seconds later, Brophy saw the night-fighter pulling up from below. "He's coming under us," Brophy warned. As he wheeled his turret to take aim, the Junkers flashed by with cannons blazing. Both port engines were knocked out and the wing tank caught fire. Another burst tore into the fuselage, starting a fire between Mynarski's turret and Brophy's.

The attack also put the intercom out of business. De Bryne pushed the button that turned the red light on at all stations, the signal to bail out. "A" for "Able" was done for.

Brophy recalled looking at his watch at that very instant; it read thirteen minutes past midnight on June 13!

All of the crew got out safely except Mynarski and Brophy. Mynarski slid down from the mid-upper turret and made his way to the rear escape hatch, about fifteen feet from the rear turret. Just as he was about to jump, he glanced around and spotted Brophy; one look told him that his buddy was trapped. The turret's hydraulic system had been shot away and the manual system wouldn't work. He was unable to make it pivot to get out. Mynarski turned away from the escape hatch and, because the pilotless aircraft was lurching so wildly, got down on his hands and knees and crawled towards the rear through a wall of blazing hydraulic oil. By the time he reached the turret, his flying suit was on fire from the waist down.

Brophy shook his head. "Don't try!" he shouted. But over the roar of the rushing air and the whine of the engines he couldn't be heard. It wouldn't have made any difference if he had. Mynarski grabbed a fire axe and began chopping at the turret. It gave slightly but not enough. In desperation he tore at the doors with his hands. By now he was a mass of flame. Brophy screamed, "Go back Andy! Get out!" and waved him away. Mynarski hung his head as though he were ashamed, but he knew he could do no more. Crawling back through the fire again, he looked back in anguish. When he reached the escape hatch, he stood up and slowly came to attention. Standing there, his clothes on fire, he saluted. Just before he jumped he said something. Brophy couldn't hear, but it was clear to him what that something was. Loud and clear. "Good night, *Sir.*"

Mynarski's descent from the bomber was seen from the ground. His clothing and parachute were on fire. He was alive when he landed but so badly burnt he died later of his injuries. Miraculously, Pat Brophy survived, and thankfully too — otherwise the saga would never have come to light. When the Lancaster crashed near the village of Gaudiempre, close to Amiens, the impact freed the jammed turret and Brophy was thrown clear, uninjured. However, his harrowing ordeal had taken its toll. When he took off his flying helmet a tuft of hair came with it — along with the four-leaf clover!

Brophy said later, "I'll always believe that a divine providence intervened to save me because of what I had seen, so that the world might know of a gallant man who laid down his life for a friend."

BUD Hornell's demise was no less horrific, but it was an ordeal by water instead of fire. This was his sixtieth mission and, tragically, his last; he had logged 600 hours of submarine patrol time. Though U-boat sightings north of the Shetland Islands had been reported more and more frequently over the past week or so, on this particular patrol of June 24, which had already lasted a long, tiresome ten hours, Hornell and his crew of Canso *9754 "P"* had not so much as seen a gull. Bored and fed up, they set course for Wick some 1,000 miles away. Suddenly a surfaced German submarine — U-1225 — appeared off the port beam travelling at full speed. Hornell sounded "Action stations!" and swerved in at right angles to attack. However, the submarine opened fire first. Then, as the Canso's gunner took aim, one of the forward-firing guns jammed. Nevertheless, he raked the submarine's conning tower and killed most of the crew on deck.

But *U-1225*'s fire had also taken its toll. Cannon shells had torn two gaping holes in the starboard wing and had set that engine and the fuselage on fire. The aircraft had

David Hornell, Royal Canadian Air Force

become almost uncontrollable from the violent vibration. Nevertheless, Hornell pressed home his attack. Swooping down at deck level, he dropped depth charges in a perfect straddle that blew holes in the submarine's hull. The U-boat's bow lifted majestically out of the water and then the vessel slowly sank beneath the surface. Some of the crew, however, had managed to escape and were bobbing in the sea.

With the Canso's weight alleviated by the release of the bombs, Hornell managed to climb back up to 250 feet. But that was it. By this time the flaming starboard engine had dropped right off and stability, such as it was, was gone entirely. Turning the aircraft into the wind as best he could, Hornell prepared to ditch. He bounced the plane off the surface twice before it finally settled in a heavy rolling seven-foot-high swell. All eight of the crew were able to get away from the battered hulk with the two four-man dinghies before it sank. However, only one of the dinghies would inflate — the other one exploded when the valve was turned on. That left them with a raft that could uncomfortably hold seven, one man taking turns in the water clinging to the side.

Before they crashed, the radio operator had tapped out a distress signal. No one received it; the wireless set had been too badly damaged when the aircraft was hit by the submarine's fire. But, after four hours in the sea, the crew spotted another Canso on patrol. Desperately they fired off one, two, three and the last of their flares. The final one caught the pilot's attention. The flying boat, manned by a Norwegian crew, signalled to the life raft by Very light the welcome news that it had radioed for help and that a high-speed air-sea rescue launch was on its way. But a long wait still lay ahead; the ordeal was far from over.

By this time, the waves had risen to twenty feet with the wind gusting to thirty knots. Overcome by the cold, Hornell became seasick. Then the waves got worse, fifty feet high, and the wind blowing now at fifty knots. To ride out the waves, the crew had to shift in unison. Then, after fourteen hours in the sea, the dinghy capsized on the crest of a wave. With what strength they could still summon, the airmen righted it and climbed back in. One of the crew, the 2nd flight engineer, died of delirium. His body was lowered overboard with the sombre realization that they would no longer have to take turns in the water.

They had been in the sea for sixteen hours when a Warwick transport aircraft attempted to drop an airborne lifeboat to them. But it landed 500 yards away and the dinghy could only be seen when it rode the crest of a wave. Despite the condition of the sea and the distance, Hornell, who at this point was going blind, wanted to go after it. One of his crew restrained him.

Thankfully, the sea and the wind finally began to subside, but not before another one of the crew, the flight engineer, succumbed to the ordeal and Hornell had lapsed into unconsciousness. Twenty hours and thirty-five minutes after they had ditched, the rescue launch at last arrived, pulled alongside the dinghy and took the six survivors aboard. But although Hornell was given medical treatment, he died three hours after being rescued.

Ian Bazalgette, Royal Canadian Air Force

AUGUST 4, 1944, about two weeks before the Allied breakout from Normandy, German buzz-bombs launched from missile sites in northern France were still raining down on London. Not until September, when the Canadians overran northern France, would this inhumane menace be curtailed. In the meantime, there was only one way in which to try and fight it; strike at the source by bombing the launching pads themselves, though these were portable and easily concealed in woods, as well the as the bases of supply. One such source, uncovered by British intelligence, was a V-1 flying bomb depot at Tossy St. Maximim in the Beauvais area.

On this particular summer morning, "Baz" Bazalgette flew his Lancaster as master bomber in a raid on that supply base. His job was to mark the target with incendiary bombs as a beacon for the bombers that followed. As he neared the depot, his aircraft came under severe anti-aircraft fire. Both of the starboard engines were knocked out. The bomb-aimer had his arm and part of his shoulder torn away. Smoke and flames overcame the mid-upper gunner who had to be given a shot of morphine. But there was no turning back. Because the deputy master bomber had been shot down, the raid depended on Bazalgette, and what was left of both his crew and his aircraft. He had to press on, which he did, marking the target accurately and precisely, ensuring the raid's success.

But after dropping the bomb load, the plane went into a dive, spinning out of control. Bazalgette had to wrestle to put it back on even keel and then the inner port engine packed up; worse, the starboard wing quickly turned into a mass of flame. At 1,000 feet and with no hope of regaining height, with a fire on his hands and two of his crew knocked out of action, he could only hope to put the aircraft down somewhere to rescue what was left of the situation. He ordered the remaining crewmen to bail out; then, doing his best to avoid crash landing in the French hamlet of Senantes, he was spiralling down towards an open field when the aircraft exploded, killing all aboard.

ANDY Mynarski is buried in Méharicourt Cemetery of the French hamlet that bears its name. In 1981, the surviving members of his crew, along with his sister, Stephanie Holoway, and her husband, visited the grave and donated a bronze commemorative plaque to be attached to the cairn in that village. His Victoria Cross, the property of Mrs. Holoway, is on loan at the Air Command Headquarters Bishop Building in Westwin, Man., displayed in a room that bears his name. A group of lakes in Manitoba and a junior high school in Winnipeg are named in his honour. A "Mynarski Trophy" is awarded annually to the Canadian Forces air station married quarters community that provides a high-calibre youth program.

Bud Hornell lies in Lerwick Cemetery in the bleak Shetland Islands, his grave a solemn monument to his valour and sacrifice. In March 1991, his Victoria Cross was placed on permanent display in the Bishop Building. Some members of his crew and his brother were present at the ceremony.

Ian "Baz" Bazalgette was buried in Senantes Churchyard, not far from Beauvais. His tombstone reads, appropriately, "Greater love hath no man than this. That a man can lay down his life for his friends." But he is also suitably remembered at home in Canada. In 1949, a mountain in Jasper National Park was named after him.

Chapter Thirty-Eight

THE SOUTH ALBERTANS LAY SEIGE TO ST. LAMBERT

ON July 25, 1944, the United States 1st Army broke out of the Normandy invasion bridgehead in France at St. Lo, sweeping south around the German 7th Army to trap it in a scissorlike grip by wheeling left to tighten the vise, with the 2nd Canadian Corps advancing on Falaise from the north. Most of the burden in closing the "Gap" fell to the Fourth Canadian and First Polish Armoured Divisions. David Vivian Currie's C Squadron of the 29th Canadian Armoured Reconnaissance Regiment (South Alberta Regiment), a mixed bag of tanks, PIAT guns and infantry, was given the task of blocking the Germans' way through the village of St. Lambert-sur-Dives, a key point in the Chambois-Trun escape route.   On the evening of August 18, after encountering stubborn German resistance, Currie entered the hamlet alone and on foot to size up the situation. He made a swift decision typical of him – take the place and hold it.

Currie was born in Sutherland, Sask. on July 8, 1912. From 1913 to 1939, his family lived in Moose Jaw where he was educated at King George Public School and Central Collegiate. He also attended Moose Jaw Technical school and became an automobile mechanic and welder. In 1919, he joined the militia, and on January 30, 1940 enlisted in the regular army with the rank of lieutenant. In April 1941, he was promoted to captain and assigned to the Royal Canadian Engineers training school at Dundern, Sask. Six months later, he was posted to the Canadian Armoured Corps training school at Camp Borden, Ont. In May 1942, Currie was attached to the 29th Armoured Reconnaissance Regiment and went overseas in August. In March of 1944, he was promoted to the rank of major. He and his unit landed on the Normandy beaches on D-Day.

That morning of August 18, Currie led his squadron with a company of Argyll's to the outskirts of St. Lambert-sur-Dives where its lead tanks were badly hit by enemy fire. By that afternoon, he was the only officer in his unit who had not become a casualty. He requested permission to mount an attack to rescue the two disabled tanks. Despite heavy mortar fire, he personally directed the evacuation on the firing line until the men got clear.

Next morning, with a small force of tanks, infantry and anti-tank guns, but with no artillery support, Currie organized an all-out assault on the village. In the face of determined opposition from German tanks, guns and infantry, by noon he and his men had succeeded in seizing and consolidating a position halfway inside the village. For the

Tank movement in Falaise, 1944

next thirty-six hours, the enemy launched one counterattack after another in a desperate attempt to dislodge the Canadians. In Currie's own words, "It was one hell of a mess. They threw everything but the kitchen sink at us." However, Currie had arranged his defences so skilfully that the attacks were repulsed with heavy losses to the enemy.

At dusk on August 20, the Germans tried to mount a final decisive assault to break their way out. It failed miserably. The attack force was routed before it could be deployed. Seven German tanks, twelve 88-mm guns and forty vehicles were destroyed; 300 Germans were killed, 500 wounded and 2,100 were captured. Currie promptly ordered an attack and completed the capture of the village, effectively blocking that part of the Chambois-Trun escape route and denying it to the Germans trapped in the Falaise pocket.

Throughout the three days and nights of almost continuous fighting, Currie seemed to thrive on danger. He not only directed his men, but he took part in the fighting himself. On one occasion, he personally directed the fire of his command tank on to a German Tiger tank and knocked it out. During a subsequent attack, he used a rifle from his gun turret to kill enemy snipers. Another time, even though his unit's artillery fire was falling within fifteen yards of his tank, he ordered it continued because of its devastating effect on the Germans. Currie had virtually no respite during the battle; in fact, just one hour's sleep. When relief finally arrived he was so exhausted that he fell asleep on his feet and collapsed.

There is a picture of Currie taken on August 20, 1944 at St. Lambert, revolver in hand, accepting the surrender of a German officer: "He was a cocky little bugger. He didn't want to surrender to a lowly major." The noted Canadian pioneer military historian, Colonel Charles Peter Stacey, described the scene "as close as we are likely to come to a photograph of a man winning the Victoria Cross." Currie put bravery and dignity at a premium and threw in modesty and humour for good measure.

After the war, Currie spent eight years in Baie Comeau, Que. as maintenance superintendent for the Quebec North Shore Paper Company. In 1953, he moved to Montreal where he held management positions with Bonnar Equipment and National Harvester. In 1959, Prime Minister John Diefenbaker appointed him sergeant-at-arms of the House of Commons, a position he occupied for seventeen years. Known as "The Colonel," he led the parade of House of Commons officers through the Hall of Honour into the chamber during sittings, ceremoniously shouldering the heavy gold-gilded mace, the symbol of parliamentary government.

In later years, Currie served as vice-chairman of the Victoria Cross and George Cross Association (Overseas), and every two or three years he led a delegation to England. Of his own award he would simply say, "It is an honour, and you carry it for a lot of people who aren't here anymore."

David Currie died on June 20, 1986 in hospital in Ottawa after suffering a heart attack. After a memorial service in the capital city, he was buried in Owen Sound, Ont. the home of his wife, the former Isabel Civil. A provincial plaque commemorating Currie was unveiled at Queen's Park in that city on July 1, 1989. His Victoria Cross is in the custody of his family.

David Currie, 29th Armoured Reconnaissance Regiment

Chapter Thirty-Nine

A One-Man Army

BRILLIANT and often inspired leadership is needed in any military operation, but when the chips are down, victory or defeat depends on the private soldier — Johnny Canuck, the backbone of the army. How that soldier reacts in the heat of battle determines the outcome. On the night of October 21/22, 1944 in Italy, Ernest Alvia "Smokey" Smith of the Seaforth Highlanders of Canada proved to be private, NCO and officer all neatly wrapped up into a one-man army, a human dynamo who said afterward, "I was scared the whole time. Who wouldn't be?" For his deeds, Smith became the first Canadian private to win a VC in World War II.

The objective of the Canadian Corps was to get across the raging Savio River, the biggest obstacle the Canadians had encountered in northern Italy. One hundred yards wide, the embankment facing the Canadians had been cleared to allow the German gunners a clear field of fire. In the first attempt to cross it, two companies had been wiped out.

Weather conditions could not have been worse. It was cold, wet and miserable. Torrential rains had caused the river to rise six feet in five hours. The soft, vertical banks made it impossible to take tanks across. But somehow the Highlanders, who spearheaded the attack, managed to establish a toehold. The right forward company was in the process of consolidating its position on the crossroads at Pievesestina, three miles from San Giorgio di Cesena, the immediate objective, when it was suddenly set upon by three German Mark V Panther tanks supported by two self-propelled guns and about thirty infantry. Situation impossible. But not to Smokey Smith, who led his two-man PIAT team across an open field under heavy fire from the tanks to a roadside ditch that afforded the cover and range he wanted. Posting one man on guard with a PIAT, he crossed the road armed with another anti-tank gun accompanied by the other Highlander.

Almost immediately a German tank came rumbling down the road, firing its machine guns into the ditches on either side. One of Smith's two men was wounded. Fully exposed to the enemy fire, from thirty feet away Smith took dead aim, fired his PIAT gun at the tank and put it out of action. Then ten German infantry quickly jumped off the back of the tank and charged Smith with their Schmeissers and hand grenades. Without hesitation, Smith leapt into the middle of the road and opened fire with his Tommy-gun at pointblank range, killing four of the enemy and scattering the rest.

Then a second tank appeared and opened fire supported by more German infantry which began to close in on Smith's position. But Smith steadfastly held his ground, firing back with his automatic weapon until the Germans finally gave up and withdrew in disorder. By this time a third tank had loomed in the distance, sweeping the area with fire from longer range. But Smith, still showing utter contempt for the danger, helped his wounded companion to cover behind a church where he obtained medical aid. He

Ernest "Smokey" Smith, The Seaforth Highlanders

then returned to his post to await the possibility of further attacks.

None developed. As a result, by dogged determination and courage, this private so inspired his comrades that they held firm against all further enemy fire until — by which time the river had subsided — their own tanks arrived some hours later. Thus the advance was able to continue with the eventual capture of San Giorgio di Cesena and a further march on the Roco River.

Smokey Smith — he doesn't know how he got the nickname — "With a name like Ernest, I guess that should be good enough" — was born in New Westminster, B.C. on May 3, 1914. He was the second soldier from that city to be awarded the Victoria Cross (the other being John Mahony), and one of four British Columbians to receive the medal. By coincidence, Mahony and Smith were born on the same street, a fact that found its way into Robert L. Ripley's *Believe It Or Not*.

Smith first went into action when his regiment landed in Sicily in July 1943. "I was the only guy who fought the whole Sicily campaign for nothing," he once wise-cracked. "I was docked twenty-eight days' pay just before we started. I was an NCO nine times. I got broke nine times. When you had a stripe, you could take off for three or four days and have a booze party and all they did was take away the stripe, not your pay." He never mentioned that during the Sicilian and Italian campaigns he was wounded twice.

For some time following demobilization, Smith worked for a photographic studio in New Westminster and dabbled in insurance. When the Korean War broke out in 1950, he re-enlisted in the Permanent Force, retiring in 1964 with the rank of sergeant as a member of the RCAF recruiting unit in Vancouver. He then joined his wife Esther as a consultant with Holiday Travel Consultants Ltd. of Vancouver, a job that entailed world travel. One of his many trips took him back to Pievesestina, the crossroads where he won his VC. Thirty pounds heavier than when he was last on the scene — "You've got to remember most of it is muscle" he laughed — he was greeted by Don Emilio Zolfoli, priest of the church, now rebuilt, and by school children waving Maple Leaf banners and asking for his autograph. For a brief moment Smokey relived the battle. "I had a big tank knocked out right here. I killed four Germans for sure. I know ... they were laid out right here."

On December 18, 1944, after King George pinned the VC he had won for that feat on his tunic, Smith recalls that the monarch handed him the leather-covered case that had held it with the words: "Here's a little present for you from me."

He has another memory of those days. "I had a brother Jack in the Canadian Scottish. He was in Northwest Europe and an officer comes up and says, 'You've got a brother named Smokey?' He says, 'Yes.' And the officer says, 'He's won the VC — you better get a machine gun and go out and win one for us.' And all my brother says is, 'I've got a crazy brother.'"

At the time this book was written, Smokey Smith was one of two Canadian VCs still alive, the other being Cec Merritt, who also resides in Vancouver.

Chapter Forty

BELATED TRIBUTE

AT twenty-three years old, he was killed by a German sniper's bullet after an heroic action that won him the Victoria Cross — the only Canadian soldier in World War II to receive the award posthumously — in which he killed some twenty Germans and took an equal number prisoner. Yet when his home town wanted to name a bridge after him, the Ontario government refused permission, a typically Canadian political attitude towards its wartime veterans. His name was Aubrey Cosens. He was born in Latchford, Ont. on May 21, 1921, the son of an army veteran of World War I.

Shortly after his birth, his family moved to Porquois Junction where he attended school. On graduation, he was employed by the Temiskaming and Northern Ontario Railroad. On November 12, 1940, Cosens joined the Argyll and Southern Highlanders of Canada (Hamilton Regiment) which in 1941 sailed to form part of the Canadian force in Jamaica. It returned in May 1943 and went overseas to England two months later. After a year there, Cosens transferred to the Queen's Own Rifles of Canada which he joined as a replacement during the tail end of the Normandy fighting and was soon promoted from corporal to sergeant.

It was during the clearing of the Rhineland which began on February 8, 1945 that Cosens won his VC. The objective of the Canadian army, along with the British and Americans, was to clear the Germans out of the area west of the Rhine. This meant capturing the Reichwald Forest, breaking the Siegfried Line and seizing the Hochwald Forest defences. By February 21, they had cracked the Siegfried. But still barring their way to the Rhine were the Hochwald Forest and the Balberger Heights. An assault was launched to open a sixteen-mile-long corridor to the river. It had been calculated that, with the overwhelming force at hand, a quick, sharp victory could be achieved. But the February thaw, the quagmire that clogged the roads and the cloud that restricted air cover turned the campaign into a nightmarish thirteen-day battle that killed or wounded 3,638 Canadians — 214 alone slaughtered on the first day of the battle which began on the early morning of February 26.

The Queen's Own Rifles were chosen to launch an attack on the German hamlet of Mooshot, thereby capturing ground vital to the development of the campaign. Aubrey Cosens' platoon, supported by a pair of Sherman tanks, assaulted three German strongpoints in farm buildings but were twice beaten back by fanatical enemy resistance and were themselves fiercely counterattacked. One of the tanks was knocked out and the platoon suffered heavy casualties, including the platoon commander who was killed.

Cosens immediately assumed command. Gathering the four survivors together, he announced: "I'm going to get a Hussar tank to bust its way through the wall of the main farmhouse. I'll go through the hole and take the Jerries in the rear. Cover me until I get to the tank. When I run into the house, I want you to give me plenty of covering fire. If you can keep them busy, they might not see what's happening."

Placing his men in key positions to cover him, he raced across the open ground under heavy German mortar and shell fire while his comrades kept up a steady fusillade of rifle bullets aimed at the farmhouse windows. Reaching the one remaining Sherman tank, Cosens took up a position behind the turret to direct its fire.

Cosens got the tank rolling and as it roared forward he fired high explosives from the 75-mm cannon. Then, leaping from the tank, Sten gun in hand, Cosens ran ahead while the Germans tried to shoot him down from the farmhouse. Then, like a Juggernaut, the tank crashed through a wall of the farmhouse. With bricks falling all around him, Cosens plunged into the building. While his four rifleman continued to engage the Germans, Cosens was literally cleaning house inside, shooting his way from room to room, killing or wounding the surprised enemy.

After clearing the main farmhouse, Cosens charged the second and third buildings, routing, killing or wounding more Germans who, watching him charge about in the face of a hail of machine-gun fire and small-arms bullets, must have thought he was invulnerable to their fire. Cosens quickly reorganized his small band, placing the men at key points and stationing the tank in a position to launch a fresh attack. He then started out to report to his company commander when an enemy sniper's bullet struck him in the head, killing him almost instantly.

Cosens is buried in Groesbeck Canadian Cemetery War Cemetery at Nijmegan in Holland. After the war, in 1963, the officers and men of the 1st Battalion of the QOR serving with the regular army in Germany erected a bronze plaque at the site. It reads:

In Commemoration
of
SGT AUBREY COSENS V.C.
1st Bn The Queen's Own Rifles of Canada
who on the night of
25/26 February 1945
led the survivors of his
platoon in the capture of
these farm buildings which were
vital to the success of future
operations of the
8th Cdn Inf Bde
For his gallantry, initiative and
determined leadership
Sgt. Cosens was
posthumously awarded the
VICTORIA CROSS

On August 29, 1965, a provincial commemorative plaque was unveiled in his memory on Highway 11 south of the north intersection with Highway 67 near Porquois Junction. A tourist steamer plying Lake Temagami is named after him, as is the Latchford branch of the Royal Canadian Legion. Also, Cosens's Victoria Cross is displayed at the Glenbow Museum in Calgary, Alta. His Sten gun was nickle-plated and preserved.

Yet on Thursday, October 3, 1985, the *Ottawa Citizen* broke with the headline: "ONTARIO TOWN IRKED BY REFUSAL TO NAME BRIDGE AFTER WAR HERO". The story went on to say:

> LATCHFORD (CO) - Residents of this tiny town bristle when they think of how the Burlington Skyway in southern Ontario was renamed after a politician but they can't get politicians to name a bridge named after their wartime hero.
>
> This community 120 kilometres northeast of North Bay was the home town of Sgt. Aubrey Cosens, posthumously awarded the Victoria Cross after he was killed in action in Holland during the Second World War while serving with the Queen's Own Rifles.

Aubrey Cosens, The Queen's Own Rifles

> But the Ontario government has denied a request from Latchford residents to name a 91-metre-long bridge across the Montreal River on Highway 11 after Cosens.
>
> The government doesn't name bridges after people, Transportation Minister Ed Fulton said in a letter to Latchford officials.
>
> But as the residents are quick to note, the Burlington Skyway spanning Hamilton harbour was recently renamed Burlington Bay James N. Allan Skyway in honour of James Allan, former Conservative member of the legislation for Haldimand-Norfolk and Ontario treasurer. Allan was transport minister when tenders for the skyway were called.
>
> Fulton's letter said motorists might be tempted "to slow down or stop on bridges or their approaches while they ponder the significance of the bridge name or search for further information about the event or person named."
>
> Fulton suggested instead that the province pay to have a cairn bearing Cosens' name installed in a roadside park adjacent to the bridge.
>
> But Mayor George Lefebvre described Fulton's reasons for not naming the bridge after Cosens as "really ridiculous."

Fulton had been warned by his staff of discerning public servants that any such recognition would open the floodgates because there were 2,800 bridges in Ontario. (For the

Mud encrusted tank

record, twenty-one Canadian VCs came from Ontario.) The issue came to a head when Gus Goutoski, a leading real estate man in Halton County and a veteran of the QOR, backed by a resolution unanimously passed by 2,500 delegates of the Royal Canadian Legion's Ontario Command, persuaded Fulton to reconsider. According to Goutoski, he eventually "caved in."

The result was that in 1986 prominent signs were installed at both ends of The Sgt. Aubrey Cosens VC Memorial Bridge, and a cairn was erected. At the inauguration ceremonies, Fulton cut the ribbons. In attendance were Lieutenant-Governor Lincoln Alexander and Veterans Affairs Minister George Hees. Brigadier Ben Dunkleman, Cosens' company commander who recommended him for the VC, unveiled the commemorative cairn.

Fred Tilston, The Essex Scottish Regiment

Chapter Forty-One

THE WHIRLING DERVISH

OF war Fred Tilston once said, a characteristic smile on his face, "I enjoyed it. It was like a game of Cowboys and Indians. The only difference is that we were using live ammunition."

It was just such live ammunition to which he referred so cavalierly that cost Tilston both legs below the knees, later an eye and very nearly his life when a bullet pierced a lung and lodged close to his heart. It was typical of Tilston that he took it all in stride. His sense of humour never deserted him. When asked what quality was important in winning the Victoria Cross, he replied unhesitatingly with a grin: "Inexperience!"

Frederick Albert Tilston was born in Toronto on June 11, 1906, and moved to Chicago with his parents at age eight. When his father was killed in an accident, Tilston, his mother and two sisters moved back to Toronto. His mother took a job to support them. Fred attended De La Salle High School and took a paper route to help out with the finances. On graduating he worked as a delivery boy for a downtown pharmacy. His ambition was to become a doctor, but without enough money to study full time he had to settle for a job as a pharmaceutical apprentice, working in a drugstore by day and studying in the evening.

After a three-year apprenticeship, he spent two years alternating between the Ontario College of Pharmacy and the

University of Toronto. To keep some money coming in, he took part-time jobs at drug-stores, working on the night shift or all day on weekends. He finally got his degree, grad-uating second out of a class of 105. He first went to work as a dispensing pharmacist in a drugstore and then went on the road as a travelling salesman with the Canadian arm of the giant American pharmaceutical firm Sterling Drug, manufacturers of Bayer Aspirin. This eventually took him out west where he met his future wife, Helen Adamson, a hairdresser in Edmonton, Alta. By 1939, Tilston had become Sterling Drug's sales manager with headquarters in Windsor, Ont., and it was there that he joined the Essex Scottish Regiment when war broke out.

He enlisted as a private, but because of his age — he was thirty-three — education and managerial experience, he was quickly promoted first to sergeant and then to an officer, although on the drill square he was a disaster, seemingly unable to co-ordinate his arms with his legs on parade. However, he was soon posted to Camp Borden, Ont. for field training which was much more to his liking.

Overseas, Tilston was spared from participating in the Dieppe raid of August 19, 1942 in which the Essex Scottish embarked thirty-two officers and 520 other ranks. The regi-ment was decimated, with only three officers and forty-nine other ranks escaping the casualty list. That December, during a training exercise in Sussex with live ammunition used to add realism, a mix-up in orders and signals resulted in Tilston taking a bullet in the back that dropped him like a log. When his men rushed to help him, he opened one eye and grinned: "Custer's last stand." But the wound was serious; it came within a frac-tion of killing him. The bullet had passed through a lung and entered the pericardium, the muscle around the heart. It called for intensive care and precise, delicate surgery but Tilston recovered and was back with his regiment within four months, this time as adju-tant — the principle administrative officer — with the rank of captain. He asked for a transfer to field duty, but the CO had found him so proficient as his righthand man that the request was denied.

During the Battle of Normandy in the summer of 1944, the Essex Scottish, which played no part in the landings, was designated as part of the break-out forces. In August, the regiment was one of those which had fought its way into Falaise. But it had moved so far so fast that it lost contact with the brigade headquarters. Tilston and a driver were dispatched by jeep to advise HQ of the regiment's position. On the way back, the vehi-cle drove over a German land mine which exploded. "The jeep went one way in the air and I another," Tilston later wrote. Fortunately, the floorboards had been sand-bagged for protection, otherwise both occupants would have had their legs shattered. But Tilston's wounds were severe enough to put him back in the hospital. He had concussion and both ear drums were blown, and his right eye was damaged by shrapnel splinters. For many years his sight was unaffected, but the minute particles of shrapnel eventually became dislodged and the eye had to be removed, After two months of medical treat-ment and rest, Tilston returned to the regiment.

By February 1945, Tilston had managed to get himself assigned to a rifle company, but to his disgust, when the regiment attacked the road between Goch and Calcar in the fight to the Rhine, he was left behind. However, in the fierce and bloody fighting, the company commander was killed, so that on the morning of March 1 Tilston found him-self in command of C Company with the rank of major.

At this time, as part of the Second Canadian Division, the Essex Scottish had been given the task of breaking the German defence line north of Udem and clearing the northern half of the Hochwald Forest, a thick coniferous wood several miles square in area which guarded the approach to the town of Xanten, the last enemy bastion west of the Rhine protecting the Wesel bridge escape route.

The plan called for the battalion to attack with two companies — A Company under Paul Cropp on the right flank and Tilston's C Company on the left. The start-line was at the edge of a group of farm buildings about 500 yards from the forest across a stretch of level farmland that offered no cover whatsoever. This attack, the first Tilston had led, and which would also be his last, was supposed to be supported by tanks. However, the softness of the soil on the left made it impossible for them to go forward; they could only advance on the firmer terrain on the right. This left Tilston's flank completely exposed. In any case, the tanks were slow to get under way. The assault was scheduled to start in the half light of the early morning at 7:15. a.m., but it wasn't until nine o'clock that the Canadian artillery barrage began bursting along the edge of the start-line.

As the shells began exploding ahead of them, the Essex Scottish began their advance across the field. Tilston, with his wireless operator, was slightly ahead of the first two forward platoons, with one following up in reserve. They had not gone far when German machine-gun fire started coming from across the field from two directions, left and right. Men began falling, including Tilston who was hit in the head, but he got up and rejoined his men as the company continued forward.

Now the German mortars opened up, adding to the Canadian casualties. With an open left flank and no tank support, C Company had no choice but to keep walking ahead as shells and machine-gun bullets tore huge gaps in their flanks. Halfway across the field, they ran into the first line of German trenches. Tilston went running into the attack and blew up a machine-gun nest with a hand grenade. Their Bren-gun carrier, which had the company's reserve ammunition supplies, turned back to evacuate the worst of the wounded.

When the company reached the edge of the wood, they encountered barbed-wire entanglements strung with anti-personnel mines. At night that would have been devastating, but in daylight the defence was soon surmounted. Tilston next found himself face-to-face with an 88-mm gun. He threw a hand grenade at it and one of his platoon commanders followed suit. By the time they reached it, the enemy gun crew had fled.

By this time, the Canadians had reached a network of enemy trenches and dugouts at the edge of the woods. Before the Essex Scottish got to them, the Germans had ducked back inside the bunkers and now began sniping at the Canadians from the rear. But they had left a pile of grenades unattended and C Company began flushing the enemy out with the enemy's own weapons. It was just as well. With the Bren-gun carrier gone, the unit's ammunition supply was becoming desperate.

Meanwhile, A Company had reached its objective, a group of farm buildings on the edge of the forest to the right. They had fared better than their left-flank counterparts. With proper tank support, they had suffered fewer casualties and had expended less ammunition. Dividing the two companies was a stretch of open ground and a road which the Germans were hammering unmercifully with mortar bombs and machine-gun fire. Tilston had been wounded again, this time in the hip. Knowing that something had to be done about his company's critical ammunition situation, he nonetheless instructed his men to hold their position while he set off by himself to replenish it with a supply from

A Company. As he approached, ignoring the enemy fire around him, the other company commander, Paul Cropp watched him in awe:

> I saw him coming across, no worries, just a smile on his face ... and in he sauntered, more or less, and said, "We are short of ammunition, what can we have?" So we supplied him. He was, of course, bleeding from a number of wounds and we patched them up for him and sent him back. But the thing that really struck me about Fred was that this man was really enjoying the war. Here am I, terrified by what's going on most of the time and here is a man who is totally enjoying what is happening.

Tilston ran back through the hail of German fire, this time loaded down with hundreds of rounds of ammunition and two boxes of grenades, just in time to help his men ward off an enemy counterattack. That kind of fighting went on all afternoon. One of his platoon leaders, Charlie Gatton recalled:

> He [Tilston] had no regard for enemy fire. He must have been beyond caring, I suppose, because he never got down into the trench. He just stood on the parapet or squatted beside it and just discussed our problems as if we were at a board meeting. He was absolutely cool. Fred made several trips across the road under fire and brought us grenades and boxes of ammunition.... I can't remember how many boxes of grenades we used up. You wouldn't believe it — it was just like a snowball fight really.

Gatton collected a load of ammunition from A Company himself and two other men went across during the afternoon. But Tilston made a total of six trips. This had allowed the company to hold on until the rest of the battalion arrived to advance through their lines to push further into the woods.

It was on the sixth and final run that Tilston was wounded for a third time that day. He described it:

> Between our position and Paul Cropp's headquarters was a very large crater. I was just passing through it when a mortar shell landed and I was at the wrong place at the wrong time. It got me. So I never made that final trip. I made myself as comfortable as possible under the circumstances. I simply undid my webbing, got into a reasonably comfortable position, gave myself a shot of morphine and waited. I think I became unconscious, you know, intermittently.

One of Tilston's legs had been completely blown off below the knee. The other was so badly shattered he couldn't move. When his men found him, he refused to be moved until he was sure that the last of his command could still hold their ground. Only twenty-seven of the 103 men who had started out with the company that morning were still alive to fight.

Tilston was taken to a field-dressing station, then shipped back to the Canadian Military Hospital at Horley in Sussex. Doctors fought desperately to save his shattered leg, but it was a losing battle and it had to be amputated below the knee. Before returning to Canada, Tilston travelled to Buckingham Palace to receive his VC in a wheelchair from King George VI.

In July 1945, Tilston arrived in Toronto to be greeted with a hero's welcome at which 15,000 people turned out. He entered Sunnybrook Military Hospital where he was given artificial legs. One night Tilston, along with fellow VCs John Mahoney and Paul Triquet, got permission to go out on the town. They did not get back until 4:00 a.m., all three singing lustily, much to the chagrin of the hospital staff. "But," explained Triquet, "we had something to celebrate. We'd gone to a nightclub and Fred had had his first postwar dance."

Fully recovered and rehabilitated, Tilston got his old job back at Sterling Drug and married Helen Adams after a thirteen-year courtship. They had one son, Michael. Tilston rose to be president of his company, which moved its headquarters from Windsor to Aurora, and eventually chairman of the board. He also became honourary director and past-president of the Canadian Foundation for the Advancement of Pharmacy, as well as director and past-president of the Proprietary Association of Canada. In 1965, he was made "Man of the Year" by the Independent Druggists' Association of Montreal.

In 1963, Tilston became honourary colonel of his old regiment, which had been renamed the Essex and Kent Regiment. And he was named honourary president of the Colonel Fred Tilston Branch of the Royal Canadian Legion in Aurora. Fred Tilston died in Toronto on September 23, 1992. His VC was presented by his family to the Royal Canadian Military Institute in Toronto.

Chapter Forty-Two

THE GALLANT ORDERLY

OPERATION Varsity: the final major undertaking of the war in Europe. Beginning at eleven o'clock on the morning of March 24, 1945, a vast aerial armada of 1,589 carriers and 1,337 gliders — flying from scattered bases throughout France and Great Britain — started dropping and landing airborne troops near Wesel on the east bank of the Rhine. As part of the 6th British Airborne Division, the 1st Canadian Parachute Battalion alighted just north of Dunford Wood. During their descent, the paratroopers were peppered with German machine-gun and sniper fire. Twenty-three Canadians were killed, forty wounded and two taken prisoner.

Among the injured was Frederick Topham, a medical orderly who was shot in the nose. Though bleeding profusely and in excruciating pain, that did not stop him from tending the wounded under savage enemy fire for the next six hours in a series of actions that won him the Victoria Cross, the second-to-last Canadian VC to be awarded.

Frederick George "Toppy" Topham was born on August 10, 1917 in Toronto and was educated at King George Public School and Runneymede High School. Before enlisting as a paratrooper he was a hard-rock miner — a "mucker" — in the Wright Hargreaves Mine at Kirkland Lake, Ont. When he went to enlist in the airborne, on which he had his heart set, he was rejected. The recruiting officer was prepared to accept his six-foot, two-inch height but he was thirty pounds too heavy for the parachute troops. For weeks Topham ate practically nothing and ran for hours every morning. When his weight fell to 175 pounds, he applied again. This time he was accepted and went overseas with the 1st Canadian Parachute Battalion.

During 1944, the number of army casualties had been far greater than had been anticipated and an urgent appeal was made for volunteers to serve as orderlies in the medical corps. It was dangerous work, much of it under enemy fire, and volunteers were advised that the guns with which they were issued were to be used solely to protect their patients — not themselves. Topham, who held the rank of corporal, was one of the first to volunteer.

Frederick Topham, 1st Canadian Parachute Battalion

Almost immediately after he had parachuted onto German soil that March morning in 1945, he heard a desperate cry for help from a wounded comrade out in the open, dangerously exposed to enemy fire. Two medical orderlies from a field ambulance unit rushed forward to his aid, but as they knelt down beside the stricken parachutist, German machine-gunners cut them down. Topham dashed forward to take their place. It was while attending to the man's wounds that he was struck in the nose by an enemy bullet.

Having rendered first aid to the injured paratrooper, Topham laboriously carried him from the field through furious enemy fire to the shelter of the wood. During the next two hours, he dismissed all offers of medical help for himself and continued to bring in casualties from the field without regard for the accurate and heavy German fire all around him. Only after all the wounded had been cleared did he consent to have his bleeding nose treated. He was then told that he could evacuate, but he insisted on returning to his post.

On his way to join his company he came across a gun carrier that had received a direct hit. Mortar shells were bursting all around and the vehicle was ablaze, its own ammunition exploding. All three of its crew were wounded and in grave danger. Despite orders to stay clear, Topham ran to the rescue and, ignoring the danger of flames, detonating ammunition and German mortar fire, managed to bring the three men across open ground to safety, though one later died from his injuries.

The citation to Topham's VC reads:

> This NCO showed sustained gallantry of the highest order. For six hours, most of the time in great pain, he performed a series of acts of outstanding bravery, and his magnificent and selfless courage inspired all those who witnessed it.

Topham's own comment was: "I don't believe that one boy in the outfit wouldn't have done the same."

On August 10, 1945, as tens of thousands of Torontonians cheered him, Toppy Topham was driven in a convertible up a flag-festooned Bay Street, streamers flying, to be officially welcomed home on the steps of city hall. Several months later, on November 10, he laid the cornerstone for Sunnybrook Memorial Hospital. At the same time, the County of York township presented him with a government annuity to provide him with $100 a month after he reached age fifty. Topham married and he and his wife Mary lived in Etobicoke. Topham took a job as an emergency troubleman with the Toronto Hydro Electric System. He died suddenly on March 31, 1974 at age fifty-four. At his wife's request, his funeral was private.

On November 9, 1980, a provincial memorial plaque in Topham's honour was unveiled at the Etobicoke Civic Centre at Highway 427 and Burnamthorpe Road. In attendance were his wife Mary and members of the Canadian Airborne Regiment. His VC, retained by his family, is presently on loan to the Canadian Airborne Forces Museum, CFB Petawawa, Ont.

Chapter Forty-Three

CANADA'S LAST VC

IN Sakiyama Peace Park on Northern Honshu, a cairn and memorial plaque overlook the site where Robert Hampton Gray won the Victoria Cross, the last Canadian to do so, the only Canadian fighter pilot to whom it was awarded in World II, and the only member of the Royal Canadian Navy and sole Canadian naval airman to receive it. The memorial, erected by the Japanese in 1989, is the only one made to an Allied officer or serviceman on Japanese soil.

"Hammy" Gray won his VC for a successful attack on a Japanese warship in Onagawa Bay, in which he lost his life, only an hour before the Americans dropped the second bomb on Nagasaki which brought the war to an end. He was one of 4,000 Canadians who at one time or another were "on loan" to the Royal Navy from the RCN during that conflict.

Born in Trail, B.C. on November 2, 1917, the son of a Scottish immigrant and veteran of the Boer War, Gray received his public and high school education in Nelson, B.C. He then spent a year at the University of Alberta in Edmonton followed by three years at the University of British Columbia in Vancouver where he became associate editor of the university year book Totem and joined the Canadian Officers Training Corps. After graduating with an arts degree in the class of 1940, he enlisted in the Royal Canadian Naval Reserve in Calgary on July 18, was mobilized as an ordinary seaman and sent to HMCS Stadacona in Halifax.

On August 3, he was selected as one of seventy-four candidates for duty with the Royal Navy and sailed for England for basic training on HMS Raleigh. He then volunteered for the Fleet Air Arm, was accepted and began his pilot training. Gray became one of 2,629 Fleet Air Arm pilots to earn their wings through the British Commonwealth Air Training Plan in Canada. Graduating in October 1941 with a sub-lieutenant's commission, Gray returned to England the following month for operational training before being posted to 757 Squadron at HMS Kestrel in Worthy Down. In May 1942, he began a tour in Kenya, South and East Africa with several squadrons as well as a stint aboard the British aircraft carrier HMS Illustrious.

After a period of leave in Canada, on August 6, 1944, Gray joined 1841 Squadron aboard HMS Formidable, which was engaged in launching air strikes with Corsair fighter-bombers and Barracuda torpedo-planes into Norway's Alten Fjord against the German battleship Tirpitz that was holed up there. On August 29, Gray led his section in an attack on three Narvik-class destroyers anchored in the fjord. Despite intense fire from the shore batteries and the destroyers, the Corsair pilots pressed home their attacks. A shell hit Gray's aircraft and shot away most of the rudder. But Gray returned to his ship and coolly circled for forty-five minutes while Formidable manoeuvred into position, then made a deck landing without incident. He was Mentioned-in-Dispatches for his "undaunted courage, skill and determination in carrying out day attacks on the German battleship Tirpitz."

By this time, as senior squadron pilot, Gray had already become something of a legend for his aggressiveness, bordering on the reckless, in the air, in contrast to his rather mild, quiet, innocent manner in the wardroom. But as one of his mates put it, he was "a rare hand in a crap game."

In April 1945, *Formidable* joined the British Pacific Fleet off Saskishma Gunto, a small group of islands between Formosa and Okinawa, to prevent Japanese planes from reaching the invasion area of the latter. By July the war had swept northward and the carrier became engaged in striking at the Japanese mainland. On July 18, Gray's flight found itself busy strafing Nipponese airfields. On July 28, Gray led an attack over the inland sea and made a direct hit on a merchant ship which was later reported

Robert Hampton Gray, Royal Canadian Volunteer Reserve

to have been sunk. For "determination and address [sic] in air attacks on targets in Japan," Gray was awarded the Distinguished Flying Cross.

At eight o'clock on the morning of August 9, five days before the war ended, Hammy Gray sat strapped in the cockpit of his Voight Corsair with his engine running awaiting the green light for take-off. One section of Corsairs was already in the air. Gray was to follow with his two sections of eight aircraft as soon as *Formidable* turned into the wind. The target was Matsushami airfield. However, at the last minute he was given fresh orders — verbally — to avoid breaking radio silence. Now his flight was to attack Japanese shipping in Onagawa Bay.

The unit was well suited for such an assignment. The Corsair was one of the most manoeuvrable fighter-bombers built. Designed to out-class the Japanese Zero, its cranked inverted gull wings gave it a lethal look. With a top straight-and-level speed of over 300 miles an hour, it carried two 500-pound bombs.

Gray climbed his section to 10,000 feet, flying west, and after 150 miles over the sea crossed the Honshu coast north of Kinksan. As the planes proceeded inland, the pilots could see the town of Matsushima and the airfield, their original target, on their left. The new objective Ogawana Bay now loomed on the right. Several major ships were moored there including the 1,000-ton ocean escort sloop *Amakusa*, two minesweepers, a training ship, several smaller submarine-chasers and shipping vessels.

The Corsairs reached a point northeast of the bay, then turned 180 degrees. They began losing height and picking up speed, racing down the harbour valley to the harbour mouth. They crossed the shoreline around 9:45 at low altitude and in sight of their targets. This was a skip-bombing attack, assuring maximum accuracy but also rendering the planes highly vulnerable to anti-aircraft and general fire from both the ships and the shore batteries. Suddenly, a curtain of intense fire enveloped the Corsairs.

Gray took aim on *Amakusa*, anchored in the middle of the harbour. As he swept in a cone of fire — from everywhere it seemed — zeroed in on him. Ack-ack shrapnel struck the aircraft, knocking one of the bombs away and setting the Corsair on fire. But Gray persisted in his attack, holding a steady course. Flames streaming behind him, he closed to within fifty yards before releasing his remaining bomb. It was a perfect strike amidships. Gray's plane turned slowly to starboard, then rolled over on its back and dived into the water. Neither the pilot nor the Corsair were ever found.

One hundred and fifty-seven Japanese were killed in the raid, seventy-one aboard *Amakusa* when it sank.

In addition to the memorial at the Sakiyama Peace Park, countless other tributes have been paid to Hammy Gray. Buildings, a mountain, institutions and organizations have been named after him and displays put up in his honour. The dependants' school at Canadian Forces Base Shearwater, N.S., home of the RCN Air Service, is named after him. The Canadian War Museum has a memorial display in his honour that displays his VC. A restored Corsair with Gray's markings is on show and flown by the Hamilton Wartime Heritage in Hamilton, Ont. A swimming pool in Nelson bears his name as do the Nelson Sea Cadets. Lake Gray, 103 miles north of Edmonton, was named in his memory as late as 1983. And like all Canadian sailors who lost their lives in World War II, his name is inscribed on the Sailors' Memorial at Point Pleasant Park in Halifax, N.S.

In recommending Gray for the VC, Vice-Admiral Sir Philip Vian, commander of the RCN Pacific Fleet Task Force wrote: "I have in mind firstly his brilliant fighting spirit and inspired leadership; an unforgettable example of selfless and sustained devotion to duty without regard to safety nor life and limb." In February 1946, in Ottawa, Gray's Victoria Cross was presented to his parents, John Balfour and Wilhelmina, by the Earl of Athlone, governor general of Canada.

Monument to commemorate Robert Hampton Gray, erected in his memory, Sakiyama Park, Onagawa Bay, Japan. It stands directly opposite where Gray's Corsair crashed into the water in the action that won him the Victoria Cross

VC ASSOCIATES

IN June 1866, Private Timothy O'Hea of the Rifle Brigade of the British army became the only person to win the Victoria Cross on Canadian soil. O'Hea extinguished a fire on a railway car loaded with ammunition at Danville, Quebec, an action that saved many lives. O'Hea was badly burned.

By strict definition according to the standards set down at the beginning of this compendium, O'Hea does not qualify as a Canadian VC even though his deed took place in Canada. He was not a Canadian, never lived in Canada and did not serve with a Canadian unit. It is also noteworthy, though it is certainly in no way to his discredit, that the action that won him the decoration was not even made in the face of the enemy. However he does, by any measurement, deserve Honourable Mention. The same applies to a group of others (fifteen) who are Canadian VCs by association. They won the medal as non-Canadians, but later made the Dominion their home. They are:

Barry Churchill Beet
Dennis Dempsey
Raymond de Montmorency
Benjamin Handley Geary
Robert McBeat
John McGovern
John Pearson
George Richardson
Robert Ryder
Henry Harvey Robson
John Sinton
Ronald Neil Stuart
Joseph Tombs
Charles William Train
Thomas Orde Lawder Wilkinson

To all, a hearty salute!

LOCATIONS OF CANADIAN VCs

RECIPIENT	MEDAL	BURIAL
ALGIE, Wallace Lloyd	Sold at auction, 1995	Niagara Cemetery, near Cambrai, France
BARKER, William George	Canadian War Museum, Ottawa	Mount Pleasant Cemetery, Toronto
BARRON, Fraser Colin	Family	Prospect Cemetery, Toronto
BAZALGETTE, Willoughby	RAF Hendon Museum, England	Senantes Churchyard, I a n Oise, France
BELLEW, Edward Donald	Royal Canadian Institute, Toronto (stolen)	Military Hillside Cemetery, Kamloops, B.C.
BENT, Philip Eric	Ashby-de-la-Zouch Grammar School, England	No known grave, Polygon Wood, France
BISHOP, William Avery	Canadian War Museum, Ottawa	Greenwood Cemetery, Owen Sound, Ont.
BOURKE, Rowland Richard Louis	National Archives Ottawa	Royal Oak Burial Park, Victoria, B.C.
BRERETON, Alexander Picton	Family	Three Hills, Alberta
BRILLANT, Jean	Le Musée, Royal 22e Regiment, Quebec City, Que.	Villers-Bretonneux Military Cemetery, Fouilloy, France
BROWN, Harry	Canadian War Museum, Ottawa	Noex-les-Mines Communal Cemetery, France
CAIRNS, Hugh	Canadian War Museum, Ottawa	Auberchicourt British Cemetery near Douai, France
CAMPBELL, Frederick William	Unknown	Boulogne-Eastern Cemetery, France
CLARKE, Lionel Beamaurice	Family	Etratat Churchyard, Le Havre, France
CLARKE-KENNEDY, William	Family	Mount Royal Cemetery Montreal
COCKBURN, Hampden Zane Churchill	Upper Canada College, Toronto	St. James Cemetery, Toronto

COMBE, Robert Grierson	Province of Saskatchewan Archives, Regina	No known grave, Vimy Ridge, France
COPPINS, Frederick	Winnipeg Rifles Memorial Branch, Winnipeg, Man.	Oakland, California
COSENS, Aubrey	Canadian Rifles, Glenbow Museum, Calgary, Alta.	Groesbeck Cemetery Nijmegen, Holland
CROAK, John Bernard	Canadian War Museum, Ottawa (on loan to Army Museum, Halifax, N.S.)	Hangard Wood Cemetery, France
CRUICKSHANK, Robert Edward	London Scottish Museum	Leicester, England
CURRIE, David Vivien	Family	Greenwood Cemetery Owen Sound, Ont.
DE WIND, Edmund	Family	No known grave, near Grougie, France
DINESEN, Thomas	Family	Leerbeck, Denmark
DOUGLAS, Campbell Mellis	Canadian War Museum, Ottawa	Wells Cemetery, Somerset, England
DUNN, Alexander Roberts	Upper Canada College, Toronto	Senafe, Ethiopia
FISHER, Frederick	Family	Near Poelcapelle, Belgium
FLOWERDEW, Gordon Muriel	Framlingham College, England	Namps-au-Val British Cemetery, France
FOOTE, John Weir	Royal Hamilton Light Infantry	Union Cemetery, Cobourg, Ont.
GOOD, Herman James	Royal Canadian Legion, Clinton, Ont.	St. Alban's Cemetery, Branch Bathurst, N.B.
GRAY, Robert Hampton	Canadian War Museum, Ottawa (on loan from the family)	No known grave. Crashed into Onagawa Bay, Japan. Body was never recovered.
GREGG, Milton Fowler	Royal Canadian Regiment of Canada, London, Ont. (stolen)	Snider Mountain Baptist Cemetery, N.B.
HANNA, Robert	29th Battalion, Vancouver, B.C.	Masonic Cemetery, Burbank, B.C.
HALL, Frederick William	Family	No known grave, near Ypres, Belgium
HALL, William Edward	Nova Scotia Museum, Halifax	Hantsport Baptist Church Grounds
HARVEY, Frederick Maurice Watson	Family	Fort MacLeod, Alberta

HOBSON, Frederick	Canadian War Museum, Ottawa	No known grave, France
HOEY, Charles Ferguson	Lincolnshire Regiment Museum, England	Taukhyan Cemetery, Rangoon, Burma
HOLLAND, Edward James Gibson	Upper Canada College, Toronto	Cremated, ashes on Island 17, Temagami, Ontario
HOLMES, Thomas William	Royal Canadian Legion, Owen Sound, Ont. Branch	Greenwood Cemetery, Owen Sound, Ont.
HONEY, Samuel Lewis	Canadian War Museum, Ottawa	Quéant Cemetery, France
HORNELL, David Ernest	Air Command Headquarters, Winnipeg, Man. (on loan from the family)	Lerwick Cemetery, Shetland Islands
HUTCHESON, Bellenden	Toronto Scottish Fort York Armoury	Mount Carmel Cemetery, Mount Carmel, Illinois
KAEBLE, Joseph	Le Musée, Royal 22e Regiment, Quebec City, Que.	Wanqueten Communal Extension Cemetery, France
KERR, George Fraser	Family	Mount Pleasant Cemetery, Toronto Ont.
KERR, John Chipman	Canadian War Museum, (on loan to Provincial Museum of Alberta)	Mountain View Cemetery, Vancouver, B.C.
KINROSS, Cecil John	Family Lougheed	Soldiers Plot, Cemetery, Alberta
KNIGHT, Arthur George	Glenbow Museum, Calgary, Alta.	Dominion Cemetery, Hendicourt-lez- Cagnecourt, France
KONOWAL, Filip	Canadian War Museum, Ottawa	Notre Dame Cemetery, Ottawa
LEARMONTH, Okill Massey	Governor General's Foot Guard Museum, Ottawa	Noix-les Mines, France
LYALL, Graham Thomas	Family	Haifa Sollu War Cemetery, Egypt
MacDOWELL, Thain Wendell	University of Toronto Memorial Tower	Oakland Cemetery, Brockville, Ont.
MacGREGOR, John	Family	West Korah Cemetery, Sault Ste. Marie, Ont.
MacLEOD, Alan Arnott	Air Command Headquarters, Winnipeg, Man. (on loan from the Canadian War Museum)	Kildonan Cemetery, Winnipeg, Man.
MAHONY, John Keefer	Family	Cremated, London, Ont.

McKEAN, George Burdon	Canadian War Museum, Ottawa	Brighton Extension-Mural Cemetery, England
McKENZIE, Hugh	Canadian War Museum, Ottawa (on loan to Princess Patricia's Canadian Light Infantry Regimental Museum, Calgary, Alta.)	No known grave, Friesland, Belgium
MERRIFIELD, William	Family	Cranbrook Lake Cemetery, Powell River, B.C.
METCALFE, William Henry	Family	Bayside Cemetery, Eastport, Maine
MILNE, William Johnstone	Canadian War Museum, Ottawa	No known grave, Vimy Ridge, France
MINER, Harry Garnet Bedford	Clinton Branch, Royal Canadian Legion	Crouy-sur-Mere British Cemetery, France
MITCHELL, Coulson Norman	Royal Canadian Engineers Museum, Chilliwack, B.C.	Montreal, Que.
MULLIN, George Henry	Princess Patricia's Canadian Light Infantry Regimental Museum, Calgary, Alta.	South Cemetery, Legion Plot, Moosomin, Sask.
MYNARSKI, Andrew Charles	Air Command Headquarters, Winnipeg, Manitoba	Méharicourt Cemetery France
NICKERSON, Arthur Herbert Lindsay	Family	Cour, Kintyre Argyll, Scotland
NUNNEY, Claude Joseph	Cornwall Armoury Cornwall, Ont.	Aubigny Communal Cemetery, France
O'KELLY, Christopher	Canadian War Museum, Ottawa	Drowned in Lac Seul, Ont. Body was never recovered.
O'LEARY, Michael	The Irish Guards	Paddington Cemetery, London, England
O'ROURKE, Michael James	British Columbia Regiment, Vancouver, B.C.	Forest Lawn Cemetery, Vancouver, British Columbia
OSBOURN, John Robert	Canadian War Museum, Ottawa	No known grave, Hong Kong
PATTISON, John George	Glenbow Museum, Calgary, Alta.	Lachaudière Military Cemetery, Vimy Ridge, France
PEARKES, George Randolph	Canadian War Museum, Ottawa	Victoria, B.C.
PECK, Cyrus Wesley	Canadian War Museum, Ottawa	Cremated, Family Plot, New Westminster, B.C.
PETERS, Frederick Thornton	Sold by auction in the United Kingdom in 1944	No known grave. Drowned off Plymouth Harbour.

RAYFIELD, Walter Leigh	Canadian War Museum, Ottawa	Soldiers Plot, Prospect Cemetery, Toronto, Ont.
READE, Herbert Taylor	Gloucester Regiment, City Museum, England	Locksbrook Cemetery, England
RICHARDSON, Arthur Herbert Lindsey	National Archives of Canada, Ottawa	St. James Cemetery, Liverpool, England
RICHARDSON, James Cleland	Family	No known grave. The Somme, France
RICKETTS, Thomas	Family	Anglican Cemetery, St. John's, Nfld.
ROBERTSON, James Peter	Family	Tyne Cot Cemetery, Passchandaele, Belgium
RUTHERFORD, Charles Smith	Family	Colborne, Ont.
SCRIMGER, Francis Alexander Caron	Family	Mount Royal Cemetery, Montreal, Que.
SHANKLAND, Thomas William	Family	Mountain View Cemetery Vancouver, B.C.
SIFTON, Ellis Wellwood	St. Thomas Military Regional Museum, Ont.	Military Cemetery, Vimy Ridge, France
SMITH, Ernest Alvia	Living	
SPALL, Robert	Princess Patricia's Canadian Light Infantry Regimental Museum, Calgary, Alta.	No known grave. Near Amiens, France
STRACHAN, Harcus	Not known	Vancouver, B.C.
TAIT, James Edward	Family	Fouquescort Military Cemetery, France
TILSTON, Frederick Albert	Essex and Kent Regiment, Windsor, Ont.	Toronto, Ont.
TOPHAM, Frederick George	Canadian Forces Base Petawawa Museum	Toronto, Ont.
TRIQUET, Paul	Le Musée, Royal 22e Regiment, Quebec City, Que.	Quebec City, Que.
TURNER, Richard Ernest William	Royal Canadian Dragoons Museum, Camp Gagetown, New Brunswick	Mount Hermon Cemetery, Quebec City, Que.
YOUNG, John Francis	Family	Mount Royal Cemetery, Montreal, Que.
ZENGEL, Raphael Louis	Royal Canadian Legion, R.L. Zengel Branch	Rocky Mountain House Alberta

ILLUSTRATION CREDITS

Victoria Cross (Canadian War Museum) - pg. 2

The grave of Alexander Dunn (National Archives of Canada, PA147996) - pg. 3

Alexander Dunn, 11th Regiment of Dragoons (National Archives of Canada) - pg. 6

"Balaclava" by Augustus Butler (Army Museums Ogilby Trust, London) - pg. 7

Herbert Reade, 61st Regiment of Foot, Sketch by Helmut Rath (National Archives of Canada, C33487) - pg. 10

William Hall, Naval Brigade, Royal Navy (National Archives of Canada) - pg. 11

"The Storming of Delhi", Artist unknown (National Army Museum) - pg. 12

Campbell Douglas, 24th Regiment of Foot (National Archives of Canada) - pg. 13

Arthur Richardson, Lord Strathcona's Horse. Photo from J.C. Ridpath, *The Story of South Africa* (Guelph, World Publishing Co., 1902) - pg. 16

Liliefontein gun on display at the Canadian War Museum - pg. 17

Richard Turner, The Royal Canadian Dragoons (National Archives of Canada, PA6315) - pg. 20

Villagers admiring Michael O'Leary's VC (*The Sphere*, January 20th, 1917) - pg. 23

Canadian troops in the trenches taking their rest before the next assault (National Archives of Canada, PA2468) - pg. 25

A detail from "The Battle of Second Ypres".

Painting by W.B. Wollen, rendered from a photograph. The original is with the Princess Patricia's Canadian Light Infantry (Canadian War Museum) - pg. 26

"The Rescue" (Canadian War Museum) - pg. 27

Fred Fisher, 13th Battalion. Painting by George J. Coates (Canadian War Museum) - pg. 28

An illustration of a parados, an elevation of earth behind fortifications to secure them from attack from the rear (Canadian War Museum) - pg. 29

Francis Scrimger, Canadian Army Medical Corps, 14th Battalion (National Archives of Canada, PA6771) - pg. 30

A detail from "The Battle of Second Ypres" by W.B.Wollen (Canadian War Museum) - pg. 31

Frederick Campbell, 1st Battalion (National Archives of Canada, C11195) - pg. 33

Climbing out of the trenches (National Archives of Canada, PA648) - pg. 35

Leo Clarke, 2nd Battalion (National Archives of Canada) - pg. 36

James Richardson, 16th Battalion (National Archives of Canada) - pg. 41

Frederick Harvey, Lord Strathcona's Horse, at his investiture by King George V (National Archives of Canada) - pg. 43

Vimy Ridge Memorial (National Archives of Canada, C7492) - pg. 44

Thain MacDowell, 38th Battalion. Portrait by Harold Knight (Canadian War Museum) - pg. 46

The field of battle at Vimy Ridge (National Archives of Canada, PA1020) - pg. 49

Ellis Sifton, 18th Battalion (National Archives of Canada) - pg. 50

Robert Combe, 27th Battalion. Portrait by R.M. Morgan (National Archives of Canada, C33100) - pg. 52

Billy Bishop, Royal Flying Corps. Painting by Alphonse Jongers (Canadian War Museum) - pg. 54

Canadian troops in the trenches, (National Archives of Canada, PA2468) - pg. 57

"The Runner's Last Stride" (Canadian War Museum) - pg. 58

Michael O'Rourke, 7th Battalion. Painting by Ernest Fosbery (Canadian War Museum) - pg. 59

Frederick Hobson, 20th Battalion (National Archives of Canada, C33053) - pg. 60

Okill Learmonth, 2nd Battalion. Painting by James Quinn (Canadian War Museum) - pg. 61

Robert Hanna, with fellow VC winner Michael O'Rourke (National Archives of Canada) - pg. 61

Filip Konowal, 47th Battalion. Painting by Ambrose McEvoy (Canadian War Museum) - pg. 62

Artist's impression (Canadian War Museum) - pg. 66

Christopher O'Kelly, 52nd Battalion (National Archives of Canada) - pg. 68

Thomas Holmes, 4th Canadian Mounted Rifles (National Archives of Canada, PA2352) - pg. 70

An attack on a pillbox (Canadian War Museum) - pg. 72

George Pearkes, 5th Canadian Mounted Rifles Battalion (National Archives of Canada, PA2364) - pg. 73

James Robertson, 27th Battalion (National Archives of Canada) - pg. 74

Cecil Kinross, 49th Battalion, (National Archives of Canada) - pg. 76

Harcus Strachan, Fort Garry Horse (National Archives of Canada, PA6744) - pg. 81

Battlefield (National Archives of Canada, PA2195) - pg. 83

Edmund De Wind, 31st and 15th Battalion. From *Letters from the Front* (Cdn. Bank of Commerce; 1920) - pg. 84

Gordon Flowerdew, Lord Strathcona's Horse (National Archives of Canada, C33344) - pg. 85

George McKean, 14th Battalion. Painting by F.H. Varley (Canadian War Museum) - pg. 86

Joseph Kaeble, 22nd Battalion. Pencil drawing by Alfred Bastien (Canadian War Museum) - pg. 88

Alan MacLeod, Royal Flying Corps (National Archives of Canada) - pg. 92

Fighting the Flying Circus. Illustration by William Wheeler from *Knights of the Air* (Macmillan, 1963) - pg. 94

Rowland Bourke, Royal Naval Volunteer Reserve (National Archives of Canada, PA161003) - pg. 95

Victoria Cross (Canadian War Museum) - pg. 99

John Croak, 13th Battalion (National Archives of Canada) - pg. 102

Herman Good, 13th Battalion (National Archives of Canada, PA6663) - pg. 103

A battle scene typical of World War I (National Archives of Canada, PA884) - pg. 104

Raphael Zengel, 5th Battalion (National Archives of Canada, PA6796) - pg. 108

A bayonet attack (Canadian War Museum) - pg. 109
Storming a trench with bombs and bayonet (Canadian War Museum) - pg. 110

James Tait, 78th Battalion (National Archives of Canada, PA6710) - pg. 111

John Mahony, The Westminster Regiment (National Archives of Canada) - pg. 168

The Memorial to Canadian Airmen (Courtesy the Jackman Foundation) - pg. 170

Andrew Mynarski, Royal Canadian Air Force (National Archives of Canada, PL38261) - pg. 172

David Hornell, Royal Canadian Air Force (National Archives of Canada, PL25355) - pg. 174

Ian Bazalgette, Royal Air Force (National Archives of Canada, PL37038) - pg. 175

Tank movement in Falaise, 1944 (National Archives of Canada, PA132719) - pg. 178

David Currie, 29th Armoured Reconnaissance Regiment (National Archives of Canada, PA140875) - pg. 179

Ernest "Smokey" Smith, The Seaforth Highlanders (National Archives of Canada) - pg. 181

Aubrey Cosens, The Queen's Own Rifles (National Archives of Canada, PA166764) - pg. 185

Mud encrusted tank (National Archives of Canada, PA113675) - pg. 186

Fred Tilston, The Essex Scottish Regiment (National Archives of Canada) - pg. 187

Field medicine (Canadian War Museum) - pg. 192

Frederick Topham, 1st Canadian Parachute Battalion (National Archives of Canada, PA131823) - pg. 193

Robert Gray, Royal Canadian Volunteer Reserve (National Archives of Canada, PA133296) - pg. 196

Memorial to Robert Hampton Gray, Onagawa Bay, Japan (Courtesy Stuart E. Soward Collection) - pg. 197

Soldiers advance (National Archives of Canada, C46606) - pg. 198

BIBLIOGRAPHY

Arbuckle, Graeme. *Customs and Traditions of the Canadian Navy.*
Halifax: Nimbus Publishing Limited, 1953.

Creagh, Sir O'Moore and E.M. Humphries. *The V.C. and D.S.O.*
London: The Standard Art Book Co. Ltd.

Lucas, C.E. *Victoria Cross Battles of the Second World War.*
London: Heinemann, 1973.

Machum, Lt.-Col. George. *Canada's VCs.*
Toronto: McClelland & Stewart Ltd., 1956.

Melville, Douglas A. *Canadians and the Victoria Cross.*
St. Catharines, Ont.: Vanwell Publishing Ltd., 1986.

Nasmith, Col. George N. *Canada's Sons and Great Britain in the World War.*
Toronto: Thomas Allen, 1919.

Naval Officers Association of Canada. *Starshell.* December 1962.
Victoria, B.C.

Smyth, Brig. The Rt. Hon. Sir John. *Great Stories of the Victoria Cross.*
London: Arthur Barker Ltd., 1977.

Swettenham, John. *To Seize the Victory.*
Toronto: The Ryerson Press, 1965.

Swettenham, John (ed.). *Valiant Men.*
Toronto: Hakkert, 1973.

Turner, John Frayne. *VCs of the Army 1939-1951.*
London: George G. Harrap & Co. Ltd., 1962.

Turner, John Frayne. *VCs of the Air.*
London: George G. Harrap & Co. Ltd., 1960.

Winton, John. *The Victoria Cross at Sea.*
London: Michael Joseph Ltd., 1978.

Discovery magazine. November 1987.
Toronto: Terrace Publishing Ltd.

For Valour: *The Victoria Cross in Action.*
London: Methuen, 1985.

The Globe and Mail, Toronto, Ont.

The Toronto Sun, Toronto, Ont.

NAME INDEX

WORLD WAR II

VC ASSOCIATES

OTHER BOOKS BY ARTHUR BISHOP

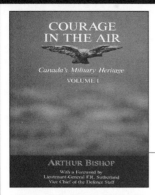

COURAGE IN THE AIR
CANADA'S MILITARY HERITAGE, VOLUME I
Arthur Bishop

These biographies bring to life the stories of those who fought in the air in the most spectacular of modern wars, World Wars I and II, and Korea.

0-07-551376-5

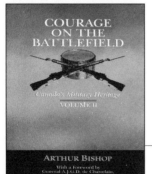

COURAGE ON THE BATTLEFIELD
CANADA'S MILITARY HERITAGE, VOLUME II
Arthur Bishop

These exciting narratives bring to life the stories of soldiers who fought in the War of 1812, in the Crimea, the Indian Mutiny, the Boer War, in World Wars I and II, and in Korea.

0-07-551556-3

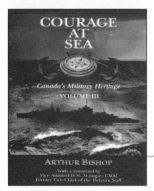

COURAGE AT SEA
CANADA'S MILITARY HERITAGE, VOLUME III
Arthur Bishop

These are the stories of Canada's war heroes who fought at sea during two World Wars, as well as the Royal Canadian Navy's role in Korea.

0-07-551640-3

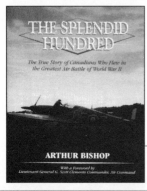

THE SPLENDID HUNDRED
THE TRUE STORY OF CANADIANS WHO FLEW IN THE GREATEST BATTLE OF WW II
Arthur Bishop

The untold story of the 100 Canadian Fighter Pilots who flew during the Battle of Britain.

0-07-551683-7

These books are available at bookstores across Canada. If a book is out-of-stock, ask your local bookstore to order it from MCGRAW-HILL RYERSON.